Crane Island Journal Part Three

Vor (Spring)

A Memoir of a Remarkable Daily Life on a Small Island in the Salish Sea

By John Ashenhurst

Walt's Third Blessing

Afoot and light-hearted I take to the open road,
Healthy, free, the world before me,
The long brown path before me leading wherever I choose.

Henceforth I ask not good-fortune, I myself am good-fortune,
Henceforth I whimper no more, postpone no more, need nothing,
Done with indoor complaints, libraries, querulous criticisms,
Strong and content I travel the open road.

The earth, that is sufficient,
I do not want the constellations any nearer,
I know they are very well where they are,
I know they suffice for those who belong to them.

(Still here I carry my old delicious burdens,
I carry them, men and women, I carry them with me wherever I go,
I swear it is impossible for me to get rid of them,
I am fill'd with them, and I will fill them in return.)

From Song of the Open Road by Walt Whitman

Vor (Spring)	1
Dedication	3
Introduction	4
One-hundred-eighty-four: Vast	10
One-hundred-eighty-five: Transitions	15
One-hundred-eighty-six: Circle Route	22
One-hundred-eighty-seven: The Springs	29
One-hundred-eighty-eight: Return	33
One-hundred-eighty-nine: Happy Birthday to Me	36
One-hundred-ninety: Orcas Heights	40
One-hundred-ninety-one: Loss, gain, change	44
One-hundred-ninety-two: Too Cold, Too Long	48
One-hundred-ninety-three: Spring Dump Run	52
One-hundred-ninety-four: Meeting the Ferry	57
One-hundred-ninety-five: Jones Island Picnic	62
One-hundred-ninety-six: To the Ferry	67
One-hundred-ninety-seven: Fixing	71
One-hundred-ninety-eight: It's A Hoot	75
One-hundred-ninety-nine: Cinco de Mayo	79
Two-hundred: Out They Go	83
Two-hundred-one: Spring Clean Up	88
Two-hundred-two: New Science, New Religion: Part 2	92
Two-hundred-three: Dinner Guests	97
Two-hundred-four: Carrying On	101
Two-hundred-five: Red in Tooth and Claw	105
Two-hundred-six: Bambi Goes Home	108

Two-hundred-seven: No Wake	111
Two-hundred-eight: Catchment	115
Two-hundred-nine: Kayakers	119
Two-hundred-ten: Clean up	123
Two-hundred-eleven: To Harstine Island	126
Two-hundred-twelve: On the Road Again	130
Two-hundred-thirteen: Los Osos	134
Two-hundred-fourteen: Projects	137
Two-hundred-fifteen: First Birthday Party	140
Two-hundred-sixteen: Elfin Forest	143
Two-hundred-seventeen: On the Road Yet Again	147
Two-hundred-eighteen: Jiggety Jog	150
Two-hundred-nineteen: Making Choices	153
Two-hundred-twenty: A Kind of Life	156
Two-hundred-twenty-one: Two Steps Forward	160
Two-hundred-twenty-two: Short Cut	163
Two-hundred-twenty-three: Guests	166
Two-hundred-twenty-four: Memorable Day	170
Two-hundred-twenty-five: Customer Service	174
Two-hundred-twenty-six: More Boat Troubles	178
Two-hundred-twenty-seven: Try, Try Again	182
Two-hundred-twenty-eight: Ripening	187
Two-hundred-twenty-nine: Not again?	192
Two-hundred-thirty: "I Want to Do Everything"	197
Two-hundred-thirty-one: Gemütlichkeit	203
Two-hundred-thirty-two: Trophy Case	207

Two-hundred-thirty-three: Trapped	211
Two-hundred-thirty-four: Boys in Transit	214
Two-hundred-thirty-five: Turnaround	218
Two-hundred-thirty-six: Budget	222
Two-hundred-thirty-seven: Flower Sunday	227
Two-hundred-thirty-eight: What Goes Around	231
Two-hundred-thirty-nine: Grind	235
Two-hundred-forty: Welcome Home	239
Two-hundred-forty-one: Good Deed	244
Two-hundred-forty-two: Purple Grains	247
Two-hundred-forty-three: Timberrrr! Uh-oh....	251
Two-hundred-forty-four: Seven Hundred Pounds	255
Two-hundred-forty-five: Helpmeet	260
Two-hundred-forty-six: Summer Solstice	264
Two-hundred-forty-seven: Pirate Booty	268
Two-hundred-forty-eight: Remodel	272
Two-hundred-forty-nine: Wheels	276
Two-hundred-fifty: Blooming	282
Two-hundred-fifty-one: Let's Get Together	285
Two-hundred-fifty-two: Refulgent Summer	289
Two-hundred-fifty-three: Off on a Tangent	293
Two-hundred-fifty-four: How It's Done	296
Two-hundred-fifty-five: Long Days Burning into Night	300
Two-hundred-fifty-six: Six Big Firs	304
Two-hundred-fifty-seven: Parade	308
Two-hundred-fifty-eight: Another Parade	313

Two-hundred-fifty-nine: Fourth Open House	319
Two-hundred-sixty: Plumbing Help	322
Two-hundred-sixty-one: Sympathy	326
Two-hundred-sixty-two: Operational	330
Two-hundred-sixty-three: The Details	334
Two-hundred-sixty-four: Short Strokes	338
Two-hundred-sixty-five: Grand Opening	342
Two-hundred-sixty-six: Reid Harbor	348
Two-hundred-sixty-seven: No Winds	353
Two-hundred-sixty-eight: It's the Berries!	357
What's Next?	360

Vor (Spring)

Vor (Spring)

A Memoir of a Remarkable Daily Life on a Small Island in the Salish Sea

By John Ashenhurst

Crane Island Journal is a four-part memoir beginning with *Haust* and *Vetur* and continuing with *Vor* and *Sumar* (autumn, winter, spring and summer in Old Norse)

Publisher: Classics Unbound

V1.00 12/10/2024

Copyright © 2024 by John Ashenhurst

ISBN 978-0-9904563-4-6

All rights reserved. Created in the United States of America. No part of this book may be reproduced in any manner whatsoever without written permission except in the case of brief quotations embodied in critical articles and reviews. For information, address Classics Unbound, 5615 24th Ave NW, #43, Seattle, WA 98107

All photographs are the property of the author unless otherwise indicated.

For more information see www.craneislandjournal.com.

Dedication

Our parents and siblings: Opal Dragstedt LaTour, Anthony LaTour, Ronald LaTour, James H. Ashenhurst, Elin Barkman Ashenhurst, Marcy Ashenhurst McNeill, Julie Ashenhurst Andrews

Introduction

Vor (Spring) is Part Three of the *Crane Island Journal*. See Part One, *Haust (Autumn)* for the story of how we came to live on Crane Island and Part Two, *Vetur (Winter)* for the island's history. Part Three, *Vor (Spring)* and Part Four, *Sumar (Sumer)* follow *Vetur*.

Deer Harbor Hamlet (98243) lies close to the southwest corner of Orcas Island and boasts two marinas (one allows transient moorage), whale watching, a dock store, two restaurants, a Post Office, fire station, and the Worldmark Deer Harbor resort. The dock store sells boaters gasoline and diesel and provides a pump out service and public restrooms and showers.

Deer Harbor has a population of about 300, with a median age of 57, 60% male, and with an average household income of about $155,000. Sixty percent have a college degree and more than half are married. One-third of the occupied housing units are rented. (See https://www.point2homes.com/US/Neighborhood/WA/Deer-Harbor-Demographics.html)

Deer Harbor is accessible by driving from the ferry landing or if you rent a car on the island from the Eastsound airport by rental car. If you want to fly to Deer Harbor directly, you can by Kenmore Air float plane, a 75 minute trip from Lake Union in Seattle. Friends that visited sometimes came by float plane and on the way back from picking them up in Deer Harbor in our Sea-Sport, Yvonne would pull up her crab pot, let our friends pick out the big Dungeness males and throw the rest back in the water. Once home on Crane Island, and with a glass of wine handy, at Yvonne's direction, our friends would knock the crabs carapace's off and they'd go into a pot for dinner.

Kenmore Air float plane leaving Deer Harbor

We bought a house in Deer Harbor in the fall of 1997, when we were living in Boulder, Colorado, thinking of it as an Orcas summer house, and didn't spend much time there until 2000 when we began to make improvements.

Introduction

Yvonne and 'Mantha Moo Moo

The house is on the side of a hill and draped in clematis

Introduction

We turned the one-car garage into a studio and bunk house

And added decks and doors off the two bedrooms.

Introduction

In 2006 when we'd done just about everything we could think of with our house in Deer Harbor, we began to look around for a house on the water we liked and could afford. A realtor friend took us to nearby Crane Island and the visit was eye-opening — beautiful, a house with good bones, a view, a pocket beach, the community dock nearby, and lots of possibilities.

With Al doing a first look - exciting

We sold our Deer Harbor house one day and bought the Crane house the next, renting back the Deer Harbor house for a few months while we prepared the Crane house for our move and occupancy.

And then we got to work - some of that described in *Haust* when we put in a new kitchen. One of the first things Yvonne did, after redecorating, was to work on enclosing a garden area, intending to develop beautiful and productive gardens as she had in Deer Harbor. It was a challenge.

Introduction

And the garage could be a studio with a loft. Yes!

We were a mile from our house in Deer Harbor but now in a different world
— magical. Every day.

And that's what the *Crane Island Journal* is about.

Now turn the page to get started on this, the third volume — *Vor (Spring)*
JCA, December 4, 2024

One-hundred-eighty-four: Vast

"The woods are lovely, dark and deep, But I have promises to keep, And miles to go before I sleep, And miles to go before I sleep." - Robert Frost

We were back in Boulder, where we'd lived for 25 years and raised our kids before moving to Orcas Island and then Crane Island, now staying with friends we'll be with in Chimayo, New Mexico for our 19th Good Friday pilgrimage.

Yvonne woke up earlier than usual; she had slept well and would want to leave once she got up and showered, some time around 8:00. Did she want oatmeal? No. Yes. At 7:30 she came into the kitchen where Tessa and I were talking and I was finishing up an email to Jens on the matter of image permissions. Tessa was on her way out to her swimming session at the South Boulder Rec Center. Where was the oatmeal? I hadn't made it yet. But she wanted to go very soon and eat breakfast right now. Then let's have bagels. We left the house about 9:00, first having to talk with Alan and Tessa about when they'd leave Boulder and when they'd appear in Taos. They thought not before noon and before 6:00.

I-25 approaching downtown Denver was stop and go for miles; we should have taken the express lanes; and then the traffic eased and we made good time through Castle Rock, Monument, Colorado Springs (where we'd return Saturday afternoon), and Pueblo, a cloudy 34 degree day suggesting snow, the mountains to our right and the plains to the left, a route we'd traveled many times on our way to southern Colorado or New Mexico, less interesting but faster than Route 285, the route we took the year before when we entered the mountains south of Morrison, to Kenosha Pass, where we descended into South Park, through Fairplay, and on to Salida where Yvonne shopped for yarn and I bought Merwin's *The Shadow of Sirius*, and where we met Alan and Tessa for dinner, and then over Poncha pass and to the Great

One-hundred-eighty-four: Vast

Sand Dunes National Park — a place we'd camped with the kids many times — overnight at a motel — and then south through the San Luis Valley, Fort Garland, San Luis, and into New Mexico, passed Taos to Espanola and then east to Chimayo.

We turned off I-25 at Walsenburg, a mining town that had seen better days, and spotted Dean's Lexus at George's Drive Inn. Barb and Dean had arrived only minutes before. We had a chance to talk and for me to ask the cashier where I could find a Radio Shack store to buy a cable to attach my iPod or Yvonne's iPad to the radio in the rented Versa (the FM iPod to radio transmitter hadn't worked) but Walsenburg didn't have one though the Family Dollar store might — and it did. Heading west out of Walsenburg, the summits of the Spanish Peaks, to the left, were hidden in clouds and as we approached La Veda pass we could see a snowstorm over the Sangre de Cristo Range. Yvonne had found some NPR programs to listen to through her iPad, one a Codrescu commentary, and in order to listen we'd each worn one earphone. Listening, now, through the Versa's radio/CD system was much more satisfactory. At Fort Garland I turned south and Yvonne reclined her seat and started a nap that would last almost until the New Mexico border. She slept through San Luis, as far as I could see unchanged, a town where Alan had taught for a year before going to grad school. Emma's Hacienda looked like it might be open. We'd stopped there, sometimes all of us converging at the same time, Alan talking with some of the locals he still knew, but Emma was gone, and Joe was gone, once a boxer in the tradition of Jack Dempsey from the nearby town of Manassa. The sky was now mostly blue with puffy clouds arranged roughly in north-south curves and the sun through the windshield was hot. The Sangre de Cristos were now on our left and a variety of volcanic remnants on our right with occasional views of distant snow-capped peaks. South of Questa the rolling road entered piñon pine and Utah juniper forest, eventually emerging above the Rio Grand Valley, Taos to the left, and an extraordinary hundred-mile view to the south and west.

One-hundred-eighty-four: Vast

184A: Dinner at Orlando's, north of Taos: Yvonne, Tessa, Alan, John, Barb, Dean

At 3:00 we drove slowly through Taos Plaza, the historic center of the town, where we'd spent a few hours three years before, our bonus daughter Corrina with us, bereft at the loss of her mother. Today Yvonne wanted to buy a book on Mabel Dodge Luhan and we parked in a lot north of the Plaza, close to Moby Dickens where I sat outside typing and Yvonne shopped. Then on to the Mabel Dodge Luhan House east of the Plaza and bordering Taos Pueblo land, open all the way to the mountains. Dean and Barb had already checked in and we saw them a bit later as Yvonne and I walked around the grounds getting a sense of what life was like here 80 years before when Dodge Luhan presided over an itinerant group of writers and artists, a personality that had helped create the culture of Taos. Alan called when they crossed the New Mexico border in their Prius. His GPS system told him they would be in Taos before 5:30 so we made arrangements to meet at Orlando's, a Mexican food restaurant on the road north of town, and they arrived before we did. Good food, laughter, and back at the Mabel Dodge Luhan House we had a tour of one another's rooms. Alan and Tessa were on the second floor, with the use of the D.H. Lawrence bathroom — where he had painted the windows in colorful, mostly abstract patterns.

184B: Bathroom in Mary Austin room; writing desk between two half walls on right

One-hundred-eighty-four: Vast

Dean and Barb were in the Robinson Jeffers room that backed up to the Taos Pueblo land and a clear view to the east. We were in the Mary Hunter Austin room that featured among other things a writing nook conveniently located between an old-fashioned bathtub and the toilet. We all found ourselves very comfortable in this run-down, shabby, elegant, memory-laden, haphazard adobe structure parts of which were more than 200 years old.

Sitting in the comfortable Rainbow room, ready for visiting, the evening veered off in an unexpected direction when Alan decided to call Dave and Ann to see whether they could pick up his camera and the cross Ann had found years before on Mount Sanitas above their house in Boulder and which one of us wore each year during the Chimayo Good Friday walk. Alan was clearly unhappy about leaving these items at home and here in the Mabel Dodge Luhan House he decided to call Ann and Dave and walked into the living room with his cell phone, coming back with a story about how they had agreed reluctantly and would call from the Davis driveway at 8:20 in the morning for instructions about how to enter the house and where to look. But maybe that was too much. When someone pointed out that the trip to the Davis house was out of the way for the Phillips who would be going straight south on Broadway out of Boulder, Alan began to reconsider and then called them back and told them he didn't want them to stop after all - the right decision.

One-hundred-eighty-five: Transitions

"In every change, in every falling leaf, there is some pain, some beauty. And that's the way new leaves grow." — Amit Ray

Breakfast at the Mabel Dodge Luhan House isn't casual, continental, or light. A chaffing dish held long thick strips of crisp bacon, another pork sausage, and a third a spinach frittata sixteen inches across and four inches high. Sliced fruit was displayed at the end of the serving table and another had stacks of small home-made corn flour muffins. Coffee and hot water with eight kinds of tea covered a third table. The dining room was nearly filled leaving only scattered seating so the three couples couldn't sit together but split up to three different tables. Almost all the happily chatting people at the tables were women, at the House to attend a painting workshop, one of many workshops on the arts, writing, knitting, leadership and other topics conducted by outside contributors held during the year. We joined a couple and a single woman and soon found that the couple would be staying at the Hacienda in Chimayo over the weekend arriving after we left. They hadn't realized that Friday there was the most important day of the year. The single woman was a writer in residence from Berlin who was observing the American scene and recording it. Susan and Bob, from Connecticut but now living in Washington, Maine, Unitarians as it turned out, talked about living in a small town where the natives made a difficult living quarrying the gravel on which the town stood while newcomer retirees were looking for untouched charm, the conflict coloring the life of the town. Like Barb and Dean, Yvonne and I, their's was a blended family, yours, mine, and ours.

After sitting outside in the warming sun, the lilac buds struggling to burst in this very dry climate, we made our way to the little Penitente Morada church, La Morada de Nuestra Señora de Guadalupe, not far away across the sagebrush covered sandy soil but accessible only by road and then a path. We'd crowded into Dean's car and once he parked next to a Hispanic ceme-

One-hundred-eighty-five: Transitions

tery with one new grave, the dirt piled high on top of it, and many older graves, some more than 100 years old, many with fading plastic flowers and a few with fresh spring flowers, we walked along a narrow drive toward the church, a weathered pole fence on our left and the cemetery on our right, crossing a dry irrigation ditch and arriving at the church, not a large building, unusual in its lack of windows. Pueblo property, covered in sagebrush, but otherwise unbroken, stretched north toward Taos Peak and east toward the Sangre De Cristo foothills, and to the west, about a quarter of a mile away, the profile of the Mabel Dodge Luhan House was clearly visible.

185A: La Morada de Nuestra Señora de Guadalupe

A gentle south breeze flapped the brown fabric, a shirt perhaps, draped around the black ten foot high cross at the point where the horizontal and vertical members met. A walkway about twenty feet wide bounded by a barbed

One-hundred-eighty-five: Transitions

wire fence that separated it from Pueblo land led from the church grounds to a white cross several hundred yards north. At intervals along the way, rocks arranged into crosses lay in the sand among the sagebrush, headed by a larger gray rock, a headstone with a black stenciled number, 1 to 14. A hundred feet into this stations of the cross processional, but on the left, sagebrush branches had been arranged in the sand to create a heart shape (it seemed to me, anyway), with quartz stones laid in the middle and three small bird feathers, brown on the outside with a core of blue. Georgia O'Keefe had done a painting of the white cross many years before, probably an earlier version. This cross was set into a concrete foundation and wobbled in the wind, a white painted steel bar embedded in the concrete bolted to the cross and holding it in place. Was the cross sometimes lowered and then raised with a Penitente tied to it?

Leaving Mabel Dodge Luhan we made our way to the Taos Square and then to the shops immediately north where we spent an hour finding gifts and a card to mark Ann's birthday Saturday. Leaving Taos and using her iPad, Yvonne directed me toward the Taos/Sante Fe High Road and we turned southeast, to follow the tracks of Kit Carson, Bishop Jean Marie Latour (Jean-Baptiste Lamy) of Cather's story, and untold native Americans who used that north/south route, high above the Rio Grande Valley, which historically, in places, was very difficult to pass through. The High Road winds its way through white pine forest or sometimes piñon and juniper, flatter than one would expect, crossing bench land below the Sangre de Cristo before it splits into canyons and arroyos that can only be crossed by ravens and eagles. Coming out of the forest land we passed through Peñasco and several other small towns, brown adobe houses with red roofs planted in green fields. Spring was slower coming here and in places in the shade snow hung on. Life had to contend with cold here, more so than in the valleys below, closer to the Rio Grande, but at least water was less scarce, at least as snow melt.

At Truches, the little town the setting for John Nichol's *Milagro Bean Field War*, we turned west, downhill toward Chimayo, Years ago the eight of us had walked from Truches (Trout) to the Santuario, fascinated by the local cemetery and the many cars that had been driven off the road into the arroyos below over the years, probably as a form of disposal. But things had changed. The town looked more prosperous with some new large houses under construction. The road was now wider and safer, the junked cars gone; a 21st century

One-hundred-eighty-five: Transitions

New Mexico. Before going to the Hacienda, Yvonne and I drove on and parking near the square walked to the El Santuario de Chimayo. The New Mexico State Police were on hand but not in the number they would show Friday. The Lowlow's Lowrider Art and food stand and the Peregrino restaurant nearby was open for business but had no customers. A scattering of people were entering the Santuario and we decided to do that now rather than wait in line for hours on Friday afternoon at the conclusion of our walk. The "Little Priest," Father Casimiro Roca, welcomed visitors, some to look and others to pray. Yvonne and I spent fifteen or twenty minutes in a pew, meditating I suppose for want of a more appropriate term, finding the quiet center of the world where the spinning stops. On the way out, Yvonne took some of the sacred soil from the sipapu in the anteroom floor, holy since before the Spanish arrived and the Santuario was built. The Tewa Indians frequented this healing spot centuries ago and I rubbed some on my back, aching, perhaps from sitting so long in the Versa the day before. Perhaps 50 crutches hung from two bars, testimony presumably, to healings at the Santuario. Two poster-sized cardboards each held more than 100 photographs of the young and old, uniformed and civilians, dead and alive, loved, missed, and hopefully blessed. A small sign attached to the poster explained that new pictures were to be left at the church office, not added spontaneously, a prescription we hadn't seen before.

Coming out into the bright light we walked toward the back of the church and looked down into the grounds below, spruced up from years past with an alter and benches for outside services. We went over to an area for leaving lighted candles, a place of hope, sorrow, and resignation, where in 2008 Yvonne had lit a candle for her brother Tony the morning after she received a call here at Chimayo from her brother Ron from the VA hospital in San Diego where Tony, in a physician induced coma, was near death.

At 5:00 Yvonne and I with Alan and Tessa and Dean and Barb walked across the road to the Rancho de Chimayo, sister business to the Hacienda de Chimayo where we were staying. The Rancho had once a farm house and was now a lovely adobe building strung with Chimayo red chile ristras. Nearly three years ago it had suffered a fire that closed the restaurant for a year but the interior had been refreshed without being barbarously remodeled. The bar was empty and orderly and we immediately rearranged three tables at the western French doors anticipating that our party would soon grow to 9, ordering a pitcher of margaritas (lemonade for me), nachos, quesadillas, and guacamole from a welcoming, efficient, and robust young woman who was very attentive to us until we left after 7:00.

185B: Rancho de Chimayo: Dave, Sara, Ann, Barb, Tessa, Yvonne

Dave, Ann, and their daughter, Sara arrived soon, having met at Poncha Springs where Sara had left her car after coming over Wolf Creek Pass from Gunnison where she now worked for Western Colorado University in student services. She had spent years in Moab, much of it outdoors and often river rafting and when I asked her whether she had seen *127 Hours* she replied that she had and liked it but that the opening scenes of the hikers' play in the Blue John Canyon were completely unrealistic. She knew the two women who had been portrayed and the real scene wasn't anything like what Danny Boyle had shown. Standing water in Utah was anything but attractive.

Crowding into room seis, where Dean and Barb had hosted our gatherings at the Hacienda now for many years, snack bounty was unloaded onto the big low table we sat around and the conversation begun in the Rancho continued here. Eventually I suggested that we direct our attention to the walk tomorrow, first deciding which route to follow and then to share the focus for our walk. Yvonne and I had talked about the possibility of what we called the circle route, one that started at the Hacienda and headed north, against the stream of pilgrims and then east up the road toward Truchas, turning south and then west and eventually north, a thirteen-mile circle that eventually arrived at the Santuario. The other three possibilities were to drive up to Truchas and walk back, something we'd done many years ago but which we found challenging to our knees and legs because it was downhill all the way, or to drive to Española, and then walk up the valley road, a route we'd done once, interesting because we walked through the local community the whole way but not much fun because of the intense traffic on a narrow road, or finally from the Cities of Gold Casino, south of Española at the head of the High Road to Taos that goes through Chimayo. After some discussion we all agreed that given the ideal weather forecast the circle route seemed most appropriate.

We went on to talk about why we were walking this year, each pilgrim describing briefly someone who was suffering and wanted healing. I cited my ex-brother-in-law Karl who was recovering from his second cancer of the mouth operation and daughter-in-law Natasha's brother, Justin who was struggling to create a successful life with the mother of two of his children who herself was struggling with an overwhelming addiction. Yvonne talked about her niece, now 41, whose kidneys were failing, suffering the effects of drug addiction. Alan said that this year he was walking for himself, unsure for the first time in many years what to do with his worklife and on the verge of needing to decide whether to continue along a path that was becoming less satisfying or to strike out in a new, less conventional academic direction. Having heard him say for years that he couldn't imagine doing anything different from being a teacher, a professor of education, I was surprised at this change. Dean too was walking for himself, needing to make a decision in a few months whether to give up the practice of medicine. Dave also had to confront

One-hundred-eighty-five: Transitions

retirement and Ann talked about her concerns. Barb had just retired and was trying to adjust to the change. In past years each of us was usually concerned about transitions in the lives of our children, parents, family, or friends. This year the focus on our own transitions was more prominent.

One-hundred-eighty-six: Circle Route

Come, come whoever you are,
   Wanderer, worshiper, lover of leaving.,
   Ours is no caravan of despair,
   Come, yet again come - Rumi

We gathered in Barb and Dean's room, seis, bringing in additional chairs from outside to seat the nine of us, and the Hacienda staff brought in our continental breakfasts on folding, wood, TV tables. Snacks from the evening before remained on the table in the center of the group including brown hard-boiled eggs Tessa had brought from Boulder. After breakfast we formed a circle on the grass in the courtyard that faced the road where a steady stream of peregrinos flowed south toward the square and Santuario. We took stock of our feelings and intentions, sang three songs we were familiar with from our Boulder Unitarian Universalist Church background ("Go Now in Peace," "All I Ask is that Forever You Remember Me," and "Listen, Listen, Listen to My Heart Song") then gathered our packs and water and filed out the gate in the wall, down the wooden stairs to the road, turning left against the human current, heading north, away from the Santuario. Mostly the road was crowded with people but occasionally a car or two or sometimes a motorcycle would pass but by the afternoon cars would clog the road forcing walkers to the shoulders. At the turnoff to Route 76, we swung right, following the road uphill, leaving the stream of pilgrims behind, since virtually all were coming up the valley road from the direction of Española, not downhill from Truchas, six miles up the steep road.

Looking around I counted seven, with me, eight. Someone was missing. Back at the intersection, two hundred yards away, Dean was bent over, his arms stretched out in front of him, hands on his legs holding himself up. He was having an asthma attack. I walked quickly back to him, followed by Barb, and he stood up wheezing and then squeezing the cap of his inhaler to squirt relief into his throat but he continued to wheeze. He wanted to go on, saying he thought he would recover as the drug took effect. I went ahead to tell the rest of the group what was happening where they'd stopped a few hundred yards ahead and then returned to Dean and Barb, with Alan, who wanted to help if possible. I offered to return to the Hacienda to fetch Dean's Lexus so that he could follow us by stages in the car, joining us for a picnic lunch along the way but he turned me down. We walked very slowly but it was clear he could hardly breathe, he was almost suffocating, and without enough oxygen he could barely walk. Dean said he would return to the Hacienda, that he would be OK and he and Barb started back downhill and Alan and I walked on, reluctantly, without our friends who I knew were disappointed not to be part of this walking stage of our pilgrimage.

    I wanted to talk with Alan about his career quandary, to understand what had changed, what he thought his options were, and what he thought about my suggestions of the evening before. Throwing more light on the context he explained how two of his college friends, each pursuing PhDs in education at the same time, optimistic and confident, had become nationally recognized leaders in their specific fields while he, though highly respected by his colleagues, students, and doctoral candidate advisees, had not become a full professor, had not written the books he imagined he would, and had lived with broader priorities including deep family, church, and community involvement. He now had to admit to himself he would never catch up with them. His five year grant would expire in another year, the funding that allowed him to do research and buy out of a five class teaching load, teaching just two classes so that he could pursue his research. He would need another grant or be assigned five classes, something inconsistent with how he thought he could best contribute. A grant would commit him to five years and restrict him to basic research just as he was coming to realize his interests were broader, he had a wider understanding of the problems and potential solutions of education problems and now knew his role should be to synthesize, write, and report on the bigger picture, expanding his collegial pool to principals, school boards, teachers, and other educators who were actively trying to make the educational process more successful. Dave joined our discussion and agreed that it seemed to make sense that Alan widen his horizon from satisfying his professional discipline to those the discipline was intended to serve.

One-hundred-eighty-six: Circle Route

Once off the Truchas road and following Cundiyo Road (503) and entering a hamlet at the foot of the hill we would soon climb, we encountered two small, very friendly German Shepherd mix dogs. We were wary because in the past dogs had at times made us very uncomfortable. This was different and welcome. We bid the dogs goodbye but were soon joined by a third, again very sweet and eager to befriend us, another German Shepherd mix, continuing with us through the hamlet and up the steep, winding, and narrow road, more or less south. Though we tried repeatedly to shoo her away, she wouldn't leave us so we let ourselves enjoy her company and we warned her of approaching cars when we saw them. Alan began a conversation with Ann and I questioned Dave about his, so far vague to me, retirement plans. It was clear to me soon that he really did not want to retire; he would cede direction of the association to his successor but badly wanted to continue to have an office with the group and to serve on an ongoing basis as an advisor, an emeritus director, recounting stories that demonstrated that what he knew and who he knew had continuing value and was perhaps even crucial to the continuing success of the organization. Did the Board see things the way he did? Yes, without a doubt. Would the incoming director, who the Board, not he, would appoint, be comfortable with the former director hanging around? That was the question. David, 77, did not really want to retire. His identity was in his role. Alan, 64, did not want to retire but he was determined to change his role.

Before noon we left the road where two streams formed the Santa Cruz River, cutting through green pastures populated with a handful of tan (and one brown) steers lazing in the midday sun, setting up our picnic on the bank of the stream in a grove of head-high willows, Lucy, my name for our canine companion, wading in the creek, taking a drink and finding a cow pie to roll in. No cars passed while we shared our crackers and cheese and other finger food. The intensely blue sky above was background to two circling turkey buzzards and across the road a raven flew midlevel along a steep cliff and then found the place it wanted to alight. Quiet, peace, beauty, friends, love.

Then on up the hill through Cundiyo, another hamlet, and up and down over a series of ridges as we turned west on our way back to Chimayo. Finally, a mile away, we could see the High Road to Taos turnoff (Rt 98) for the Santaurio, glutted with cars in both directions and thousands of pilgrims walking downhill on the final leg of their short or perhaps very long pilgrimage, from Albuquerque, for instance. On the left side of the road, below, someone had dumped four large tires and scattered trash among the juniper and piñon pine. A lone turkey buzzard circled above to the right and two ravens floated at a higher level farther north keeping their eyes on the buzzard who might lead them to a feast.

186A; Lucy joined us the whole route

Over the next rise the Rio Grande Valley lay to the south and north, the river hidden but its gifts evident in the greening willows and cottonwoods on its banks. Across the valley, Los Alamos was almost visible and the Jemez mountains, the remnants of a huge volcano, rose facing the Sangre de Cristos behind us. Somewhere down along the river Pueblo Indian groups occupied reservations on the land they'd had for centuries, through Spanish, Mexican, and then American administration, and some would have Easter dances this weekend. Above and a quarter mile east of where the High Road turns downhill to Chimayo, we left the road and gathered against a barb wire fence for a better view while Tessa found the passages in the Jefferson Bible she wanted to read. Jefferson had created his own edition, excising passages he had found unacceptable, especially those describing miracles, leaving the New Testament much shorter but more acceptable to himself and other late enlightenment deists.

186B: Circle route, Jemez Mountains to the west across the Rio Grande River

Yvonne and I walked most of the last mile and a half together, sometimes hand in hand, Lucy with us more than the others, both of us having a sense that Samantha, our black dog gone, was with us as Lucy, the little Shepherd nosing Yvonne's legs from time to time. As the foot and wheeled traffic thickened many people began to notice Lucy, who was friendly to everyone, and it seemed to us she was looking for someone familiar. A woman in a car moving away from Chimayo, on hearing Lucy wasn't ours advised leaving her with animal control, not something we were likely to do.

186C: Pilgrims waiting to enter the Santuario de Chimayo

My feet in my new Keen's were beginning to hurt and I could tell the top layer of skin on the ball of my left foot had detached itself from the layer below and would fall off once I took my socks off. The line waiting to enter the Santuario stretched south, maybe a thousand souls waiting, the end of the line more than an hour from the door. None of us would wait in line now. At the Vigil store, Sara and I waited outside while the others went in, including Lucy though she didn't stay long, and joined Sara who sat in the shade on a log to the side while I sat on a post to observe the rich passing scene. Soon the others came out joined by Elizabeth Kay, author of *Chimayo Valley Traditions*, local artist, and partner to Raymond Bal, the store's owner, to take our picture to add to her growing collection of local photographs. We discussed Lucy and after Elizabeth looked her over, she declared Lucy non-local, guessing that she'd been abandoned and would soon become a victim of the coyotes who roamed the area. The best bet, she said would be to take Lucy back to where we first met her and hope for the best. Back at the Hacienda, with Lucy in the Subaru wagon's luggage area, Sara drove the car repeating our walk, saying goodbye to Lucy, who was comfortable, perhaps even really at home in the hamlet where she first joined us.

Later after rests and showers, we crossed the road to the Rancho de Chimayo for dinner. Dean was energized, at least compared to those of us who had made the 13 mile walk, by the progesterone he had consumed to mitigate his asthma. The dinner was delicious, not only because we were very hungry following our exercise; Dave pronounced the chile rellenos the best he had ever tasted - because of the light batter they had been dipped in. Still around the table at 9:00, we were among the last to leave what had been a crowded Friday dinnertime at the Rancho. We'd been talking off and on five days now and hadn't run out of things to say, ask, or laugh about. Tomorrow we'd reluctantly separate, to see one another occasionally over the next year but not for extended periods until our 20th walk next year — which we hoped would include many of those who had joined us in the past.

One-hundred-eighty-seven: The Springs

One's destination is never a place, but a new way of seeing things."
– Henry Miller

The Rancho de Chimayo opened for breakfast at 8:30 and the nine of us were first in line this Saturday morning. Yvonne and I wanted to be in Colorado Springs by 3:00, probably a six hour drive, so we encouraged the early start for the group. Because we had stayed in the associated Hacienda, breakfasts at the Rancho were half price, a bargain on top of already reasonable prices. The restaurant had been restored to its pristine state after the fire and the staff was eager to serve our morning gustatory needs. Though we had eaten big meals the evening before everyone felt empty and was ready to start again — except for Yvonne and me — so we shared a huevos ranchero, over easy, and were entirely satisfied with half-portions or probably more accurately two thirds/one third portions.

Back at the Hacienda we assembled in the courtyard for our group picture, easily convincing Viola, Hacienda manager, to take the group's picture — the women seated and the men behind — as we'd done now 19 times, with the forsythia in the background, usually golden but now because Easter was so late, partly leafed out with the flowers long gone. More songs in our circle, "Go now in peace," and then hugs, the car loaded, and we were driving past the Santuario square, south toward Santa Fe and then to curve around to the east and then north, this route longer in miles than retracing our steps through Taos and San Luis and Fort Garland and Walsenburg to I-25 but faster because the speed limit was 75 instead of 60 and passing not the problem it would be on a two-lane road.

The pilgrims were still coming — perhaps because they weren't able to get off work on Friday — 300 on the High Road between Chimayo and the junction with Route 285 south of Espanola. All the vendors were gone and just a few porta-potties were awaiting pickup. These peregrinos would walk as we had walked when we did our first pilgrimage — thousands along the highway, on their own, without any of the comfort-making infrastructure provided free by volunteers that had begun appearing in earnest about 2003 — who knows why. Our circle route the day before had been bare-boat except for the final mile and a half and that was just fine.

187A: In the Hacienda courtyard - Dave, Dean, John, Alan, Sara, Ann, Barb, Yvonne, Tessa

Rather than go through downtown Santa Fe and out the Old Santa Fe Road to reach I-25, we took the Relief Route, a piece of beltway around the

One-hundred-eighty-seven: The Springs

western part of Santa Fe, going out of our way a few miles but not being caught by lights or traffic. Speeding east on I-25, we flew by the Clines Corner turnoff we'd taken the year before to visit Yvonne's high school friend Deb and her husband Bart who on retiring and at his insistence had fled Seattle's grey skies and drizzly rain for high desert New Mexico's bright sun and persistent drought. Surely New Mexico is one of the most beautiful habitable deserts on the planet and Santa Fe one of the most beautiful towns but for us it was too dry and too far from family.

Then on to Las Vega, NM to stop for gas and sandwiches to eat while hurtling north, the land east of the mountains flattening out until the ridge that divides Raton and New Mexico on the south from Trinidad and Colorado on the north came into view. Ann had explored this ridge and area years ago, finding tarantulas wherever she looked. I'd spent two weeks with the Boy Scouts, south and west of Raton, at Philmont in 1957 hiking and camping in the mountains that I'd come to love and that called me back in 1975 when I moved from Elgin, Illinois to Boulder, Colorado.

We had gotten a late start, a 9:30 departure had become 10:30 but by 3:30 we were pulling up in front of my sister Julie's house, she coming out to meet us and inviting us in for tea, with son Cooper, who had been busy in the house with clean up and painting projects.

Julie and Cooper, Yvonne and I then met my sister, Marcy, her husband Paul, her son Matt and his wife Lindsay — with Matt's children Aelias and Alana — and Julie's daughter Phoebe and her husband Alan at a new BJ's restaurant, a chain reaching out from California, a sophisticated machine with advertising playing all around the room on giant screens — a thoroughly different experience from what we'd just had in New Mexico — that satisfying and this a dadaist joke.

But it wasn't up to us. Aelias, age 12, was seated on my left and we talked about computers and operating systems; he was a fan of Linux and provided user support to other students in the computer lab in his middle school. Matt, seated on my right, and I talked about concepts of the multiverse, something with his math and computer background he found interesting. Seating and time made it impossible to talk with Phoebe who was intent on becoming pregnant and Alan, a Springs brewmaster.

187B: Colorado Springs - Phoebe, Yvonne, Lindsey, Matt, John, Aelias, Marcy, Cooper (by Paul McNeill)

    Then a cookie with a dab of vanilla ice cream and a lit candle on top appeared and it was my birthday — cards, a folding sack/backpack, a billed cap, and a picture of me, age two, sitting in my father's lap. As we left the restaurant, I used the snow brush provided by Advantage Rent A Car to sweep an inch of snow from the car, more snow coming thick and fast — springtime in the Rockies.

One-hundred-eighty-eight: Return

"Home is not where you live, but where they understand you." – Christian Morgenstern

Though more than an inch of snow had fallen, the roads were clear and only wet and we encountered little traffic driving north on I-25 up Monument Hill, past Greenland Ranch, and then Castle Rock, turning northeast to bypass most of Denver on our way to DIA. Denver had no snow but the sky was cloudy, the Front Range not visible. The Versa was nearly out of gas as we pulled into the filling station at the airport. We had used about 30 gallons and driven 882 miles, averaging less than 30 miles per gallon. I wasn't impressed. The airport was busy but not crowded on this Easter Sunday and we ate our lunches, chicken and noodles from Panda Express for Yvonne and a Quizno turkey sub for me. The Frontier flight to SeaTac was uneventful except for one substantial bump that the flight attendant near me reported was the result of crossing the contrail on another plane.

The rain in Seattle had stopped before we arrived, the streets drying out, and we walked across International Blvd to the Radisson to get our van — which had eight "parking tickets" on it, each demanding a $76 payment. The front desk attendant told me she would take care of the problem and we began our drive north to Burlington and Costco — which turned out to be closed — and then Taco Time for take-out dinner — which was closed. Crossing the twin bridges over the Swinomish Channel, we'd navigated years ago in the *Gumption*, our pocket trawler, we turned off the highway to buy gas at the tribal Chevron station — their discounted rate $3.85 per gallon. Gas would be well over $4.50 on Orcas now. A stop at Food Pavilion for some groceries and Subway for a sandwich for me and we were soon in line at the Anacortes Ferry Terminal reading the *Sunday Seattle Times*. The two sections of the Orcas Island Food Bank building were scheduled to board the ferry mid week and be installed on their site next to the Community Church in Eastsound the middle of the coming week. Yvonne would take pictures for the Food Bank website and a reporter from the *Islands' Sounder* was expected to be on hand.

188: 2003: Going south from Anacortes, approaching Twin Bridges in Gumption

Initially almost empty, the two lanes devoted to Orcas began to fill up and when the *Chelan* departed at 6:25 perhaps 60 cars were waiting to board for Shaw and Orcas. Arriving on Orcas at 7:30, a gentle rain was falling intermittently from a dark sky. While we were gone, the deciduous trees had leafed half out, the tulips had flowered, and many of the rhododendrons were covered with blossoms. Back at the marina with Crane dimly visible across Pole Pass, we walked down the ramp, the dock cart full, Yvonne wheeling the two suitcases, greeted by the overpowering fragrance of flowering Madrona and

One-hundred-eighty-eight: Return

we knew we were nearly home. The water was calm except for a small wake coming into the little marina from a boat now long gone. Unbuttoning, unzipping, and unbungying Margaret's boat, we loaded it with our travel gear and new groceries and made the ten minute trip through Pole Pass to the Crane Island Association community dock. We'd seen Jim and Nancy's boat on the Orcas side though their van was still in the lot. Perhaps Jim and Nancy were having dinner with Steve and Pam, at their house above. On the Crane side Lou's boat was parked on the west leg of the dock, something he was beginning to do though I couldn't understand why and Cabot's *Kelper* was right behind it, so we had to park farther from shore than we normally did.

Apparently there had been little rain while we were gone because the path across Och's meadow had dried out, no longer muddy with water from the field uphill from it draining down. Yvonne turned the hot tub up to 103 and I turned on the water, propane, unlocked the remaining doors, and turned off the "hold" on the seven thermostats, and the house, now at about 58 degrees began to warm up. Yvonne watched the first installment in a series on the Kennedys while I sat next to her reading Alexander Waugh's *The House of Wittgenstein: A Family at War* that I had picked from the sale table at the Elliot Bay Bookstore in Seattle the Saturday before. Then to the 103 degree hot tub and bed, Yvonne halfway through a history of the Mabel Dodge Luhan House and me finishing my second reading of Bering's *The Belief Instinct* in preparation for the talk I would give to the UU group in two weeks. We had had a wonderful trip but were very happy to be home. We both had a great deal to do in the coming week.

One-hundred-eighty-nine: Happy Birthday to Me

"Grow old along with me! The best is yet to be." – Robert Browning

The rain lasted all morning, by noon had stopped, and the evening was clear, a not uncommon pattern for Crane Island in the spring. James called twice during the day, the second time to officially wish me a happy birthday. He and Keith had just set up an elevated platform for the kittens and he had baked baklava for the first time. Jen and Corrina called later, laughing and giggling, Corrina explaining that she and Kelly would be coming up to Crane for the weekend. Noah and family and then Eric and family each called when I was talking to James, leaving a voice mail of them singing happy birthday. Yvonne made my favorite — spaghetti — for dinner — with carrots, salad, and a baguette — with a very chocolate bundt cake for dessert. Ann had left a birthday message and Barb an email. A very nice 68th birthday.

Right after lunch Yvonne dropped me at the West Sound Marina so that I could pick up the *Huginn*. Ian was coming back from lunch, a mug of coffee in his left hand, and we talked briefly about what he found with the boat — basically nothing. It was in good shape. They didn't have time to patch the fiberglass and gel coat on the starboard aft swim platform corner; I would do that when the weather warmed up and dried out. Betsy had ordered and received the waxed twine Yvonne was looking for. The *Huginn* was parked right below the raised deck working area accessible by walking along tippy dock sections and I made a special effort not to fall into the water. The boat was hemmed in by other boats and dock so I made a special effort not to crash into anything as I backed out and turned around to go to the fuel dock to buy the ration specified by Yvonne, our comptroller. At $4.70 per gallon I limited myself to 15 gallons, after which the fuel gage still didn't read half full. They addressed the sticky idle — it didn't always drop when it should have — by tightening the throttle — changing its feel and my ability to subtly adjust it.

The pressure washing, bottom painting, zinc changing, and fluid changing and topping up had cost less than $700, one of our lowest boat repair charges ever — not even one full boat unit. Accelerating away from the fuel dock I was back at the Crane Island community dock in 20 minutes, experimenting with the outdrive trim adjustment — finally understanding, I hoped, the relationship between the position of the outdrive — close to or far from the transom — and how the boat behaved in the water. Close to — brought the bow down and was more stable. Farther away brought the bow up a bit with less drag on the hull — or so it seemed to me.

189: 2003: LaConner for lunch

With our self-imposed publishing deadline for *The eNotated Metamorphosis* approaching, I had invited Chris over to discuss our status and consider next steps and picked him up at the Orcas dock about 2:30. Lynn had finished proofreading Jens annotations and supplementary pages, not finding much but noting some expressions that felt more German than English in their construction. We talked about the image permissions situation and then about the cover, using Google image search to see what others had done over the years. We were stumped. I sent Jens an email asking if we could visit with him the next day to cover these items as well as provide Chris an opportunity to take some pictures and video. He could and we would.

After dinner, Yvonne reminded me that I had asked her whether she'd like to go for a walk around Crane later and now that it was later she would. The flowering current next to the hot tub was 80% leafed out and the ocean spray had turned green in our absence. A raven perched in a tree over Yvonne's compost bins looking for anything interesting and not seeing promise flew north toward Orcas. I'd seen Gary at the dock midday on his way to Jones Island, a state park where he was responsible for the water system and he said that he'd finished his work at well house #4, not by repairing the leak — which he couldn't find but by laying new pipe from the main. The system was now tighter than it had been in some time and he'd had to turn off the pumps to prevent the tank from spilling over. As Yvonne and I passed the tank, I noted that its level was 13 1/2 feet, just shy of the overflow mark. Six deer looked at us from inside the fence in the Becker's pasture and then bounced away to the east and into Steve's woods. I heard what sounded like an osprey and Yvonne though she saw movement in the nest. A chick or two? The maples were in full flower as were the madronas — which also seemed to be suffering a blight. Many madronas had brown and grey lower leaves that didn't look like the normal early summer pattern of new leaves forcing off old ones and she'd found discussion on the internet of a blight apparently connected with the prolonged winter's cold. Along the way Yvonne shared what she was learning about the Mabel Dodge Luhan House and Dennis Hopper's tenure as owner in the 70s. The house was a touchstone of American artists culture for the last 90 years. A deer on the airstrip. Josh and someone else were at Ilze's house — having carried over sheets of plywood earlier in the day by fishing boat from the Orcas dock — a lot of work. A scent of methane, as usual, from the area below the earthen dike that formed one side of the pond behind the Och's house. Four deer, two yearlings, watched us cross the Och's meadow to home.

Earlier in the day, returning from Orcas after taking Chris back, walking along the Crane dock and then up the ramp, across the parking lot, through

One-hundred-eighty-nine: Happy Birthday to Me

the split rail fence and then on the path to our house, I was filled to overflowing, something that happened not infrequently with what I can only describe as a feeling of love — for a place — understanding what people sometimes talk about but which I hadn't before known. It's real.

One-hundred-ninety: Orcas Heights

"The best view comes after the hardest climb." - Unknown

I left the house just after noon and as I docked at Orcas was greeted by Jan and then Dan, coming to Crane for the rest of the week, with their son, daughter-in-law, and two grandchildren, clearly very happy at the prospect of spending time on the island on this very sunny, warming day — that had defied the weatherman's predictions of rain. I asked Dan whether anything interesting had happened at the Saturday Board meeting I'd missed while in New Mexico. No — but he had written and Martha had distributed to the membership a recounting of the unattended burn pile Yvonne and I had come upon in March, how Tom and Liz had brought the fire engine, the property owner's caretaker who had come from Orcas in the dark to help, and the attendance of two carpenters who had been working at a house nearby — and the problems we'd had getting the pumper to pump. Dan wanted to use the story to prompt members to pay more attention to fire and safety issues and to sign up for first aid and fire engine training classes — to overcome a casualness or lassitude that didn't well serve the island. Then I was off to the Deer Harbor Post Office, flowers there and across Jack and Jill Lane, at the Resort, where they were in great abundance (especially bright colored tulips) to drop off and pick up, and then on to Chris' to see whether he wanted a ride to the other side of Orcas — but he'd need to drive separately in order to do a multitude of errands. At the Eastsound airport I dropped off a return shipment at the UPS agent's site and then stopped at the Eastsound Post Office to mail a CD of Chimayo photos to Alan and Tessa — since they had forgotten to bring their camera and had only the use of a pre-digital disposable camera they'd bought on their way down to Chimayo.

One-hundred-ninety: Orcas Heights

190: Piling at dawn

One-hundred-ninety: Orcas Heights

Orcas Highlands is a housing development on the east side of East Sound (the fjord), a few miles south of Eastsound (the village), on the west flank of Mt Constitution, a 2400' mountain mostly contained in Moran State Park. In 2008 Jens found out about Orcas Island from a magazine article and then he and Susan visited Orcas and bought a home they were now occupying during his sabbatical from teaching at Wellesley, while she continued her web work. So far he was happy with Orcas but Susan had found the lack of sun over the winter problematic. Chris and I were visiting Jens today to go over details for *The eNotated Metamorphosis*, Kafka's striking "little story" Jens was annotating and which we expected to publish in the next few weeks.

Our house is right on the water with views to the east. Jens and Susan live at about 800 feet above sea level with views to the north and west, of Orcas Island, Waldron and then Saturna behind it (in Canada) and Point Roberts and perhaps even Vancouver far to the north, Stuart Island, Jones Island, San Juan Island to the west, with Vancouver Island far to the west. Because Orcas has so much coast line and so much vertical relief, many properties have outstanding views of one sort or another.

Jens and Susan had brought their love bird, Walter, an affectionate mini-parrot, cross country when they drove from Massachusetts in January after Jens finished fall semester and today he perched on Chris's shoulder, the tallest shoulder in the room until Susan picked him up on her finger and put him in the bathroom.

Lynn had proofread Jens' notes and essays and I'd added comments from David. Jens would add his own markup and either make changes to a text file I'd given him that I could import back into the database or hand me back the 100 paper passages with his instructions about what to change and what to leave as is. We talked about image permissions and then looked at cover designs. Because Chris and I had spent more than a hour the day before scouring the web for design ideas without finding anything we were taken by, we had fallen back on the quick layout I had done more than a month before that used the cover of the 1916 edition as a graphic on our cover, Chris having added embellishments to what I'd done. Jens didn't feel qualified to recommend one of the half-dozen versions over another and so called in Susan who after a period of discussion suggested the design be kept simple, our new text kept clearly separate from the text of the cover original and that cover background color have more contrast with the color of the original.

One-hundred-ninety: Orcas Heights

Back home I put on my work clothes, in this case nearly rags, and with the dock cart moved log sections from the driveway where they'd lain for several weeks after Yvonne and I had brought down 10 trees, to the firewood area outside the fence of the decorative garden on the north side of the house. Five cart loads — or two and a half weeks of firewood, once it was split and dried out. A number of trunks, mostly thin that we might want to use for the Borgfest — our name for our family gatherings — treehouse project remained — to be moved another time. I wouldn't know for sure until I'd split the wood piled in the firewood area but with the trunks that had escaped from a log boom and which I cut and moved from the community beach, the three trees Tim had cut down and moved to the front, and these recent additions, we might now have seven weeks of potential firewood — out of the 28 or 30 we needed for the next winter. More collecting would probably have to wait on having our pickup on the island to carry cutup deadfalls back to our lot.

One-hundred-ninety-one: Loss, gain, change

"Loss is not the end, but the beginning of a new chapter." - C.S. Lewis

The buffleheads and mergansers were gone; at least I no loner saw them every morning on either side of the community dock, the former to the left and latter to the right. Perhaps they were following the warming temperatures and strengthening sun to the north. Light from the morning sun, below the horizon, was now visible well before 5:00 and lingered in the evening at least until 9:30.

I'd missed the Greybeards the week before because we had been traveling and I was eager to share a cup of tea in Howard's "honeymoon cottage," our clubhouse, I suppose ("No girls allowed"), to listen and share. Brian took the floor today — deliberately and with aforethought. He wanted to talk about loss and he handed Howard a steno pad to use to record any suggestions we might have. A few weeks before, induced by his Parkinson's Disease medications or the medications that were intended to deal with unwanted side effects, he had fallen asleep at the wheel of his Volvo and driven it into a ditch, totaling it. His medications caused narcolepsy. His daughter, Dawn, concerned that he would hurt himself or others, had gotten him to agree that he wouldn't drive beyond Deer Harbor, certainly not to Eastsound, ten miles away, but Brian had physical therapy sessions twice weekly in Eastsound and needed to shop for groceries. How would he get back and forth from town? He'd made the cabin next to his house available gratis to a young women who agreed to help him from time to time but after the first four-hour trip back and forth to town made excuses about doing it again and clearly wasn't a reliable source of help. He had a hard time walking, his back bent forward and he moved very slowly, this morning telling us that even when allowing extra time, his slowness was making him late. He could no longer write though he could make out with a keyboard. He was very unhappy. He had lost much of his physical mobility and now was losing his mechanical mobility. Howard had spent time with him the previous day, responding to a sense that Brian was very depressed and discouraged. Brian was looking for suggestions — it seemed to me both practical and emotional/spiritual.

191: Food Bank back half ready to roll

Regarding the first category we suggested he change his "cabin for indefinite services" to cash in both directions. She should pay for the space; he should pay her or someone else for helping him with errands. Second, he should contact "Hearts and Hands," the local volunteer service. Third he could talk to Jim Allen, who, with MS, has even more severe problems getting to town; perhaps Jim and Brian could share the expense. I told Brian I would be happy to be his driver once a month. Finally, Taylor, a high school student, a few doors south of Brian, was looking for ways to earn some money. Regarding the second category we pointed out that we were all losing — everyday; it was everyone's lot, though we admitted that his losses were more dramatic than ours — at least for now. I talked about Yvonne's observations — coming from years as an activities director at a senior residence — that diminished lives are still full lives — even if that isn't evident to the oblivious. And then we talked about how Bob Harris, initially so unhappy being in a nursing home had accepted it and was making a life that had friends and satisfactions. At the start of our session Brian was teary; at the end, I think, determined to cope. What's the alternative, after all?

Yvonne had errands to run in Eastsound — and the first half of the new Food Bank building was due to arrive at its site by about 4:00 — which she wanted to see. Jens announced in an email that he had finished his review of Lynn's proofreading of his annotations and essays and wanted to get together, so Yvonne and I headed for town after lunch and after I'd had time to open the donation envelops for the Pole Pass No Wake Zone committee (for which I acted as treasurer), write thank you notes, and let the other committee members know where we stood; we'd have about $3500 to spend this spring on maintaining existing buoys and adding new ones. Yvonne dropped me at Keybank and went on to the Islanders' Bank and then I walked the two blocks to the Post Office and then to meet Jens at Enzo's coffee shop in a pouring rain. Jen's had the manuscript — with Lynn's comments as well as his own and we went through them one by one; I'd make the changes to the database the next day. We talked about the faculty book "show" at Wellesley the next week and how to be ready for it and Kafka and Kafka scholarship and then he dropped me at the Community Church where Yvonne soon appeared and a crowd was gathering to greet the new Food Bank building. And then it appeared, roof first, coming up the Main Street hill by the bank and then turning left on Madrona Street, pulling into the church parking lot. Larry, Food Bank Board President, in a short sleeved shirt in the rain, as usual, and Joyce under an umbrella in a well-cut long wool coat, appeared and watched. George, standing on a truck, talked to the driver and crew and I stood close by to listen. They'd park the first half across the lot, parallel to but 50 feet from where it would be placed, then come back in the morning, put rollers under it and

One-hundred-ninety-one: Loss, gain, change

roll it sideways into the site that had been prepared for it. The second, front half of the building would appear about 4:00 the next day. By Saturday morning the building would be on the site, the two halves joined, ready to receive power, water, and phone connections. What fun!

One-hundred-ninety-two: Too Cold, Too Long

"Nature does not hurry, yet everything is accomplished." - Lao Tzu

Martha's first round of cross connection survey mailings had yielded about a 50% return. I wrote to tell her how we'd fared so far and she responded saying that she'd do a followup — and then at some point I will have to begin calling Crane Island Association members. In order to protect public water supplies, Washington State, and probably every other state, has regulations that require potentially contaminating sources to be separated from a shared system by devices that prevent the reverse flow of water. Because I was the Crane Island water czar it was up to me to move the Board and members through a process to establish a cross connect (backflow) policy consistent with Department of Health requirements, then find out which members had at-risk systems through a survey, and then monitor their bringing their personal water systems into conformance with the Association policy. We were in the survey or fact-finding stage.

About the time Yvonne left for Eastsound and Rock & Roll choir practice, I set off for a walk around the island, finding, as I expected, little activity. The tank level had fallen at bit to just under 13 feet, not surprising since Gary said he had curtailed all pumping for now. Dan, who I hadn't seen directly but whose boat and car movements suggested that he had been repeatedly on and off the island, was probably at work on a project in his wood shop. As I walked along Circle Road and approached his driveway, a boat trailer parked perpetually on the west side, I heard the sounds of what I took to be an osprey — large fishing birds, constituting their own genus, with four talons, two opposing the other two, that facilitate pulling fish from the water and holding them securely until arriving at a nest or some other preferred dining location. I couldn't see movement from the three foot wide nest at the very top of a 60

One-hundred-ninety-two: Too Cold, Too Long

or 70 foot tall tree but I could see it, with the tree, rock back and forth in the southeast breeze.

I turned into Jason's driveway hoping to drop off checks from the association bookkeeper he needed to countersign so that I could send them out. He and his family were on the island — but not as it turned out at home — just their golden retriever puppy, now nearly full sized, a replacement for their older version who had died and left them bereft. I called out, in case they were inside, but received no reply but that was enough to trouble the dog who started to bark and otherwise act protectively of the grounds though at the same time acting a bit embarrassed — wanting on the one hand to be friendly and on the other proprietary. I decided not to climb the stairs to the deck and search for a place to leave the checks and their mailing envelopes. Next door I could see the lights on in Dan and Jan's cabin, though no sign of the six of them — with son and family, probably, like Jason, taking advantage of spring vacation. No activity at Ilze's construction site — Josh probably already having returned to Seattle for the weekend.

The day before Yvonne had constructed an elaborate pole bean support structure from her supply of bamboo, a good deal remaining from her garden gate project of three years before. She'd been preparing the soil, having applied manure to the raised beds, flies appearing almost immediately (where did they come from?) but the soil was still too cold for seed planting — that demanded at least 50 degree soil temperature and in this very cool, slow spring, the soil fell short. Inside, in the studio, next to the french doors leading to the deck, she was growing seedlings that she would transplant once the outside world was adequately welcoming to the small plants. I'd seen onion sets in Howard's garden the day before, about a foot high, and their very thin brown, dried tips, didn't look encouraging to me, though what do I know about gardens?

Returning from town and choir practice in the fading light, Yvonne reported that the back section of the new Food Bank building had been rolled to its location and was waiting for the front section, to be delivered late in the afternoon, the two sections to be bound together by Saturday morning. I wanted to know how the sections were rolled — especially across the excavation that contained what looked like footings for the front half on the building. She had left me a pot of pea soup to heat up for dinner, with explicit instructions not to let it boil and she'd left a salad in the refrigerator for me to add the dressing of my choice to, needing only a piece of toast to make my meal complete. I ate while watching video of the devastation tornados had wrought across the South, grateful, perhaps smug, that Crane Island wouldn't suffer that way or by tsunami or by hurricane or excess heat or cold or probably from earthquake — but we could still complain — the drawn out spring was too cold, too long.

192: Food Bank front half being delivered

After spending the day applying the corrections Jens' and Lynn's note called for to the *Metamorphosis* database, editing two images, and making minor changes to the software, I built a new version of *The eNotated Metamorphosis*, this one, it turned out, as I inspected it via Kindle software on my Averatec Windows notebook, my MacBook Pro, my Kindle, my iPod, and Yvonne's

One-hundred-ninety-two: Too Cold, Too Long

iPad, to be a strong candidate for publication. After installing the latest iOS Kindle software, and in the case of the iPod bringing iOS up to date, image expanding worked perfectly. The book looked good cosmetically, it all seemed to operate correctly, and I'd made improvements suggested by Jens, Chris, and David. This would be our first complex publication using organizational and presentation standards evolved especially from the suggestions Jens and Susan made to the too wonderful internal linking complexity I'd elaborated beyond any normal person's ability to understand.

At 6:00 I called my sister, Julie, to wish her a happy birthday. Her daughter, Phoebe and son, Cooper were making dinner, and ex-husband, Karl had come over for the occasion, and Alan was expected. I'd been thinking of things I could do to help Julie see the economic consequences of various choices she might make, especially regarding housing. Did she want more information? Yes, it was very helpful. She added that she was beginning to let herself see the advantages of living in a smaller, newer house, rather than focus on the sense of loss associated with the thought of leaving the house she'd raised her two children in as a single mom.

At Howard's the day before I'd questioned him about his new ductless heat pump system and talked to his Mt Vernon-based salesman about it. A Fujitsu, it would work efficiently to 17 degrees and below, something I thought wasn't possible but which Chris assured me was — with Asian, rather than American technology. How can that be? With OPALCO's subsidy and a tax credit, a system that would fit our needs would cost, installed, a bit more than $4000, including tax. Compared with baseboard heating, the system would be only a third as costly to run — it was so efficient. If we heated strictly with baseboard heat and assuming a kilowatt hour rate of $.075, our seasonal heating bill might be about $2000 — a bit more than what Howard would be paying for his oil stove with $4/gal prices — but the last two winters much of our heat had come from wood — our heating cost closer to $750 for baseboard as a supplement. That meant, assuming we continued to use wood, the heat pump system would probably take eight or ten years to pay for itself. On the other hand, if we didn't use wood, it might pay for itself in three years. Am I going to continue to cut and split wood now that I've begun my 69th year?

One-hundred-ninety-three: Spring Dump Run

"What is a weed? A plant whose virtues have not yet been discovered." - Ralph Waldo Emerson

A sunny day, not warm but not cold either. About ten logs were still lying in the driveway where I'd left them weeks before. I'd cut up the heavier logs in 16" sections and moved them to the firewood area outside the front garden fence. Son Eric had suggested we could use logs for poles and the poles for something or other relating to the treehouse project when we all convened on Crane for Borgfest 2011 in late July, so I wanted to keep some of the more promising 20' logs whole. Yvonne and I carried all but two through the south gate, around the west side of the house and then out the northwest gate, laying the trunks-to-be-poles-perhaps wedged between two small firs behind the main wood pile. The last two trunks were too heavy for Yvonne to carry the light end. At my end, the bottom of the tree, the logs were about 8" in diameter, probably too large to use as poles for the treehouse project, so I got my chainsaw, filled it with gas and chain oil and cut the two trunks into 16" (more or less) sections, stacked them in the dock cart, and in two loads moved them to the firewood area out front, the driveway now clear of tree trunks but covered with sawdust.

When cleaning up the yard I'd collected several small trunks and large branches lying on the ground and useless as firewood. Yvonne and I moved two trunks to the path above our cove and laid them on the sides of the path to mark it and laid the branches on the "to be chipped" pile to be processed later.

I put the mountain bike grandson Morgan had used when visiting back in the storage tent, noting that mink had gotten in again but from the looks of what they left and the lack of strong odor, it must have been some time ago. Not a call for immediate action. But the old dishwasher was still leaning

One-hundred-ninety-three: Spring Dump Run

against a tree next to the ex-outhouse we used to store trash and recycle until we could dispose of it and next to the dishwasher leaning against another tree (we have no shortage of trees) was scraps of plywood and other debris left over from the demolition of the old kitchen counter. And the "outhouse" storage was filled almost to capacity. With house guests coming the next day and dinner guests the next week, maybe it was a good time to finish the kitchen remodel by finally taking the leftovers to the dump.

Right after lunch Yvonne left for her Friday afternoon knitting group at the Deer Harbor Community Club — today, it turned out Bev and Pam the only other attendees. Yvonne, the grounds committee chair, had asked me earlier in the day how often the lawn and rest of the grounds should be cut and trimmed with a weed whacker. Hard to say. Certainly a week before the rummage sale and several times before that so shoppers looking at items for sale on the lawn out front of the 106 year old building don't have to wade through piles of cut grass. May is the time for rapid growth in the islands, and everywhere grass that was green all winter but relatively dormant was energized, growing a measurable quarter inch a day. By July when the rains cease for two or three months the grass has become dormant again, now not from two little warmth but too little water.

I began the dump run process about 1:20 and was back home about 4:20, the round trip process requiring three hours. First I had to move everything I intended to dispose of to the *Huginn* (Yvonne had used Margaret's boat to go to Orcas) and that required four dock cart loads to be transferred to the *Huginn*'s cockpit — four trash cans (two with recycle), a big black plastic bag (I would bring home for reuse) with recycle, a dishwasher (without a door), a non-operating microwave, a non-operating shredder, and about 100 pounds of plywood and other remodeling trash. At the Orcas dock I retrieved the dock cart from its place beneath the association storage shed where some members store their small outboards and other boating paraphernalia and to which the UPS/FEDX receiving shed is attached, loaded, and then dragged four cartloads up to the parking lot. It was heavy going though as Theresa said as she watched me with Jason and their two kids from the dock — where they'd met another couple whose kids I guessed had been over to Crane and Jason and Theresa's cabin. At least the tide wasn't very far out, that is, the ramp could have been much steeper than it was.

One-hundred-ninety-three: Spring Dump Run

Panting, panting, I walked up to the upper lot above Deer Harbor Road, unlocked the F-150, popped the hood, closed the battery switch, closed the hood, got in and once on Deer Harbor Road backed the truck down the driveway to the bottom of the lower lot and began to load the bed of the truck with what I'd moved by cart, by boat, by cart, filling the bed of the truck and then securing it all with a bungee cord web. During the process, I noticed a very large, very stout spider waiting on the side of one of the trash cans, having made its living in the former privy where the cans are stored presumably by preying on the small flies that generate spontaneously from the food waste unfit for the compost pile that makes its way from the kitchen. I flicked the spider into the bed of the truck. I'd seen another when loading the cans into the cart from the privy.

Jan, who was on Crane for part of the week with Dan, a son, daughter-in-law, and two grandkids, pulled into the lot in her RAV4 and parked without me having to move my pickup. How did she like her RAV4? A lot. Mileage? 26. Hmmm. In another 15 minutes I pulled into the San Juan County Solid Waste Transfer Station and waited briefly in line to talk to the attendant. The dish washer would cost $22 to dispose of and I'd need to leave it with the other appliances on the far side of the dumping building and needed to do that before going over the scale.

As I approached the transfer building a raven flew out holding a tasty morsel found somewhere inside. At least a dozen ravens called to one another from the trees surrounding the building, each in a different voice, perhaps talking about their findings instead and eager for the humans to leave the space to them. The dishwasher joined two water heaters and two electric ranges. Again driving around the scale I passed close to a big blue van containing treasures to be left at the Exchange, a second use, pay-what-you-think-is-right enterprise behind the transfer station. I saw Arthur, always dapper in a fine felt hat, mustache and goatee, helping the driver of the big blue van unload. Then onto the scale for a "before" measurement and then to transfer building for a dump-off. A blue, metal cube at least 40' on a side with a concrete floor, and a deep slot at the rear where a transfer trailer is kept, was busy with two pickups unloading to the floor and a yellow tractor using its scorpion tail-like shovel to pack trash in the trailer below, a huge pile of trash, mostly moldy white garbage bags, about 15' across and 8' high, waiting to be pushed from the floor into the trailer using the scoop at the other end of the

One-hundred-ninety-three: Spring Dump Run

tractor. Now four trucks, tightly packed, with the tractor still working in the rear, were unloading their stinky cargo, able to forget about what would be carried by ferry to the mainland and then dumped in a landfill in Skagit County.

193: Clearing the floor into a huge open trailer

Back at the attendant's station I began filling out a check to pay my fee — $92.50 — but that can't be right! It wasn't. I was being charged for leaving a refrigerator but I hadn't. The adjusted bill $60.50; $22 for the dishwasher, $5 to leave recycle (the County had recently begun charging for it — a necessity in trying to balance the budget), and the remainder for 200 pounds of trash. With trash fees going up and recycle fees now charged, Islanders were beginning to burn their trash and recycle again as they had before our enlightened times. And soon perhaps they'll take the next step and just dump it in the water, the standard practice a century ago.

Driving by the Resort at Deer Harbor I noticed that the steep hillside where years ago James had slipped and fallen, twisting his knee, while weed whacking, leading to a dishwashing job in the kitchen that made it clear to him what a good idea going to college would be, was suddenly covered with dandelions, more yellow in our green world since the daffodils, for the most part, were continuing to hold their own, a benefit of the lingering cool weather. Back on Crane, pushing the cart carrying four empty trash cans back to the old outhouse where they wouldn't be bothered by raccoons, I saw dandelions everywhere. Where had they been hiding, these harbingers of warming weather?

One-hundred-ninety-four: Meeting Ferry

"The greatest good you can do for another is not just to share your riches but to reveal to him his own." - Benjamin Disraeli

First I swept out the cockpit, dirty after the dump run the day before and then I sat in the late April sun on one of the two removable seats now mounted on the engine compartment cover in the *Huginn*'s cockpit reading the Saturday *Seattle Times*. On a day like this in 1997 Yvonne had called me, at home in Boulder, from the Orcas Hotel above, sitting with her friend Julie, sipping a latte and waiting for the tardy ferry, telling me she wanted to return, with me and James, from Boulder in the summer, to look at property. Now she was standing on the dock talking by cell phone to Corrina, who, dropping Kelly, nearly eight months pregnant, at the ferry terminal in Anacortes, couldn't find a parking place in the nearby lots and had to drive to the lots above that were nearly as filled. Now late, she had run, more or less, to the terminal building, her Mac computer bag flappy madly against her side, among the last to board, now couldn't understand why the ferry didn't leave, its departure time having arrived, even passed, so they'd be late, due, we found out later, to a medical emergency aboard the ferry. Flowers everywhere, cool delicious air, warmth radiating from above, a slight breeze, a sense of anticipation, the dock above peopled as it hadn't been for months. We weren't in a rush.

The *Huginn* was parked on the inside of the county dock, the Orcas Express whale watching boat on the outside, more exposed to the wakes of passing boats, having begun the 2011 season the weekend before after spending the winter idle in the Cayou Quay Marina in Deer Harbor. Dan, the boat's captain, told me their opening weekend had gone well but today's bookings would barely cover their direct costs: the boat burned two gallons of fuel per mile — now at $4.00 per gallon. The 2008 season had been terrible, 2009 better, and last year more or less normal. Two years before, at this dock, when I was to pick up son Noah, Natasha, Morgan, and Opal needed but didn't have life

One-hundred-ninety-four: Meeting the Ferry

jackets for the two kids, Dan had given me two old life jackets from the Orcas Express.

Yvonne, now also sitting in the sun reading the *Times* after having made a trip to the Market on the dock above for groceries for the weekend and a turkey and cheese sandwich for us to share to compensate for now not being able to get home at a reasonable time for lunch, was a bit startled, pointing out that the Coast Guard had just moored in front of the Orcas Express, having arrived without a sound, in my experience their modus operandi. Four crew members, three young men and one young woman, dressed in red and black jump suits, locked the door to their Defender, a 25' rubber-hulled boat with an aluminum cabin and powered by three 300 hp outboards, and walked along the dock up the ramp to the market to buy lunch. Their passenger, a woman in a green uniform with a Washington State Fish and Wildlife patch, stopped to talk with Dan about the three Orca pods that spent most of their time in the Salish Sea, the primary source of income for Dan and the justification for her job.

Dan and the State official discussed the local Orca whales: Ruffles, the 60 year-old member of J Pod, also known as J-1, father of members of J, K, and L Pods, and tourist favorite easily identifiable by his wavy, six foot dorsal fin, was still missing and presumed dead, having been last seen in November off Victoria. Granny, now aged 100, was still active in J-Pod and though females sometimes lived into their 90 (or above) males had much shorter lives, rarely living into their 60s. Dan said that an Orca mother's first calf usually dies because it is part of a process of flushing contaminants from the mother's body though succeeding calves do well.

Noisy crows perched on the roof peaks above the dock, greeting the *Evergreen State* inter-island ferry, on time but now ahead of the *Elwah*, 20 minutes late leaving Anacortes. A seagull paddled to the side of the Coast Guard boat looking for handouts. A sign on the shore above identified the OPALCO cable crossing to Shaw Island and a nearby sign described available kayak tours. One end of a 2 x 12 plank against which the *Huginn* was moored flapped as the dock oscillated in the wake of a long passed boat. Eel grass, crucial fish habitat, was visible fix feet below in the clear water. The Sheriff's department boat was parked 50 feet away on the other side of the tall pier our dock was attached to by an aluminum ramp. And then the *Elwah* was coming into the ferry dock and we walked up the ramp and then driveway in front of Russell's store to wait for Corrina and Kelly to come up the walkway from the ferry. Two lovely young woman, friends from high school, Corrina soon to go to Philadelphia for an MFA in studio art and Kelly, who appeared to be carrying a basketball under her coat due for delivery June 3rd and whose husband Tim was just arriving in Paris to meet with members of his Google team, spend a week planning, and then return, with Kelly and baby to return in August for a two-year tour of duty in the "City of Light."

194: Corrina, Kelly, Yvonne

Arriving on Crane, I saw Jason and his parents at the head of the dock, not having seen them since Yvonne and I, with Alan and Tessa, who were visiting, acted as first responders to a call for help at Jason's cabin, finding both

One-hundred-ninety-four: Meeting the Ferry

Jason and his father lying on the ground in pain, Jason having fallen off the red steel roof he was cleaning onto his father who was holding the ladder. The Friday Harbor Sheriff's boat arrived within 15 minutes with four EMTs aboard, treating both victims and finding, fortunately, that neither was in a condition serious enough to require airlifting though Jason's damage to his knee eventually required surgery. I had five checks I wanted Jason, as president of the island association, to sign so that I could put them in the mail and he followed me back to the house to do so. He reported that not much had happened at the Saturday Board meeting I had missed because Yvonne and I were in New Mexico and then Colorado that day.

Yvonne was giving Corrina a tour of the new kitchen, Corrina having helped at the onset of the project by providing advice on the countertop color when shopping with us a IKEA but then not seeing the final result because of her two month photography trip to India. Then without much effort we convinced the young women a walk around the island in the afternoon sunshine was in order. Not far from well house #4 where I explained the leak discovery and fix process we ran into Martha coming the other way and she handed me a check for the No Wake Zone fund and said she would put out reminders next week to members who had not responded to my cross connection survey. Further along Circle Road I pointed out the osprey nest and Corrina quickly saw two osprey on branches next to the nest, resting perhaps after having fed one or more chicks. Later as we turned and walked to the north end of the airstrip, one of the osprey flew a figure above us but below a turkey vulture that was riding afternoon updrafts, the osprey, large though smaller than an eagle, underwings with light leading and dark trailing markings, just the opposite of the turkey buzzard, and with distinctive dark splotches interrupting the light leading edge. We passed Dave's driveway with no sense that he was hosting 14 of his mens' group members from Bainbridge Island — who managed a burn pile, disposing of what seemed to me massive amounts of dead and cut branches in his effort to be fire-wise about his property, though when we were near home I thought I could smell and see smoke coming from the west.

Yvonne supplemented the leftover cauliflower soup and made more popovers and we lingered over dinner for two hours talking about Kelly's plans for baby and Paris and Corrina's for graduate school and the right man she had yet to find. They wanted to hear about my upcoming Unitarian talk and I obliged, first talking about why cosmologists no longer saw a role for a god of the gaps, primarily because of the explanatory power of the multi-verse. Both were comfortable with the idea of the multi-verse and surprised that I had encountered objections — from Ken because it seemed to abrogate his sense that the future wasn't determined and Alan because he wanted only one universe and it with a purpose. And then we talked about Jesse Bering's book, *The Belief Instinct* and the way human beings create a theory of mind about people in general and more complex versions for individuals — all of which make it possible to more accurately predict human action than is possible by just observing behavior and extrapolating — but which in turn leads to the over-application of theory of mind, or conscious purpose that knows the contents of our minds, acting sometimes consistent with our wishes and sometimes not, having another, hidden agenda, that we try to decipher by looking for clues in natural processes and events — like storms or earthquakes. The over application of theory of mind, to invisible entities, expresses itself in different ways through different cultures and contexts but is an illusion, though sometimes a useful and comforting one. I was surprised at the young woman's lack of challenge to this way of thinking, comfortable with the idea that neither the universe nor our lives have any objective purpose, only what we conjure or accept. It wasn't news to them, it wasn't depressing, and it didn't make either cynical about individual or community life. Their earnestness remained complete — in part, they thought, because neither overestimated the ability of language to tell the whole truth.

One-hundred-ninety-five: Jones Picnic

"Live in the sunshine, swim in the sea, drink the wild air." - Ralph Waldo Emerson

Somehow I managed to stay in bed until about 7:00 after being ready to embrace the day two hours earlier. The clear sky and the calm water looked like summer weather though the temperature was about 10 degrees cooler, a harbinger of days to come. Yvonne had prepared casserole French toast the night before and baked it after she got up a little after 8:00. After frying some turkey bacon and with the girls nowhere in sight, she decided it would be acceptable for us to begin eating and shortly they were at the dining room table and Yvonne was frying more bacon, thick, crisp strips and she had warmed maple syrup and put out preserves to spread on the two-inch thick French toast rectangle she cut and served us.

I'd finished the Chimayo web photo album the night before and uploaded it to our family website but Yvonne when trying to show Kelly the pictures found only a blank page with a three line description of the album so I repeated the process, now with success. I had suggested the day before we consider a Sunday picnic on nearby Jones Island and since the day was mild and sunny, everyone was enthusiastic about the idea. Yvonne and I hadn't been to Jones for three or four years mostly because when we boated we did so with bigger boats and longer distances in mind. Today we would use our 19' SeaSport, the *Huginn*. Neither Yvonne nor I could understand why we hadn't been to Jones, a Washington State Park, more frequently.

Yvonne gathered picnic lunch makings — bread, chicken salad, cheese, crackers, and Pellegrino water — and I carried it to the Crane community dock while the others decided what to wear for our boat trip and then hike. At the head of the dock I saw about a half-dozen swallows darting back and forth in the air in the cove that sheltered the marina. They had returned and I was happy to see them. As I stood still at the top of the ramp one circled me several times, close enough that I could study its markings, face, wings, and characteristic split tail. Indefatigable, the swallows cut though the air for hours seeking flying insects and though I wasn't aware of them they must have been around or the swallows would have remained farther south longer. At our house on Cayou Valley Road in Deer Harbor a nesting pair had created an elegant mud daub nest under the eves and close enough to a kitchen window that we could watch the whole process develop over weeks — of construction of the nest, the laying of the eggs, the feeding of the young and then the launching of the fledglings. We were happy to do our part — basically to watch and not interfere — but the process was messy and left stains under the nest and in its environs so when the pair tried to start another batch (they sometimes manage three fledges in a season), I discouraged them by removing the nest and then hanging a paper over the siding trim they found sufficient purchase on to build a nest. And when the couple returned the next late spring I again hung a paper bag. After all, they'd built nests in the rafters in the wood shed for years. Why couldn't they do so again?

The three women sat in the sun in the cockpit while we motored to Jones and I refrained from taking the boat up on plane because Yvonne liked the slower, quieter pace of moving along at about 6 knots instead of 21. We weren't in a hurry. We had all day — at least until 4:00 when I had scheduled a meeting of the No Wake Zone Committee to figure out what should be done in what sequence with the money that had been donated. After 30 minutes motoring by way of the Spring Point coast, around the southwest corner of Orcas and then into President Channel and across to Jones being very careful to stay north and east of the buoys that marked the reef just to the left of the cove on the north side of the island. At just before noon only two boats were moored at what looked like and turned out to be a brand new dock, wider than normal and with a longer, less steep ramp that was intended to make the island wheel-chair accessible. In 1998 in this cove, with our new MacGregor sailboat and a serious lack of judgment I'd come too close to a friend's sailboat, smacking my boat into his, nearly knocking all the passengers off their feet with the shock. No physical damage was done but my tender ego smarted for days as I struggled unsuccessfully to rationalize what I couldn't. Today, older and wiser, I made a soft landing at the dock, Yvonne and Corrina tied us up and we walked up the dock, the women heading to the nicely kept restroom, two sets on the island provided with wheelchair ramps. While I talked to the island caretaker intent on bringing the facilities up to spec for the beginning of the season, the women looked at the scores of downed trees, mostly Douglas firs that had been blown over in the big storm of 1992 that roared out of the Fraser south of Vancouver, BC, toppling hundreds of trees on Jones, Orcas, and the other San Juans, knocking over at least 150 on Crane Island, many narrowly missing landing on cars, houses, and the water tank though demolishing a few sheds. Some trees retained their root structures, not broken by the wind but actually pulled out of the ground, the shallow, extensive root structure, now at a 90 degree angle, were more than twelve feet high. A mighty storm, it had been.

    Our goal was to walk the trail on the west side of the island, a repeat for me of the southeast half I'd done with James and two of his high school friends who had come to visit eight years before. The quarter trail across the waist of the island to the south cove was covered in fine, well-smoothed gravel, now with three benches along the way for walkers needing a rest. Next to the orchard above the south beach the park service had built two Adirondack shelters, with a top and bottom bunk to the right and left inside the doorless opening, a dry place to sleep, with wild animals and cold temperatures never a problem on the 188 acre marine park island. Walking down the wooden steps to the south beach a father and son were enjoying the noonday sun, having camped on the east side of the cove. We went west looking for the trail and came out on a headland covered in grass shorn by the prevailing southwest winds to the height of a golf green. South of the grass were bare rocks and massive bare bleached arrow straight tree trunks were everywhere caught in the rocks or thrust high on the south and west beaches, some at least having escaped from passing log booms.

    The whole west side of the island along the path was open and sunny, the beach there 10 or 20 feet below. Two campsites were devoted to human powered beachable watercraft, that is, kayaks, and near one the sign on a fenced area explained that the Park service was attempting to restore Garry oak that had been decimated by the black tail deer that live on the island and swim back and forth to Orcas occasionally.

One-hundred-ninety-five: Jones Island Picnic

195: Kelly and Corrina on Jones Island

The path cuts back to the north cove midway around the west side but we carried on to the north end, darker and higher from the water, watching a fisherman drift his boat along the island in the strong currents casting for — I know not what — but enjoying himself. Back on the dock and around a picnic table we made ourselves sandwiches and I told stories about my boating stupidity in the bay around us, now with four boats hanging from mooring buoys, one boat with two commercial fishermen opening shells of some kind I thought. During one exciting day in the cove my sister Julie, holding the line of dingy away from the prop while I looked for a place to anchor had dropped it twice fouling the propeller, the incoming waves threatening to drive us into the rocks. We survived. Another slow trip back to Crane, the women out back in the sun, me in the cabin, at the wheel, experimenting with the GPS/depth gauge system I hadn't taken the time to master in the four years we'd had the boat. Back on Crane a walk across Och's meadow and home.

At 4:00 Jim and Martha came over for our No Wake Zone meeting and we established our project priorities for the summer season: assuming the donations we'd collected were adequate, we'd put two buoys on the west side of Pole Pass, bringing the total to three and add another on the east side, giving us a total of three there as well but because the area covered was longer we looked to put in more on the east side in the coming years. And then there was an email from Tom to Jason and to me: he was worried again about the rocks he was convinced Jim had been stealing for years from island common areas and he had found three new foreign objects in his truck tire and felt compelled to file a report with the authorities.

Kelly made us a lentil-tomato soup with an arugula salad for dinner and we spent the evening taking about each of the women's plans, about babies and child raising, about books and movies and a bit about the demise of Osama Bin Laden, the President had reported on and we watched until we had had enough, then looked at photos Corrina had taken in India in December and January when she lived there with a family, putting up with a young man who she came to realize was too immature for her to enjoy but with a mother she came to admire, making trips into the field to meet Indian women in the midsts of their lives on their terms, finding them patient, wise, and happy living in what we would consider a state of poverty and deprived of what we consider necessities but aren't. Eye opening; encouraging; raising questions about the intense materialistic and competitive orientation of her native land.

One-hundred-ninety-six: To the Ferry

"I haven't been everywhere, but it's on my list." - Susan Sontag

Corrina and Kelly made an appearance just before 9:00. I had gotten up early — before 5:00 — because I had so much to do and by 6:00 couldn't wait another minute for oatmeal, toast, and grapefruit juice. By 8:30 Yvonne had had her breakfast. The girls were on their own. We sat around the dining room table until almost 11:00 — until Yvonne checked the weekday ferry schedule: 12:10 and then not until 5:10, a four hour hiatus. To make the 12:10 we'd have to be out the door before 11:30; not much time to shower and pack.

Our discussion had returned to Corrina in India, what she'd brought back and what she was going to do with it and Kelly in Paris, how she'd spend her time and what not to miss. In her two months in India, Corrina had traveled all over southern India, with her camera, computer, and journal, talking everywhere she went with women of all ages, especially those she thought were especially strong or creative, and mostly with lower and middle class looking to see how they chose to be feminists of some kind — or maybe not. For Corrina, in the United State at least, being a feminist meant trying to be like and compete with men, to have equal pay doing the same job men do, wearing a suit to work, focusing on a career. None of that appealed to Corrina. What she found in India was women dressed like women, especially in colorful saris, creating small businesses if that's what they wanted to do, wearing dresses or saris to work, not suits, fostering cooperation and caring rather than competition and selfishness; Indian women were not confined to traditional roles but were defining the way they occupied new roles rather than imitating men.

One-hundred-ninety-six: To the Ferry

196: Gander, goose, and four goslings (May 2010)

What would she do with the thousands of pictures she'd taken and the pages and pages of notes she'd made? I saw a book. She wasn't sure. She wasn't confident anyone would be interested in what she had to say or what she had to show. In India she'd met and become friends with a younger American woman who had married early, become frustrated, gotten divorced, and was now supporting herself by writing — scripts for television shows for instance, and had no interest at the moment in returning to the States. As Corrina described this young woman we both heard a story that sounded like Elizabeth Gilbert, of *Eat, Pray, Love* fame.

And then it was time to leave and I carried Kelly's suitcase to the dock in the pouring rain, the young women following a few minutes later. As I backed away from the Crane dock and turned the *Huginn* around to go out to and then through Pole Pass, I noticed two Canada geese in the middle of the channel not budging as I came closer — and then I saw two very small yellow blobs paddling furiously to keep up with mom and dad, fluffy goslings that couldn't have been more than a few days old. Last year the nesting pair had hatched six and the little ones disappeared one by one, the parents moving to other quarters before they were all gone. What a hard life. With the *Huginn* in gear but at idle I gave the geese as wide a berth as I dared; the tide was out and a nasty reef extended from the rock at the south side of the pass only a few feet below the water but now visible. Because I wanted to stop at the Post Office (on my way back), we moored the *Huginn* at the Crane dock on Orcas and walked up the ramp, in the rain, to take the van to Orcas Landing. Standing next to the open UPS locker in his head to toe yellow rain outfit was Tom — waiting for the Sheriff's deputy he explained — to make a report about the nine holes that had appeared in his pickup tires over a period of several years; sometimes in a front tire, sometimes in a rear tire, sometimes caused by a screw, or nail, or staple. We'd had two flat tires from what we'd picked up in the lot but Tom was convinced that in his case the damage had been caused intentionally and he'd had enough; he was going to the authorities about the matter. He apologized for causing trouble, for sending Jason and me emails on the topic and I acknowledged his need to seek help. As we drove out of the lot the deputy was coming in and when I returned to Deer Harbor a half hour later the deputy was driving north out of Deer Harbor. Tom had made his report.

The afternoon turned sunny and the rest of the day was mild. The sugar ants had returned to the kitchen counter and Yvonne cleared it and then put dollops of ant poison on scraps of paper and they came in droves, thousands, quickly devouring the poison and we hoped had taken it back to the nest to feed others, including the queen. The ants had also occupied my favorite chair next to the wood stove and I'd find them crawling on the arms of the chair, my MacBook Pro, or my hands.

Eric had posted photos from Jackson's sixth birthday party, a scene we'd been part of several times before. Maddie had a huge chocolate-covered strawberry in her mouth; Jackson's cake was covered with four Star Wars characters (I think). After dinner, Yvonne and I nearly finishing up Kelly's tomato-lentil soup, I called Noah, talking first with Natasha about her weekend — Sunday had been warm and beautiful and she and Morgan had gone fishing off the dock at the nearby state park and then she passed the phone to

One-hundred-ninety-six: To the Ferry

Opal who described her weekend breakthrough — she was now riding her big-girl bike — without training wheels. I congratulated her but didn't tell her that when I learned to ride I didn't have training wheels and just crashed the bike time after time until I got the hang of it. Noah had worked from home Friday because the kids had both come down with bad colds and Natasha had promised to cook omelets at their primary school — I didn't catch why. In order to deal with it's revenue shortfall for the coming year, the Olympia School District had announced that it would cut 10% of its teaching positions, increase class sizes, and drop courses from its curriculum. Heavily dependent on state revenue and given that Washington state was dealing with a nearly $5 billion revenue shortfall, all the public schools in Washington Sate would be affected, as well as all other public services. The ripple effect of the job loses yet to come in Washington and other states would result in private sector job loses as well. Daughter Jeni was in Pittsburgh for her friend, Adrienna's masters program graduation and among other sights they saw Frank Lloyd Wright's Falling Water House. James and partner Keith had been to a baseball game and then bought a new television — but wouldn't subscribe to cable — and instead capture the Los Angles broadcast signal.

One-hundred-ninety-seven: Fixing

"It's not about how to fix the problem, it's about how to fix the thinking that created the problem." - Stephen Covey

Having received the April water usage spreadsheet from Gary I posted the totals by meter to my month-by-month, year-to-date spreadsheet and sent it off to Martha for distribution to Crane Island Association members, The idea was to let them track their usage during the year so they could adjust their behavior (or that of guests and grown children who used the house). Since conservation of the island water supply is so important — over-drawing could cause saltwater intrusion and ruin a well — the Board doesn't want members to use excessive amounts of water (over 100 gallons per day) even if they're willing to pay higher rates ($.03 per gallon to 3000 gallons in a month, $.05 per gallon from 3000 to 4500 gallons and $.10 per gallon over 4500 gallons), so distributing a members usage report provides peer pressure where an added expense might not. Though I can't say definitively, anecdotal evidence suggests the strategy works. Shortly after Martha distributed the report to the membership, John M. called, saying that he and his wife hadn't been on Crane for more than a year (illness) but that April usage showed almost 600 gallons after months of zero usage. Yes, his son had been on the island briefly but something may be wrong — he may have a leak — and would I stop by his house and look to see if the meter is running? Yes — I'd check the meter but it was likely his son had used the water and nothing was wrong (other than — and I did not say this — he used a great deal of water in a very short time). Because I usually don't read meters (Wilma usually does) it took me a while to find John's meter. As I approached his driveway I could see Lou with his walking stick walking back toward his house after his morning walk with Rollie. Since he was 50 yards away I didn't want to break his reverie by calling to him and went on with my meter reading task. I'd written down the last reading from two days before — and the meter hadn't changed — but the valve in front of the meter had been left open — not a good idea since a leak in John's system would draw water through the meter and cost him $1000 or more — what had happened to more than one member who had neglected to turn off their water before leaving the island. Back home I emailed John my findings and he wrote back to thank me and assured me that his son had turned off the water at the house, though may have forgotten to turn it off at the road.

The tank level was at 12' and passing near the osprey nest I could hear the fledgling chirping its hunger. Even though well house #4 and its leak had been isolated from the system for the month of April, more than 5700 gallons were pumped than could be accounted for. Nancy J. had complained that their water was brown, even dirty. Gary's response by email was that since their water system hadn't been used since fall the brown color was the result of bio film being flushed off the wall of the pipe but Nancy had said that brown water recurred from time to time all last summer — which shouldn't happen once renewed use clears the bio film. Since Tom, who reports consistently clear water is only a few hundred feet upstream from Nancy and Jim, the problem has to be in that section or in their own system. Nancy volunteered to keep a log to track water quality and I seconded the motion. The symptoms she reported were difficult to explain but recurring brown water wasn't acceptable.

On Jones Island the day before we'd looked carefully at the madrona tree flowers, now mostly on the ground, light green bells attached to what would become bright red berry bunches later in the year. At his time of year the flowers have a characteristic fragrance one can't miss around our house, walking up the Crane ramp on Orcas or wherever this tree is found. On my walk around Crane I saw three large banana slugs, the first this season, each almost six inches long. The warming damp weather must have brought them out of hibernation or whatever it is they do over the winter.

After spending the morning double-checking that the proofreading corrections had been properly applied to *The eNotated Metamorphosis* — and finding some new typos to fix — and after making a few last minute changes Jens requested, I filled out the online Amazon Kindle Digital Publishing form, uploaded the cover art and a MOBI version of the book, and began the wait for a response from the Cloud. We were close now but because Amazon was continually making changes to their submission gate-keeping process it wasn't possible to know when the book would appear in the catalog or what other information Amazon would request before allowing it in .

197: Catchment and yard tools outside the studio

For several weeks the drain in my bathroom sink (Yvonne has her own and is glad of it) had become increasingly clogged. It was time to clean out the line. I removed the trap but it wasn't clogged. The problem was above and

One-hundred-ninety-seven: Fixing

after cleaning it with the handle of a plunger I found that the drain leaked and when trying to tighten the drain I cracked part of the chrome cylinder the plug fits into. I'd have to get a new one. At least the toxic white whiskers — blue shaving gel obstruction had been removed.

The flapper valve in the toilet in the master bath had been sticking and not reseating after a flush for many months — so it had been necessary to remove the tank lid to knock the flapper down and into place so the tank would fill and the water stut off. Watching the flipper work I could see that it got stuck when lifted too far so I adjusted the chain connecting the flapper to the handle flush bar, allowing more slack. But that didn't work; it wasn't the chain that was lifting the flapper too high; once the water level above the flapper fell below a certain level the flapper popped up and got stuck. After I cleaned deposits from the tube that provided a hinge for the flapper, it no longer stuck.

On the deck off the dining room I repositioned the latch for the gate at the top of the stairs because it had become difficult to operate, moving the latch higher to overcome the sagging of the gate. Then I opened the hot tub pump, heater, and filter compartment under the deck and next to the hot tub, surprised to find rats had been living in the 4 x 4 x 4 cube during the last 24 months since I had the door off. For months I'd been meaning to replace the filter; now I finally did. Along the way, needing to isolate the pump house from the hot tub above it, I removed the cover of the box the controls were embedded in to access incoming and outgoing hot tub valves. In doing so, I laid the cover of the box on the lid of the hot tub and then realizing that was a bad idea removed it too late to prevent a screw sticking out of the wooden cover from puncturing the vinyl hot tub lid cover. I wasn't happy — since a lid puncture, unless properly sealed, would let in water that would eventually compromise the cover. I left the pump compartment open; I'd deal with the rats later.

One-hundred-ninety-eight: It's A Hoot

"It is amazing what you can accomplish if you do not care who gets the credit." - Harry S. Truman

With a clear sky, the sun below the horizon in the northeast making the sky there pink and with the Salish Sea calm, the day felt like summer — though 46 rather a 60 degree dawn. Second to arrive at Howard's, I heard David telling a long story about Case Western Reserve University students who eavesdropped on Shaker Heights maids using a parabolic microphone. Brian appeared shortly; Chris was off-island. The main topic today: Island health care. David had just retired as president of the Orcas Island Medical Center Foundation, the group that owns the clinic building, but before doing so had, with the Board, arranged for Island Hospital in Anacortes, to take over the administration and operation of the Medical Center. Attempts to bring the two external family practice doctors back into the clinic had failed. The Center was operating with an unsustainable deficit made up by generous island philanthropists who had made it clear they couldn't continue the funding indefinitely. Island Hospital could operate the clinic less expensively than doing so locally, though some subsidy would be required from the Foundation and thus the community. With Island Hospital management the clinic had a sustainable future, with lower net costs for delivering medical services on the Island. It was a good thing but had come only through a long process of analysis and negotiation. David was now out of the hot seat as President of the Board. Howard was moving ahead with his garden. When leaving the honeymoon cottage and walking through the garden I asked him about the brown-tipped onion greens. Frost had touched the Walla Walla onions, Howard said, but they would be OK. His thermometer had read 37 today, ours, 46. In the past I'd found that we were usually warmer in the winter and cooler in the summer than Deer Harbor, also on the water and less than two miles away.

199: Seagull on railing outside living room (May 2010)

Leaving Howard's on Channel Road, I turned left rather than right at Deer Harbor Road, following David at a distance on his way to Eastsound, a beautiful morning, bushes now leafed out and deciduous trees soon to be complete. The Scotch broom was now bright yellow, pretty though considered an invasive noxious weed, hard to remove and if unchecked would spread until it took over the Islands. The lumberyard was bustling, the yard and barn crowded with contractor's pickups being loaded with lumber and other supplies. Picking out two 10′ lengths of brown, plastic gutter and getting a yard ticket, I took the gutter, hangers, joints, and ends inside, found a drain assembly in the plumbing department and then mothballs, with some help, up front in the cleaning supplies section. It had been months since I'd exercised our account and I was pleased to be able to today. The lumberyard must be suffering greatly from the downturn in construction. Two more Eastsound restaurants had folded; one, Bilbo's, had been a fixture of island life for more than 20 years.

Back home with my supplies, Yvonne was getting ready to attend a Women's Auxiliary luncheon at the Deer Harbor Community Club hosting its West Sound counterpart. Eating an early lunch and noticing that Yvonne had cleaned up the counter after the third massacre of the tiny sugar ants who appeared in force at intervals, I took my tools and the new drain assembly into the master bathroom to remove the drain piece I'd cracked during my clean out process the day before and replaced it with what I'd picked up at the lumber yard. Though I didn't see any leaks I left a white plastic dishpan underneath the drain pipes to pick up any drips that might come. Outside, after cleaning rat leavings from the hot tub pump house under the deck, I brought a piece of 1/2" hardware cloth from my shop and stapled it across the opening where the pipes pass through the wall to circulate water through the hot tub. I couldn't see any other place the rats could have gotten into this space. The 220 volt line enters the pump house through plastic conduit and I could see that something had been gnawing the lip of the conduit so I wrapped the end in hardware cloth. Then, leaving the mothballs in their plastic bag in their box, I put the box in an empty cottage cheese container and clipped the top of the bag so the moth balls would be exposed to the air and set the mothball outfit on the floor in the pump house and then closed it up, screwing the door to the frame. My thought was that the mothballs would make it very unlikely any rats would want to take up housekeeping again in the structure. Later in the day, it seemed like a less good idea. What I should do is to further rat proof the hot tub system and dispose of the mothballs. The puncture in the vinyl covering the hot tub lid was taped over but that would need better attention. I had not fully repaired everything I'd broken when trying to do repairs.

Amazon had changed its self-publishing gatekeeping process again and had sent me an email asking for information about the public domain and/or copyrighted nature of *The eNotated Metamorphosis*. Clearly they were feeling the heat from someplace for accepting electronic books into their catalog that weren't legitimate so they were struggling to create some sort of acceptable due-diligence process. Now the question was how long I'd have to wait for the book to enter the catalog or whether they'd want to know even more though I couldn't imagine what it could be.

One-hundred-ninety-eight: It's A Hoot

After dinner Yvonne suggested we go for a walk around the island. While she got ready I watched a large doe browse the yard next to Yvonne's small pond that was becoming a swamp. I'd seen this same deer in the early morning, its flanks lighter than its back. It nibbled short new grass, stretching and bending, its frame and muscles clearly visible through its coat — graceful, powerful, almost feline. As we left the house and walked down the deck stairs, the doe trotted over to the side of my shop and a deer trail through the wood to the meadow, turning to watch us. The tank was still at 12', a good thing. Just past the tank on Circle Road, something appeared coming through the trees at the left edge of my field of vision and I told Yvonne to watch the space above the road as an owl flew by not 30 feet in front of us through the trees and perched on a stub sticking out of the bark of a Douglas fir and turned its head to look at us. The owl was slightly lighter than the tree bark but speckled in a way that made it difficult to pick out and it took Yvonne a minute or so to see it even with me pointing right at it. Since it had "horns," it must have been a Western screech owl, the bane of mice, rats, and island squirrels even. Silent in their flight, the owls fly through branches other birds its size would avoid. Late last fall I watched an owl, maybe this one, struggle to carry a limp red squirrel across the airstrip into the trees. Almost home, on the path crossing the meadow, three black-tailed does watched us from 20 feet away, not moving from their day end pasture.

One-hundred-ninety-nine: Cinco de Mayo

"The universe is full of magical things patiently waiting for our wits to grow sharper." - Eden Phillpotts

Though the morning was rainy by afternoon the clouds has turned gauzy and enough sun came through to make it pleasant to be outside and Yvonne was. I spent most of the day until about 3:00 writing the draft of a talk I'd be making to the Unitarian group on Sunday with the title "New Science, New Religion, Part 2." I had reported on Brian Greens's book *The Hidden Universe* in February, explaining, to the best of my ability, the concept of the multi-verse, the theory that there are in fact multiple, perhaps an infinite number of universes and the way it answers age-old questions, such as why there is something rather than nothing, in the past assumed only addressable by religion. The second installment would look at the theologies of two different scientists, Bernard Haisch and Stuart Kauffman, who accept the new, latest science of cosmology but in it find purchase for new religious thought. The talk would conclude with a discussion of Jesse Bering's *The Belief Instinct*, a book in which he gives a plausible account for why theism, in one form or another, pervades human experience as an adaptive illusion.

I used the rest of the afternoon to begin to sort and rearrange some of my books, something I'd been intending to do for months. Books were stacked on my nightstand, in a basket on the floor, and in a box next to one of the two bedroom bookcases. The question: what categories of books stay in the bedroom and what categories exit — while leaving open what happens after that. I decided I would keep Emerson, now a full shelf, Thoreau and transcendentalism, Whitman, Rorty (a college philosophy professor whose thought I admired), Hartshorne (process theology), Campbell (just about everything he'd written), Lincoln, Jefferson, a very old Swedish family Bible, *Orme's Guide to the Colorado Fourteeners* (where I'd recorded climbs on 26 of the 52 designated mountains, when and who with), booklets about Nikoli Tesla (my father had

One-hundred-ninety-nine: Cinco de Mayo

been a fan), three copies of my great grandfather, John Johnson Ashenhurst's memoir, *Recollections of an Octogenarian*, my parents had published, books on ravens (Bernd Heinrich) and Native American raven stories, and Thomas Mann books and biographies. David Foster Wallace, W.S. Seybold, and J.M. Coetzee went into the living room, along with Pynchon's *Gravitiy's Rainbow* and a reader's companion. But there were too many books to find places for; I'd need to rearrange the books in my office and in the big living room bookcase and dispose of several boxes of books before I was done and there wasn't time today.

Before leaving for a Cinco de Mayo party with Jack and Pat on Orcas, a nine year tradition for them, I checked my email and found a note from Amazon; without any explanation they had chosen not to accept *The eNotated Metamorphosis* for publication. What? I forwarded the email to our group with exclamations and then replied to Amazon asking for a short explanation. This would be our fifth publication. The first two had been accepted directly into the catalog; the third and forth delayed while they dithered apparently on the question of whether we were publishing something in the public domain or an enhanced version with additional original writing — and eventually had accepted what we'd presented as new work. For *Metamorphosis* they'd changed their process again, now wanting to know whether it was public domain, who had translated it, whether it was original work and who held the copyright, questions about provenance and rights they asked very generally in the book upload page online with the Kindle Direct Publishing service. Since Amazon is an opaque organization or at best occasionally translucent, it was difficult to know what was going on with them but my guess was that they had decided their catalog was being contaminated by too many public domain books and they were trying to prevent the entry of more. This new round might be related to the too-many-public-domain books issue but they should have been able to see that with 25,000 words of original content, contributed by Jens, we were offering a new, significantly value-added work. But perhaps they had another issue — but hadn't offered a clue.

The Cinco de Mayo party was a bit smaller, we thought, than in previous years. I was still fuming at Amazon and not looking forward to socializing but on entering the kitchen began talking with Chase, who'd been president of the Library Board in my first year on it and then retired. An expert on penal systems and determined opponent of capital punishment, even though he'd had

One-hundred-ninety-nine: Cinco de Mayo

to conduct two hangings in Washington Sate when in charge of its penal system, Chase had spoken to our Unitarian group, describing the emotional cost to the people who carried out the executions as well as the dollar costs of death row isolation and legal costs. Now helping the state of California, at the request of the courts, to straighten out its prison mess, he saw first hand what it cost California to have more than 600 inmates on death row and 40,000 in prison for petty crimes, costing the state about $50,000 each per year to house or $2 billion a year for no good reason.

199: Raccoon in tree next to back deck (May 2010)

One-hundred-ninety-nine: Cinco de Mayo

Bob was ambulatory, having had a triple bypass in March, after feeling winded skiing at the top of Vail — at 12,000 feet — during the winter. So would I. But Bob was 80 and had been skiing since 1939 when he first took the ski train from Denver to Winter Park and a lift ticket cost $1.50. Vail this year was over $100. He told me he'd shared a lift with a 93 year old eager to get to the powder. I can't imagine. Sally thanked me again for having helped so much with the Yacht Club newsletter and yearbook years before when she was president and asked me if I missed cruising. I said no, that Yvonne and I had done as much as we had wanted to, found the endless hours it took to get someplace boring, and that we had too much to do or better wanted to do more than sit on a boat for more than a few days. Through their construction company, Sally and George had built Babette's cabin on Crane years ago and a few years ago the current owners, Cabot and Cynthia had it remodeled and enlarged. Jack and Pat, our hosts, had sold their second boat and Jack was happy to be without it, at least 90% of the time. He too found it tedious, as well as expensive and a consumer of time they'd rather spend with family. Scott had traded his sailboat for a powerboat that gulped fuel like a thirsty camel. Al, owner of a Camano Troll pocket trawler like Yvonne and I had had before we bought our 33' Nauticat pilothouse, hadn't used it in quite a while. A realtor, he reported that there were virtually no sales on Orcas. As an example, a 5000 square foot luxury house initially listed at $1.5m was down to $600,000 — still with no buyers in sight. Vern's Restaurant in Eastsound had closed, he reported, because the landlords wouldn't back off the $10,000 per month rent and now couldn't rent the building because it would need significant changes to meet code. Bilbo's would be back in business after the former owners took it back from the new owners. And he was sure that the landlord for Portofino's would open it again. Once the island had 65 realtors; now there were about half that number.

When we crossed to Crane about 9:45 it was almost dark, the tide high, the water calm, and the temperature mild. I used the spotlight from time to time to check for logs in the water, always a concern, especially in the dark. We were grateful we had a hot tub and Yvonne wondered how we could get along without one. Some reading of *All Things Shining: Reading the Western Classics to find Meaning in a Secular Age* and lights out.

Two-hundred: Out They Go

"The only way to do great work is to love what you do." - Steve Jobs

Another drizzly morning in the mid forties. No response from Amazon about why they declined to add our *Metamorphosis* to their catalog — but it was still early in the day. Since there was no telling whether they'd ever reply or if they did we needed to consider alternate publishing paths so I wrote up an analysis and sent it off to Jens, Chris, David, and Natasha. We could list with Barnes and Noble. I'd established an account some months before. They require EPUB format but I was planning to add that as an option to our book building software. Of course there was no way to know without trying whether they'd object to our public domain/original annotations model. Another possibility was the Ibis Reader, a browser-based reader for EPUB books that would work on virtually every platform, allowing both Web stored and locally stored books. Their website talked about licensing and white-labeling so I wrote them a note requesting a call. An advantage of Ibis Reader was its ability to handle HTML 5 and CSS 3 level pages, making it possible for us to create and publish much richer books than supported by Kindle and probably B&N's Nook, allowing us to provide features we'd considered from the very first but didn't pursue because of Kindle's limitations. Going to EPUB wouldn't solve the problem of how to enter the Kindle eco-system, the largest ebook world by far — but we could sell MOBI file versions of our books that could be downloaded from our website that Kindle and Kindle software users could download to their computers and then side load to their reading devices. We wouldn't be able to apply copy protection but we hadn't with the first four books anyway. Or perhaps we should be creating and publishing iOS and Android apps, one for each book. In any case, this Amazon hiccup was causing us to look harder at and then pursue Amazon alternatives.

200: A hamlet social center

Saturday Yvonne had scheduled for Deer Harbor Community Club spring cleanup — for the Post Office and Club building, so I needed to review the draft of the talk I would give Sunday morning to the UU group. I'd always been interested in philosophic and religious questions but had become skeptical about the value of taking this kind of talk very seriously for all kinds of reasons. The language of abstractions has a tenuous connection to reality, if any, but can be a seductive time waster at best and a path to ideological thinking, despair, manic states, cruelty, whatever, at the worst. The emergence of the problem with Amazon was sobering, making me question the value of spending more time, so far perhaps 1500 hours pursuing what might be a will-o-the-wisp. Two things that I enjoyed, both abstract in their ways, were unlikely to lead to much of anything — or so it was seeming. Though Sunday morning would tell, my experience over the last ten years was that very few people, even among our little congregation were interested in or understood what I was talking about — so why bother? But I would.

The day before I'd rearranged my bookcase in the bedroom and in the living room and now had stacks of books in my office, where most of my books were shelved. I'd need to get rid of some. There just wasn't room — and I didn't need, would never read, and really didn't care much about many of them. Presumably if I needed a copy for some reason I could get it through interlibrary loan, if a classic get it in electronic form for free, or in worst case buy a copy. None of our kids needed or wanted these books and it wasn't even obvious that the Library book sale would want them since I found out at the Friends Winter Book Sale in February, where I'd picked up a box of books for $1, that they were having trouble finding anyone to take the 20,000 remainders.

Yvonne had stored a number of broken down book boxes in her pantry in the studio and she showed me the packing tape before she left for Orcas, some errands and her Friday afternoon knitting session. Beginning by gleaning my philosophy books, most from graduate school in the late 60's, stacked books on the futon in my office and then began to put them in boxes for probable disposal at Half Price Books in Everett that would net a few dollars, it occurred to me to spend some time seeing which if any of these books had value high enough to make them worth selling online through Amazon or Alibris or someplace else. Using Google's Book Search I found that about half the books actually had some value, sometimes as much as $50 — they had become slightly rare books, a number out of print but classics in the field of philosophy. Of perhaps 150 books, 35 were worth enough to consider bothering with. The rest could go to Half Price Books

So it looked like I was creating another project for myself. To see whether it made sense to pursue, I'd list these books online and see what happened. Natasha had done a little online selling and had some success with it, lending me a book about online book selling that suggested having a steady inventory of about 1000 books would net, monthly, a nice source of additional income — but that's not what I had in mind. I had books that had some valve and to throw them out — basically — would be like throwing money away. Since over time we'd need to get rid of most of our thousands of books so as not to burden ourselves or our children, perhaps it would make sense to begin to cull our books, putting those that had value in online inventory and those that didn't dispensing with unless they had personal or family value. Over some years then perhaps we could clear out our books and be paid for it. A thought.

At dinner I told Yvonne about how, triggered especially by the Amazon problem and the probable lack of interest the UU group would have in my coming talk on Sunday I'd spent maybe 20 hours preparing for, that very specific, very concrete, very direct activities are always satisfying for me and the theoretic, indefinite, and complicated with unpredictable moving pieces are often not — though my tendency was to pursue them — in thought and action. So, for instance, cutting, splitting, stacking, and then burning firewood in our wood stove and then from time to time cleaning out the ashes and moving them to the compost pile, enjoying the cheeriness of the fire, the feeling of warmth in the kitchen 30 feet away from the wood stove on my skin, reducing our electric bill, is all very satisfying to body and soul, not requiring much abstract thought except to figure out techniques and solve problems in the process, to quantify and plan. Not much really. She replied that she'd known that forever and that was why she liked to cook, to care for children, to knit, to visit, and so on. Hmmm. We went on to talk about the Food Bank, staffed with volunteers who love the concrete and specific but will increasingly need to deal with the abstract and tenuous, paradoxically, so that they'll have a sustainable organization — now with its own building, an increasing population of clients, the need for grants and applications for them, and organized and sustained fundraising, for instance, through an annual donor-member fund drive, which would entail more rigorous accounting and financial planing, all activities that had nothing directly to do with the satisfaction gained by feeding neighbors in need you could see, talk to, and develop a sense of friendship with over time.

After dinner we called daughter-in-law, Natasha to wish her happy birthday and voice mail coming on, probably because the family had gone out to their favorite Thai place, we sang "Ja, må hon leva," the Swedish birthday song. My UU talk I'd give Saturday needed more work but I was enjoying *All Things Shining*, Dreyfus and Kelly's suggestion that we solve our society's crisis of meaning by returning to literary classics. James and Keith had given me the book for my birthday and I was interested in how it attempted to address the problem of how science had drained the sacred out of the world, one way of looking at what I'd be talking about Sunday, and how it could be recaptured, in part by understanding how the succession of phenomenological paradigms after Homer through today's monotheism had steadily obscured the experience of the sacred that came naturally to our ancestors. Or something like that.

Two-hundred-one: Spring Clean Up

"Many hands make light work." - John Heywood

Another rainy morning, the day Yvonne had scheduled for a spring clean up of the Post Office and Deer Harbor Community Club grounds. We didn't look forward to working in the rain; oh well. The day before Yvonne had picked up a platter of meat and cheese from Island Market and had made a big macaroni salad and chocolate chip cookies to feed lunch to the crew she hoped would show up in spite of the rain. As chair of the Deer Harbor Community Club Grounds Committee Yvonne was in charge of keeping what everyone could see attractive — and she did. At her direction I collected some yard tools and she assembled the food to take with — and the sun began to show through the dissipating cloud layer. It was going to be a pretty day after all.

Well before the effort's 10:00 a.m. starting time, Yvonne and I were at work. We moved what was perhaps an abandoned bicycle and trailer from the flower bed at the back of the parking lot against the hill with the resort's meeting room above, its lower wall facing the parking lot, slightly caved in at one point where someone must have backed a truck into a parking space. Though the daffodils continued their blooming almost everywhere, here only one hadn't begun to fade and dry, and Pam, when she followed my raking, leaf, and debris removal, with weeding and then heather planting, accidentally pulled out this last fresh daffodil stalk, and chagrined pushed it back into the wet, soft soil. Dave, Howard, and I cleared weeds that had begun to sprout from the cracks between the parking lot and the concrete retaining wall that held the hill behind it at bay and then I helped Yvonne transplant more heather pots to the bark covered planting area along the walk leading to the Post Office's front door. Bev weeded in front and Terry, who had brought his weed whacker put it to use on the small section of lawn south of the building along the other side of the parking lot. Kevin explained that Becky was at a womens' meeting of some kind at Rosario, and he went to work weeding. Guillaume and Euginia, who I hadn't meet before, pitched in as well.

201A: Bev weeds the Community Club flower garden

At the beginning there was much more conversation and leaning on shovels than work, reminding me of the stereotype of Chicago street repair crews when I grew up. Howard told how, as a youth in England, he had seen a newspaper headline that read "Worker falls off shovel, breaks arm." Years ago I would have silently objected to all this wasted time. Now, at 68, I knew the conversation and fellowship was really the point.

Two-hundred-one: Spring Clean Up

On the walkway on the west side of the Post Office, facing the marina (which Pat T. had said Wednesday night had recently changed hands), the big bench Mike had made with Clay's help and dedicated to Cal, who came to the PO shortly after we got started to get his mail, and his late wife, Clarina, both fifth generation Orcas Islanders, invited use that it rarely got. When I needed a broom, I knocked on the back door of the Post Office where Rene, in her second or maybe third part-time job, sorted the Saturday mail, putting it in boxes, though the service desk was closed. The fall clean up in October had attracted a crew twice today's size but those missing were off the island today or like Bob still recovering from surgery. But it didn't matter because though the fall session had required a substantial effort to overcome years of neglect, we were now in maintenance mode.

201B: Deer Harbor Community Club

By 11:00 the group reconvened at the Community Club, built in 1905 as a two room school house to serve the Deer Harbor Hamlet, and then sold to the

Two-hundred-one: Spring Clean Up

Women's Auxiliary in the 1920's for $150 when the Orcas schools were consolidated to Eastsound. Howard, Dave, and I began weeding along the west-facing front of the building, Deer Harbor Road 150 feet away across the front lawn, the Post Office a quarter of a mile south in the hamlet, rather than by itself, here, in space cut from the forest. Bev weeded the flower garden Yvonne had planted along the east wall of the new kitchen, an extension to the building we had replaced instead of as we had initially intended remodeling it in a project begun almost exactly five years before, Bev, the instigator and leader of the effort had watched, surprised and a little alarmed that day when a dozen men began to remove rotted portions of the kitchen addition only to find the whole structure too compromised to save, in the male crew's opinion, and the whole kitchen was soon lying in a heap on the floor, then carried to the adjacent lot, the floor torn up, and the whole shebang carried by trailer in a number of loads someplace where it would be stored and then disposed of. By the end of the day all that remained of the kitchen was the concrete posts that had supported the beams under the floor joists and a sixteen foot wide, twelve foot high opening now gaped in the side of the main building, the original school house.

    Terry and Giullaume used their gas powered weed whackers to trim around the building. I helped Yvonne transplant more heather to the slope that connected the back flower garden to the back parking lot. Eugenia and Pam worked on the southwest corner of the building weeding and Dave moved debris from the lawn, planting and graveled areas to the to-be-burned pile at the east edge of the back lot. Not long after noon Yvonne announced that we were done and that it was time for lunch. Guillaume and Eugenia couldn't stay but the rest of us made ourselves sandwiches inside and talked about coming projects — a new septic field to the north and the back parking lot extended. That May Saturday, five years before, at Bev's urging, had become the start of a resurgence for the Community Club that had become tired as an organization and facility. It had been, in a way, reborn, and Yvonne and I, without realizing or intending it, had become part of the core of the group that had accomplished it, making our contribution to the future, and that felt good.

Two-hundred-two: New Science, New Religion: Part 2

"Science without religion is lame, religion without science is blind."
- Albert Einstein

Yvonne had made coffee and chocolate chip cookies for after-service refreshments. I'd prepared an order of service and made copies and had decided to read two Native American chants I thought relevant for the subject matter of my talk. One, very familiar, from the Tewa people, who still live in the Rio Grande valley north of Santa Fe, and for whom the site of the Santuario at Chimayo was sacred:

> Song of the Sky Loom
> Oh our Mother the Earth, our Father the Sky,
> Your children are we, with tired backs
> We bring you the gifts that you love.
> Then weave for us a garment of brightness;
> May the warp be the bright light of morning,
> May the weft be the red light of evening,
> May the fringes be the falling rain,
> May the border be the standing rainbow.
> Thus weave for us a garment of brightness
> That we may walk fittingly where the birds sing,
> That we may walk fittingly where the grass is green,
> Oh our Mother the Earth, our Father the Sky!

Nineteen showed up for the service and my talk and only one fell asleep during it and not for the duration. But my talk was too long, an imposition on the group even though they insisted they hear it all. I summarized my late February talk, Part 1, focusing especially on how contemporary cosmology and theoretical physics had addressed four seemingly intractable questions heretofore only religion and positing a creator god had a claim to but that the multi-verse now provided more rationally convincing answers, what I had gleaned from Brian Greene's book, *The Hidden Universe*:

- Why is there something rather than nothing? *Some universes are nothing.*
- Why is the universe so perfectly attuned to creating life and us? *Not all universes within the multi-verse are, but this one wasn't created for us; we're the result of an undirected process that was possible here.*
- Is the universe infinite and eternal? *Inside it's infinite but not eternal; outside eternal but not infinite.*
- What created the universe or multi-verse? *A random event in the formless, quantum background.*

Given that a god of the gaps isn't necessary to explain either the universe itself or the evolution of life in it, how do some scientists who think the sacred is an important part of life bring god back into the equation? Bernard Haisch, *The God Theory*, suggests that the universe or multi-verse isn't material but a thought in the mind of god that expressed a particular distillation of the possible into the actual; god trying out a what-if and our consciousness is a fragment of god's. Our universe, our world, and everything in it is sacred because it's part of god. Stuart Kaufman, *Re-inventing the Sacred*, a sometime Crane Island neighbor, views the universe as incredibly creative, evolving to occupy what he calls adjacent possibles in ways consistent with but unpredictable by and irreducible to the laws of physics. For Kauffman, this unbounded creativity is sacred and worthy of gratitude and awe.

But whether or not these suggestions by Haisch and Kauffman have merit, most people won't be moved and will reject science rather than give up an accessible, person-like, low god for a distant, non-person-like, high god. Why?

The typical answers I've seen or thought about aren't very convincing because each has has significant counterexamples:

People are theists because:
- That's what they were taught — *but people also adopt beliefs they weren't taught*
- It's comforting in the face of pain, disaster, frustration, intimations of mortality — *but atheists in existential pain don't adopt theism to overcome the pain of fear of extinction and theists in existential pain don't adopt atheism to overcome the pain of fear of hell*
- There's a god gene — *but if there is why isn't belief all but universal?*
- It answers questions for them — *but science does that better*
- They've had a god experience — *but why call it a **god** experience; that begs the question.*
- It's needed to make people moral — *but why are so many atheists more moral than their theist neighbors?*

Jesse Bering, in *The Belief Instinct*, has a more plausible answer to the question — why do people ignore or reject science to maintain a belief in a theistic god? His answer is that human beings inherently see the world in terms of purpose, goals with minds, agents behind it. As babies, children, and then adults we develop increasingly sophisticated theories of mind about other people, putting ourselves in their shoes, or in their minds, so that we can successfully predict what they're going to do, from an adaptive point of view, crucial to our likeliness of passing on our genes. Probably unique to human beings, the tendency to create theory of mind, that is to see purpose and agency everywhere and use teleological reasoning, is so useful and so overwhelming that we over-apply it; we become promiscuous teleologists with a tendency to posit invisible persons, a god or gods where there isn't any real justification to do so, and if not gods, the secular stand-ins, like fate, conspiracies, or historical progress. Even if we try, Bering says, we can't give up these powerful adaptive illusions, though how we clothe it varies with nature and nurture.

A key take-away for religious liberals, humanists, and/or aggressive atheists is to be careful about being too self-righteous and to come to see how we all posit purpose where it doesn't belong. As Alan pointed out in response to my sending hims a copy of my talk, the question for religious liberals, the one Haisch and Kauffman are trying to answer, is how can we own science and at the same time experience the sacred, something that, except perhaps for Nietzsche, most people can't simply declare something to be.

202: Head of the Crane dock

Late in the afternoon I called my sister Marcy to wish her happy birthday and happy Mothers' Day (Yvonne had satisfying contact with our family group), and she said that our sister Julie was now talking about selling her Victorian house, at some point, and getting something smaller and less expensive to support, a development consistent with discussions Yvonne and I had had with her when visiting in April. And Paul had spent hours discussing theology with his mother, Elsie, visiting from Iowa, and very clear but from our point of view very conservative about her beliefs. I considered volunteering to send a copy of my UU talk for Elsie to read — but I didn't.

Walking Circle Road after dinner so that Yvonne could collect leaves and other appropriate flora she could use as stamps to apply paint in decorative patterns to card stock to make guestbook covers for Garden Club Garden Tour hosts, we saw what I think were a pair of nesting turkey buzzards, with large bodies and very small red heads. And late in the evening Nancy called to say that a doe had left a new-born fawn in their yard and they weren't sure what to do about it. More to come with Crane-Bambi.

Two-hundred-three: Dinner Guests

"There is no love sincerer than the love of food." - George Bernard Shaw

With daffodils now finally fading and tulips and hyacinths in full flower, I'm eager for the lilacs to bloom, late this year as everything else. Where there are deciduous trees and bushes on the island, their spaces are now again visually impenetrable. Three hundred yards off shore a small open boat draws a section of floating dock north toward the Crane marina on Orcas. I confirmed my suspicions with binoculars; it was Jim going to pick up lumber perhaps and take it back to his dock a quarter mile south of our house on Crane's east side. Tom, two doors south of Jim, uses this same technique to move what's too big, clumsy, or heavy from Orcas to Crane, both, I think using old sections of the Crane dock on Orcas replaced three years ago by Waterfront Construction. Eurus, the east wind that assails us irregularly from late October through early April, has blown itself out and small boats towing long barges that rise only slightly above the surface of the Salish Sea are safe and secure.

Taking her basket of green clippings with her, Yvonne left early for the Firehouse in Eastsound to meet with other Garden Club members to make decorative covers for guest books they'll provide hosts for the upcoming garden tours in June. My instructions were to clear all tools, boxes, and baskets from the front porch, unnecessary there until we resumed use of our wood stove in October. Following the path of least resistance, I filled the dock cart twice and pushed it to the firewood area outside the deer fence north of the house and pulled off the big tarp covering what was left of the split fire wood — not two weeks worth — so I could stack the three wooden boxes for kindling (some cedar strips remaining), two baskets (one to hold the next serving to be fed into the stove and a big one for the porch to hold bigger kindling selected from split wood), and then two splitting mauls (the newest one with a cracked head and the older one with a split handle), a ten pound sledge

Two-hundred-three: Dinner Guests

hammer, two wedges, a splitting maul hatchet and a good-looking steel-shanked hatchet. As I restacked some of the split wood I uncovered dungeness crab shells and claws left by mink who used the wood pile occasionally as their private dining room. Folding the big tarp double I put it back in place, laying three to four inch logs on top and against the sides so that summer winds wouldn't bother it.

With guests coming for dinner and parts of the path through the trees to the meadow still a bit muddy in spots where the chipped bark had sunk into the wet ground, I uncovered the chipper we shared with Margaret and Mike, put the dock cart next to its exhaust chute, started it up (with no problem) and began to break up bark I'd stripped from trunk sections I'd split — stacking the bark for possible future use — such as right now. The chipper, with a 3 1/2" feed hole, a 30 pound flywheel and a 7 hp engine makes a terrible racket but makes short work of whatever it's fed. The bark chips, a rich reddish brown and aromatic, soon sufficiently filled the dock cart and I turned off the chipper and pushed the cart to the path, dumping the chips where the path was muddiest, supplementing the chips I laid down along twenty feet of trail in the fall.

Later, on the Orcas-side dock under a cloudy sky, the wind and water almost calm, the tide low, waiting for our dinner guests to appear, I walked the dock looking for problems and found one. Though it's more complicated than this, one can think of the dock as having three sections, a bottom and two side that make a "U," the open end, the top, facing west and Warren's dock 100 feet away. Each side is connected to the bottom by two rubber hinges, eight inch diameter rubber donuts an inch thick. I'd had concerns about the inner donut on the south, or breakwater section of the dock and today when I lifted the bowed aluminum bridge that covers the gap between the bottom and the breakwater sections I could see that the donut was torn all the way through about 30% across its height. That wasn't good. It would need to be replaced. I'd have to write Blair, the Board member who is in charge of the docks this year, after I'd given up my position to become Treasurer (while also continuing to have responsibility for the water system on Crane).

Before I could complete my dock inspection Gordon and Sylvia and Jens and Susan appeared carrying wine and homemade peanut butter cookies and were soon aboard the *Huginn* with me heading toward Pole Pass, Gordon the tour director for Jens and Susan who were coming to Crane for the first time.

Two-hundred-three: Dinner Guests

Yvonne and I liked to have company and Yvonne was happy to cook a good meal, this evening her halibut Veracruze (tomato, onions, olives, oil, and more), with rice, green salad, and 18-hour, crispy, crunchy, no-knead bread, with a special chocolate mousse (mousse into cups, then into the freezer, and then taken out, popped in the oven, and served cooked on the outside, liquid on the inside.) Yum!

203: "What I love about Crane" in the community center

Jens and Susan got the complete tour — all our projects over the last four years, gratifying for us to get mileage out of all the work and I think reasonably interesting to first time visitors to Crane. Gordon and Sylvia hadn't see

Two-hundred-three: Dinner Guests

the new kitchen so that's where Yvonne started. Conversation ranged from how we all ended up on Orcas (and us on Crane), the friendliness of the community (Sylvia told a story about how she had gone out into the parking lot at the market and found two men who had been standing by her car waiting to offer to change her tire which they saw was flat and then a story about being in the checkout lane at the market, realizing she'd forgotten her wallet and the man in line behind her offering to pay her tab). Jens and Susan were especially struck at how Orcas nourishes potential in people who don't know they have it or if they do would be suppressed in larger communities where amateurs are frozen out by professionals or near professionals — having seen a series of original, locally written and acted short plays at the Grange Hall. Orcas was a small pond that frogs of all sizes could thrive in. A very pleasant evening and just before 10:00 with the light almost gone though a sliver waxing moon intermittently visible through the clouds mitigating the coming darkness, I put on my headlamp, to the amusement of our guests, and we headed out the door, through the north gate (Gordon securing it after us), walked across the meadow to the dock, and once aboard the *Huginn*, the tide now almost full, I guided the boat through Pole Pass, leaving our guests on the Orcas dock, to find their way home on the big island.

Two-hundred-four: Carrying On

"I have not failed. I've just found 10,000 ways that won't work." - Thomas Edison

On May 5th Amazon had sent me a note regarding *The eNotated Metamorphosis* saying "We have reviewed the information you provided and have determined that we will not be making the title available for sale in the Kindle store at this time." Argh!

It didn't make sense to me. I'd supplied the information they'd asked for about the source of the the Kafka translation, telling them it was in the public domain and that I'd gotten it from Project Gutenberg, and that all the other text was new, the copyright held by our company. Amazon had questioned the third Slocum book and the Dana book, each time making their process more complex and from my point of view more arcane. The *Metamorphosis* process was even more complex and since I couldn't be certain of the outcome — a decision with no explanation triggers the imagination — so it seemed to make sense to begin working on a Plan B and perhaps a Plan C.

Plan B would be to publish the book in ePub format, an industry standard, that Barnes and Noble but not Amazon supported. Though with a much smaller share, B & N was reported to have sold millions of Nooks, their alternative to the Amazon Kindle. I'd have to extend our book building software to create ePub as well as MOBI output.

Two-hundred-four: Carrying On

204: Jens' eNotated version of Kafka's classic

Plan C would be to distribute the book ourselves, from our website, in ePub format, letting users decide what reader software they wanted to use — unless we could create our own reader software and/or white label or in some other way take advantage of an existing reading platform.

Plan B looked like it wouldn't be much trouble; I would be able to modify the code I used to generate MOBI files for the Kindle process, the Kindle standard resembling the ePub standard in many ways.

Ibis Reader, a plan C candidate, provided a reading environment for Mac and Android devices and basically anything else that could run a popular browser and access the internet. And they were willing to license their technology. I emailed their "info" address, got a reply and suggested a telephone meeting in the late afternoon.

At noon Amazon replied to my request for an explanation for declining our book: "Based on the information you've provided we are not confident that this title is in the public domain and have determined that we will not be making the title available for sale in the Kindle store at this time." Hmmm. Maybe I was mistaken about the Wyllie translation being in the public domain. The Project Gutenberg verbiage accompanying the text of our first four books were very clear about our right to use the text unobstructed and I hadn't looked closely at the contract wording on this fourth book. Now I did. Wyllie held a 2002 copyright to translation. Amazon's gatekeepers were right; I was wrong. Now what to do?

Reading the contract terms carefully it looked like Project Gutenberg wanted a royalty — 20% of gross profits for sales of the book — but the other terms didn't seem appropriate to our situation — where we've created added value to the book, rather than just pass it through unchanged and charge people for what was free. I sent an email asking for permission and suggesting terms. I'd have to wait for a reply and once we had permission could resubmit the book to Amazon, now with a much better story.

Yvonne had gone to Eastsound for Food Bank meetings, especially interested in helping create job descriptions and procedures for the volunteers for the environment in the new building, occupancy expected in June, and was pleased at the response she got. The Food Bank was in transition, having gone from a very small, very casual organization, to one much larger, with more clients, handling more money and food, and now with a brand new building. Much had been accomplished but much more was needed — so that within a few years the organization could be self-sustainable and independent of all of the current volunteers. It needed some kind of predictable source of revenue — memberships perhaps and a more rigorous budgeting and reporting system — and that's the direction Yvonne was nudging the Board in while their focus, necessarily, was on the next day, week, or month.

About 8:00, Jeni called Yvonne to complete their delayed Mothers' Day talk. She was making plans to bring a crew of friends we knew and liked up to Crane over Memorial Day weekend. Corrina had experienced a melt-down because, though she'd be in grad school in June, for now she felt a bit useless. And Jeni was Skyping her friend DJ who had been in Afghanistan on business for more than month. I'd talked with Jen a few days earlier about her new role as union negotiator — and was very impressed and confident she would be very good at it.

Two-hundred-five: Red in Tooth and Claw

"Nature, red in tooth and claw." - Alfred Lord Tennyson

As I approached the community dock, having crossed the meadow just north of our house, I saw Howard's (from Bainbridge Island) old, tan Explorer turn from the head of the dock into the lot and park ahead of the Fire and Rescue vehicle, and then spied backpacks, bags, and boxes and two old dogs at the place the vehicle had left. Howard had been on Crane, apparently, and was on his way off. As I got closer to the head of the dock so did he coming out of the parking area and his dogs, indeterminate breed — one black and white and the other brown — came forward to say hello. I told Howard it had been quiet on Crane and he replied that he had been so busy for the last two years with his business on Bainbridge Island that he hadn't had much time to come up to Crane — but at least they'd had two good years at Bay Hay and Feed — best ever — even if it had meant twice as much work. I told him that we had some excitement on Crane and he assumed I was talking about the unattended burn pile story that had been reported to all Association members — but I was referring to the abandoned fawn Jim and Nancy had found next to their house. Then he told me that when he and CeAnn had been walking near Lou's the day before they had scared up an eagle from the ground who then watched them impassively from an overhead branch, and then a raven, and then a vulture — a turkey buzzard — and on walking over to where the birds had come from they found the remains of a fawn. When Yvonne and I had seen the two turkey buzzards I thought they were a nesting pair two days in the same area but they may have been in line for a meal.

Monday evening when I'd talked about the lot 8 fawn, Jens said that a doe had dropped two fawns near their house a few days earlier, one that was still wet having just come into the world and he and Susan had been able to watch the doe caring for and nursing her two babies. Jens added that that same doe had chased off her two yearling daughters only a week before, having intimations of imminent births.

205: Seal basking in the sun close to Crane dock

At the Greybeards gathering in Howard's honeymoon cottage 20 minutes later, he said that he was surprised the fawns were coming so early here — compared to June in Oregon. He added that he and Sheila had recently cruised over to Speiden Island to observe the colony of bachelor Stellar sea lions that hang out there, having been driven away from their rookeries — to which they won't return until adults. Several years before when cruising out to what we called Seal Rock, west of Waldron, we saw an adult male Stellar sea lion surface and were amazed at how big it was. Then a few years ago in

California we observed a rookery north of Morro Bay and again were impressed at the big males that could weigh more than a ton.

In Monterey, two years ago, walking along the a path fenced from the beach just north of the Monterey aquarium we watched mother seals instructing their pups about the ways of the water, the pups, for the most part, sticking very close to their food supply and protection. At Seal Rock we saw the same mother/child behavior, and watched an eagle perched on the rocks above the seals taking in the whole scene, waiting perhaps for a mother to leave her pup long enough for the eagle to carry it away. Though rare in this area, where Orcas feed especially on salmon, they do sometimes pull seals from rocks. Ken reported to me that a group of Orcas Island third graders had seen an Orca bifurcate a seal that had hopped onto the swim platform of their whale watching boat thinking that it was escaping.

Hard rains came in the afternoon while Yvonne worked on her myriad of administrative tasks in her studio and I sat in my favorite wicker chair in the living room working step by step on creating an ePub version of our Kafka book. At 5:00, cold from looking at the rain outside, Yvonne asked me to build a fire in the wood stove so I retrieved some kindling and wood from what remained of the stack outside and we were soon enjoying the radiant warmth of the stove. Yvonne had begun to pack for our upcoming trip to Harstine Island and Los Osos and she made chicken soup for dinner from leftovers, with a green salad — with walnuts, gorgonzola cheese, and balsamic vinegar dressing, and crusty 18-hour bread from Monday's dinner party. We talked more about the Food Bank evolution, how she had written Eric an email wondering why both my birthday and Mothers' Day had been mostly ignored by Eric and family, and *All Things Shining*. Eric called shortly, apologized, and explained that the drama of departmental politics at CalPoly continued to usurp his attention — not just from us — and that he was trying to understand how to cope better. And then we finished watching *Blue Valentine*, feeling like voyeurs to the disintegration of a marriage, engaged, sad, and seeing what was only too likely and common, especially with couples who carry so many disadvantages into their marriages, such alcoholism, drugs, or dubious family cultures. This film, well-directed and acted, seemed both accurate and almost uncomfortably intimate.

Two-hundred-six: Bambi Goes Home

"Because I could not stop for Death, He kindly stopped for me; The carriage held but just ourselves and Immortality." - Emily Dickinson

Yvonne had left for Rock on the Rock choir practice, the sun was shining, and I needed a walk, so I put the check from Jim and Nancy in my wallet, put on my blue Carmel, California jacket, bought there five years ago on our way to Los Osos and where, on our anniversary, I bought Yvonne a respectably-sized diamond engagement-type ring — then out the dining room door and down the deck stairs, closing the gate at the top of the stairs, intended to keep the deer out. Jim, one of four members of the ad hoc Pole Pass No Wake Zone Committee wanted to contribute to the effort to put in more No Wake buoys and had given me a check — I was treasurer — but the check had been made out to the Crane Island Association instead of me or the No Wake Zone — so I couldn't deposit it — and was looking for a substitute. I had another purpose in going to see Jim and Nancy. I wanted to know what had happened to the fawn abandoned by its mother in the salal next to their house.

As the raven flies or the kayak paddles, their house is about a quarter mile south of ours, on the water, facing east — but getting there by foot — conveniently — is roundabout, requiring walking west on Eagle Lane, more path than road, to Circle Road, more like a driveway than a road, south to the Rocky Road turnoff and then back east and north to Jim and Nancy's, probably a mile walk. Though windy at the water's edge, inland, amongst the trees, the wind wasn't noticeable and the sun was warm, everything glowing and green. At the Rocky Road junction I noticed what looked like bark shavings scattered under a Noble fir and looked to see the cause. A hundred yards along Rocky Road another scattering of shavings, quite regular: bark, about 1/2 across by 3 inches long. It wasn't the result of some natural bark shedding process. Some animal, perhaps human, had left the shavings, spread out in a way that suggested they had fallen from some height above.

206: What was stripping bark from branches all over the island?

Passing Tom's house I could see the partially finished shop he had been working on but no sign of him. Two lots north, I walked down Jim's driveway and around a big black high-sided trailer and yelled, Hello, anyone home, into the under-construction shop from which I could hear a radio playing. No response. Cement siding had been applied to the bottom four feet of the wall Jim later explained, as a fire-resistance measure, but no one was in back. I walked into the cavity of the two car garage and yelled up the stairs finally getting an acknowledgment from the loft where Jim had his carpentry tools and was working on a project. He wanted to write me a new check right away so we walked to the house nearby, Nancy came out, got the mis-directed check and went inside to write another while Jim and I sat on their deck looking at the water, a steel fire pit nearby.

The fawn had died and Jim had buried it in the woods. In the short time they had gotten to know the fawn, Jim holding it on his lap to keep it warm, they had fallen in love with it, a beautiful, etherial, trusting, helpless creature, abandoned by its mother for reasons unknown (because this fawn had a twin and the doe had made a choice?). Jim said he had first seen the fawn in the salal next to the house and once it had seen him it began to follow him everywhere, on very wobbly legs, , assuming Jim was its mother, perhaps never really having had a good look at her. It was small, not much bigger than a cat or small dog but with very different proportions — its rear legs much more substantial than its front. Nancy fed it milk from a bottle and they built a fire in the pit and the little fawn was soon lying next to the fire that provided some relief from its shivering. In fact it had no fear of the fire at all, and stepped into the fire pit then out — and it had no fear of Jim and Nancy, trusting and depending on them completely. Wolf Hollow, the wildlife rehabilitation center on San Juan Island told Nancy to call them in a day — suggesting that the fawn's mother might return but when she didn't and Nancy called again the next day she couldn't get anyone to pick up the phone. They wouldn't be coming to Crane to rescue the little fawn. And so it died.

Jim and Nancy then told a story about a seal pup, born apparently near their dock whose mother hadn't returned and bereft it had called out night and day for a week before expiring one night on their beach. Jim talked about how little we see now of what humans knew intimately hundreds of years ago.

Home again I took two ladders down to the front garden, with some tools, screws, and the gutter parts I had gotten at the lumber yard the week before and began to hang the gutter that would feed the 500 gallon black cylindrical water tank we'd use for a catchment system, realizing I'd forgotten to get a piece to join two sections. I'd need to go back to the lumber yard, get one or maybe two joints, some downspout and joints, and a bag of sand to put under the tank to provide a smooth level surface. At least I'd gotten started.

Two-hundred-seven: No Wake

"Adopt the pace of nature: her secret is patience." - Ralph Waldo Emerson

The winter birds are gone. When did that happen? I didn't notice until today. No more Mallards, Harlequins, Canvasbacks, Buffleheads, Goldeneyes, and no more Common or Hooded Mergansers. Even the Pelagic Cormorants are missing. The ducks have flown north — but the Cormorants? Our Crane dock Canada geese pair continues to keep us company, often coming ashore at the community dock beach though I now see no sign of their three goslings. Though the lilacs in our yard have yet to flower, inland on Orcas, where it's warmer (and colder), the fragrant bundles of blue, white, and, well, lilac blossoms are abundant. Late blooming daffodils carry on for the fading pioneers and the tulips, short-lived, are dropping petals. Dan's Albin is at the dock and he left me a cross connection survey push-pinned to the bulletin board at the dock, protected from the elements by its sliding glass cover. And Matt's came in the mail so I've had replies from all but a handful of association members; I'll need to call the malingerers.

Because Yvonne and I will be gone next Friday, Chris, David, and I met at 9:00 to review and plan Classics Unbound's doings over the last four weeks, Jens joining us at 10:00. Our main focus, *Metamorphosis*, has yet to be published and since understanding that the translation we were using was in fact copyrighted I'd written Gutenberg Foundation asking for permission but no answer was forthcoming. Ian Johnston's translation held promise; he was nearby, in Nanaimo, on Vancouver Island, retired from teaching and translator of a number of Greek and German classics we'd like to eNotate. We agreed that the paper proofreading process was satisfactory and better than a digital approach, faster for the proofreader probably and necessarily leaving an audit trail we can use to check our changes. Mechanics and technology wasn't really a problem for us but marketing clearly was. The Kindle catalog didn't help us;

no one sought out our website, activity from the two reviews had tapered off, and the Google Adwords campaign may have produced a few sales but at $9.00 a pop we were losing money on each sale and couldn't make it up in volume. We'd have *Metamorphosis* soon. We needed to do better with this potentially more salable book.

When I came home at noon, I found that Steve and Jim wanted to go out in the Pole Pass area to definitively identify positions for the three new No Wake Buoys we wanted to place that the donations we'd received would fund. And then Blair called wanting the can of anti-slip paint I'd bought about a year ago to apply to the aluminum ramp on the Orcas side. After lunch I put the paint with directions and the cross connection survey Blair hadn't completed in a box and left it under the covered bulletin board at the community dock and walked out to Steve's SeaSport, three feet longer, and in better condition than our commuter boat. Though it was a bit windy, out of the northwest, the sun was warm, and I enjoyed riding around using Steve's GPS, charts he made, and our eyeballs to choose three sites on the west side and two on the east, one just a move from one location to another nearby, and then out of the remaining four we'd actually place only three, the final decision being to forego the one off Cal's for now and instead put one off Tom's Rocks between Crane and Bell Islands.

Ready to spend time on the front garden catchment system, I couldn't because I was missing gutter joints, a downspout, and corner fittings — as well as reducers and a hose bib for the big black tank — and a bag of sand — so I'd need to visit the lumberyard again. On the Orcas side dock Blair had nearly completed painting one side of the aluminum ramp with the covering I'd given him. He'd need another quart to finish the other side of the ramp but I'd ordered only one. We talked about the tearing rubber donut hinge and the need to put a chain around the middle pile at the bottom of the U as well as water egress ladders for the Crane side.

207: The catchment tank connected to collect roof runoff

Two-hundred-seven: No Wake

The lumberyard was busier than it had been but I found an open space to pump gas into my red pickup and then drove it to the yard, loaded what I needed from outside and got a yard ticket and then parked out of the way, walking inside to find the tank parts, got some help, and then put my purchases on my account. The 100 lb. bag of sand was very heavy to lift into the bed of the truck and heavier when I lifted it out, put it in the dock cart and then took it to the head of the ramp and heavier still when I carried it down the ramp, one side impassible because of the drying non-slip covering. Heading back to Crane, a blue-hulled sailboat was also heading toward Pole Pass but at a slower, wind-dependent speed. When I'd loaded the sand bag and fixtures on the dock cart I saw the sailboat's mast over the breakwater and that it was heading right for Och's beach and then tack starboard and sailed right along the outside of the breakwater, heeled over taking the wind through the Pass. This was going to be good. I assumed they'd depend on their motor to come through the pass; the wind would be blowing directly against them. The boat was at least 35 feet long, and the navigable width of the pass much less than 100 feet; but I was wrong. The white-haired captain with his grey-haired wife tacked three times in that narrow passage — but sailed, not motored through. Terrific! I clapped and gave them two thumbs up, yelling, "Well done!" but I couldn't tell whether they'd noticed because they we very focused on their sailing. Coming west from the pass they tacked southeast, coming uncomfortably close to a submerged rock they couldn't see and then tacking to the north the wind pushed them too close to the reef near Cal's on the other side of the pass. They made it, against the wind and against the outgoing tide, in a very narrow pass, but I wouldn't have done it that way even if I had the skills.

Two-hundred-eight: Catchment

"A garden is a grand teacher. It teaches patience and careful watchfulness; it teaches industry and thrift; above all it teaches entire trust." – Gertrude Jekyll

With our trip to Harstine Island and Los Osos imminent I was determined to finish and make operational the 450 gallon catchment system at the northwest corner of the house that would provide water to Yvonne's front garden. I had the material I needed — or at least thought I did. A dry day with quite a bit of sun, the thermometer inching up toward 60. Yvonne was at work in the south part of the yard and had been raking among the Douglas fir trunks, carrying branches and leaves to the small fire she'd built in the fire pit near the rain shelter and two shops. She had trimmed a drooping ocean spray bush, removing the dead lower branches, and it lifted itself, standing straight up, proud I suppose to look so good after looking so bad.

I'd placed a ten foot section of brown, plastic, Genoa gutter running from the bottom end of the valley where the guest bedroom roof meets the studio/front walk roof to about half-way to the north end of the house but couldn't hang the remainder until I knew how things would work at the other end — that is exactly how the gutter would feed the tank and I couldn't know that until the tank was in place.

More than a year before a buck had gotten into the front garden and couldn't figure out how to get back out. I heard a crash outside and ran out the front door and saw the buck just outside the deer fence where it meets the northwest corner of the house. The buck's charge had pulled the nylon mesh fencing away from the house and along with it one of the two coaxial cables that comes down from the dish antenna on the roof, goes underground and then enters the crawl space. I screwed the board that held the fencing back against the house but never got around the remounting the dangling black coax cable. So before I could place the tank I had to remount the cable and did that using Yvonne's heavy duty stapler. Up on a ladder, trying to be reasonably careful but having to lean this way and that to reach and hold the cable against the eaves, not all of my staples fired true — some went through rather than around the cable.

The cable out of the way I could turn my attention to creating a smooth and level area for the tank to rest on and had brought home a 100 lb. bag of sand from the lumber yard for that purpose, pulling the bag of sand on the dock cart outside the fence to the tank setting location. I'd dug out a four foot diameter space next to the corner of the house, outside the deer fence, two weeks before and leveled it but because the soil was so rocky I wanted something on top — namely sand. I spread what was left of a bag of sand Yvonne had in her shed and most of my new 100 lb bag and then used my four foot long gold colored aluminum level to spread and level the sand, rotating the level around the 4 foot circle a number of times until I was satisfied. I called Yvonne away from her burn pile on the south side of the house and she helped me slide the tank — which had been sitting about 30 feet away next to the base of the tree-house-to-be — and then tip it upright and lift it onto the sand. It looked more or less plumb but because the tanks sides weren't perfectly consistent, it was hard to tell — but it would have to do. I screwed the reducers ending in a hose bib into the threaded exhaust port near the bottom of the tank facing the deer fence and garden but Yvonne thought there wasn't adequate clearance with the fence so we rotated the tank clockwise and since the fence curved off to the northwest, Yvonne was satisfied the clearance was now adequate. The tank stuck out beyond the edge of the house and the two foot roof overhang. If I put the down flow fitting at the very end of the facia, the downspout, coming off at a 112 degree angle would enter the open port at the top of the tank, not quite in the center but not too far from it. Hanging the down flow fitting and then the piece of gutter to it from the first ten foot section coming north, I now had continuous gutter to the down flow fitting. I cut a section of downspout that would carry the water from the down flow to the 16" diameter port at the top of the tank and removed the port screw on lid and tether and then stapled fine screening I'd saved for years — part of a large inventory of scraps of this and that — across the top of the port and the installed the downspout, the top end held by an angle fitting into the down flow and the bottom end held up by the screening. I was now hoping for rain.

Two-hundred-eight: Catchment

208: Moving the new catchment tank from the F150 to our house on Crane had some challenges (June 2010)

And then Yvonne told me neither television was getting a signal. The staples? Something for another day.

A bit after 6:00 Blair and Molly appeared on the stairs coming up to the deck off the dining room, having taken a shortcut across Becker's farm and coming through Mike's property two lots south. Yvonne and I had seen them Friday evening as we were leaving the Crane dock on our way to the Deer Harbor Community Club monthly potluck and Blair and Molly were arriving. Tonight Blair's hands were still black from the non-skid paint he'd applied Friday to the floor of the aluminum ramp at the Orcas dock, paint thinner ineffective on it. While Yvonne gave Molly a tour of the new kitchen she hadn't seen, Blair and I talked about dock safety ladders and then traded man-overboard and cold water stories. Molly had brought a salad to complement

Two-hundred-eight: Catchment

Yvonne's turkey chili and corn bread. We talked family — joys and challenges — and then over a dessert of baked apples stuffed with raisins Molly had contributed, a bit about pilgrimages — ours in New Mexico — and surprisingly, the new cosmology I'd talked to the Unitarians about and Molly was studying, as it turned out, with her church women's book group. A very pleasant evening — during which it began to rain in a gentle, steady northwest way. Blair and I went out on the front porch to look at the gutter/catchment system in action and it was doing what it was intended to do. At the point in the evening I would normally take our guests back to Orcas I didn't have to because Blair and Molly were also Crainians so I could finish cleaning up the kitchen after they headed out into the near-dark with their flashlight.

Two-hundred-nine: Kayakers

"Dance with the waves, move with the sea, let the rhythm of the water set your soul free." - Christy Ann Martine

The rain streamed off the roof onto the water-facing deck outside the living room. A cord that former owners, Dean and Iris had installed to move their bird feeder armature hung in a bow shape just under the eaves and caught water drops falling from above, the drops from both sides of the bow rolling downhill, meeting at the low point and dropping to the deck, a beautiful dance of drops.

With the *Huginn's* fuel gauge showing about one-eighth tank remaining, Yvonne was worried we'd soon run out of gas. Since the tank held 46 gallons (and it had been a very long time since we felt flush enough to fill it), that meant more than five gallons remained, so I wasn't worried — but more than a year before Yvonne had run out of gas (my fault) in Margaret's boat going west through Pole Pass and had been rescued by Tom and by me. She had been especially attentive (sensibly) ever since. And since it was Sunday she wanted to pick up the *Sunday Seattle Times* at the Deer Harbor Marina and then the Saturday mail at the Post Office across Deer Harbor Road. So, after she finished breakfast, about 9:30, we walked out the door into (what was for us) a heavy rain that had been filling the new catchment system since dinnertime the night before.

While Yvonne waited in the *Huginn*'s cabin out of the rain I zipped open the canvas covering Margaret's boat's cockpit, climbed in, and then checked the levels in the two five gallon red plastic fuel cans. I'd filled the spare about six weeks before — overfilled as it turned out so that fuel was leaking out that cap — and that required some decanting and cleanup — but the in-use can appeared only about half-full so I disconnected the fuel line, lifted the can out of the boat and carried it to the *Huginn*, laying it down in the cockpit.

Two-hundred-nine: Kayakers

With little wind the supersaturated air formed wispy clouds, white cotton, that drifted through the firs, cedar, and leafing maples and alder, and I half-expected them to be snagged on the branches they passed. Off Cal's dock I brought the *Huginn* up on plane, watching out for crab pot floats, flotsam, and water birds as we raised a wake speeding north toward Deer Harbor. Friday when Steve, Jim, and I were on the west side of Pole Pass reconnoitering for No Wake Zone buoy positions we had seen Cal returning home from Reef Island to the west. Steve hypothesized that Cal had been shrimping and when I saw him at the Deer Harbor potluck that night he confirmed he had caught 14 spot prawns (they can grow to 12 inches and the daily limit is 80) but wouldn't say where though the water had been more than 420 feet deep. The 1.7 mile trip, at 20 mph, takes only a few minutes and we were soon coming down off plane approaching the marina fuel dock. Yvonne pointed out that another boat was coming in for fuel, aft and to port so I chose to dock on the east side, turned the boat around, and Yvonne jumped out to secure the lines and taking her 98243 cloth mail bag walked up the dock and then ramp to the marina store to buy the newspaper and then walked the dock to the road and across to the Post Office.

Four men got off the fishing boat across the dock and on asking what they'd been fishing for and the closest replied lingcod (which is neither ling nor cod). How did you do? The reply — the other three are the fishermen and I think they'd say not well. I was wearing a yellow slicker with the hood up over the Phantom Canyon Brewing Co. blue billed cap I'd gotten for my birthday dinner in Colorado Springs from Phoebe and Alan (who is the restaurant's brew master); they were wearing thin jackets and looked soaked. I put about $85 of gas into the *Huginn* and then two gallons into the tank I brought from Margaret's boat.

Three good looking fiberglass sea kayaks were approaching from the north, probably having paddled under the deck to the street after launching in the little public park that was established a few years ago just north of the marina. Three couples, a woman in front, man in back, all wearing floppy rain hats, rain gear, and bright yellow life jackets. Where are you headed? To Jones Island. Great. It's beautiful. We were out there two weeks ago. This was a return trip for the lead boat at least and they said they weren't concerned about the rain — they had a good tent. I advised them to look into the Adirondack cabins just up from the south beach, explaining that they were new this year and would keep them drier than tent camping. They had intended to approach the island from the west, beaching below the Cascadia Marine Trail campsites where they'd camped before and which were restricted to beachable human powered craft. But it was so wet, I thought they might end up changing their minds — provided the cabins weren't already in use.

209: Kayaks above Raven's Cove waiting for action

By mid afternoon the rain had fallen off and I turned my attention to the fact that the DirectTV system could no longer pick up a satellite feed because of something I'd done when installing the catchment system — probably because I'd put a few staples through the two coaxial cables when I rehung them to get them out of the way and repair the damage a buck had done when charging through the deer fence separating the north end from the house. Eric happened to call and since he had studied engineering I asked him why staples would have a negative effect. He said he didn't know exactly but that digital systems were much more sensitive than analog systems. I brought a ladder to the side of the house, laid it against the tank, and climbed up on it, first confirming that it was heavy enough that my weight wouldn't tip it. Looking down into the top port I could see the reflection of water below, more than a foot deep — a satisfying view. I pulled out the offending staples and went inside to check reception; the system was back on the air.

I calculated that the roof area feeding the tank would provide 6200 gallons in an average year. If we captured 60% of the water than landed on that part of the roof, we could fill the tank 8 times — provided the rains and needs came at the right time — and save about $100 on our annual water bill. The system had cost about $500 to put together, so in the ideal case it would pay for itself in 5 years. We'd just have to see how it worked out for the coming dry season.

Later I called Noah to find out whether he wanted any physics and cosmology books because he'd been doing science research for a youth reader book he had in mind. He was interested so I'd pack some up and take them with when we left home Tuesday morning. That morning I'd responded to an email from Tim who had read my UU New Science, New Religion 2 paper and offered comments. It was a pleasure to have someone read it, think about it, and then offer his own ideas.

Two-hundred-ten: Clean up

"The true way to live is to enjoy every moment as it passes, and surely it is in the everyday things around us that the beauty of life lies." - Laura Ingalls Wilder

Margaret would be coming back to Crane about the 19th, when we'd be gone, so we needed to leave her boat on the Orcas side so she could get back to Crane. I had errands in Eastsound and Yvonne had a master gardener meeting later in the day, so I would take Margaret's boat, Yvonne would take the *Huginn* and when I got back to the dock I'd take the *Huginn* back to Crane and then pick up Yvonne there after she called when leaving her meeting.

The threatened rain hadn't materialized but there was a bit of wind out of the northwest making leaving the Crane dock attention-getting since the wind wanted to carry the boat away before I could properly untie it and climb aboard. On the Orcas side I moored Margaret's boat on the outer finger, one of the areas for longer term moorage, the spaces more convenient to the ramp marked with yellow (48 hours) and red (15 minutes), reserved for transient moorage.

After stopping at the Deer Harbor Post Office to drop off some thank-you notes for contributions to the No Wake Zone effort, I turned north on Crow Valley Road in West Sound and saw a pickup that wasn't going farther north drop off a woman hitchhiker and I stopped to pick her up at Frank and Liz's driveway. She was on her way to Dr. Shinstrom's office near our insurance agency adjacent to the airport and since it wasn't really out of my way I dropped her right at the door and then drove a short distance west to the NAPA store to see what I could do about the driver-side, rear turn signal light, having brought with me the tools I thought I'd need. Ray tested the bulb for me and the van was soon street legal. Making a deposit at Key Bank for the No Wake Zone Committee, I ran into Frank, who I'd seen last at a party in the winter and who had related to me in some detail his amazing World War II odyssey story. At 94 he was fit and handsome and as always very friendly and asked about James' progress on his PhD.

210: Comforting Crane Island fire hydrants

After making a personal account deposit at the Islander Bank, I parked the van near the library and walked to Roses Bakery Cafe. Jens was already at a table and I saw Bob at another. It was noon and a few tables were vacant but they would fill up soon. A bowl of homemade tomato soup and bread for me and a sandwich for Jens — which he said he would not order again. We traded stories about why we had studied what we had where and then why we did what we did where to make a living. He gave me a copy of his book on

Two-hundred-ten: Clean up

Kafka's "In the Penal Colony" story and I gave him a short, somewhat bizarre Kafka biography featuring Robert Crumb drawings. And we talked about the UU paper I'd written and sent to him at his request — which he reported he had enjoyed — finding the summarization and extension of the latest cosmology and psychology of religion interesting — though puzzled at how this atheistic orientation was appropriate for a church service — even Unitarian. His impression was that Unitarianism, at least as we practiced it was barely religious. Maybe so.

We adjourned to Enzo's for more discussion and I set him up with the software and database to begin working on eNotations for Kafka's *The Penal Colony*. After our Friday meeting he had written the rest of us a list of marketing ideas and we reviewed these briefly as well as talking about the best strategy for getting an appropriate translation and rights to the images he wanted to use for *Metamorphosis* — opening up a topic I had hoped was closed but which continued to nag. The MLA (Modern Literature Association) would be meeting in Seattle in January and we had thought briefly about getting a booth and selling there. I suggested we use that opportunity to recruit more eNotators — and perhaps try to sell books — since building our collection was critical to our success — more important in the short run than sales even.

After our meeting I drove back to the NAPA store to use the coin operated vacuums and car wash to clean the van — that had dropped below Yvonne's appearance standard for it. I'd purchased a pack of Windex wipes at Island Market and with them I was able to clean the windows, vinyl, and hard surfaces. By the time I finished 90 minutes later the van was acceptable but could be significantly improved by some effective detailing that cleaned the cloth upholstery and carpeting.

Yvonne called at 5:40 and I went over to Orcas to pick her up. Even after three meals — one with company — we couldn't finish the turkey chili — but it was better than ever — with the last of the cornbread and two slices of the banana bread Yvonne had made that morning. Tomorrow we would begin our trip to California.

Two-hundred-eleven: To Harstine Island

"Two roads diverged in a wood, and I took the one less traveled by, And that has made all the difference." - Robert Frost, "The Road Not Taken"

We were out the door and on our way to the Crane Island community dock just past 7:30. I'd set all the thermostats to 58, the hot tub to 82 and tied the lid down, put the garbage and recycle in the former outhouse, and locked the four doors. A beautiful, sunny morning — the best yet this spring. I parked the *Huginn* just to the east of the Orcas dock egress ladder and then walked up the aluminum ramp trying out the non-skid paint Blair had put down on one side of the ramp — and it seemed to work well. At the Orcas Landing market, we bought a sandwich to share for lunch, a single-shot 8 oz latte for Yvonne and a Tazo Awake tea for me — as well as the *Seattle Times* and sat parked in the ferry line, the *Elwah* late for some reason.

On the ferry, we sat with Howard and Sheila for a while — they were off to Bellingham for some shopping and to use the last of their five ride ferry ticket (before it expired — they're good for 90 days) and then climbed to the top level so I could do some writing — talked to Megan and Jane for a few minutes (to tell Megan the Greybeards intended to see Bob on the 26th). Marion was talking to Barbara (who Yvonne suspected was delusional) and Mick was reading the paper. And later, on the way down to get in our van Yvonne saw Kate (but not Ken). A big day for going to America.

Yvonne had some returns to make at Costco and I filled the tank with $3.84/gal gas and then went inside to find Yvonne shopping for gifts — one of her favorite activities — but she didn't find the jacket she wanted for Eric for his birthday so we continued down the I-5 corridor to Seattle Premium (factory) Outlets where she did. At the Union Street exit in Seattle we left the highway and parked in an underground lot and had to ask directions to find our way out to the street.

211A: Corrina, Yvonne, Opal, and Natasha

Yvonne went into H&M to find Corrina and shop while I walked two blocks to Barnes and Noble for a 10 minute demonstration of the Nook Color (I was impressed) and looked for books in the ePub format (after having had trouble making it work using Elizabeth Castro's directions) — and then the three of us were on our way to Olympia where we picked up a rental Impala ($150 for a week) for our drive to California — having determined that we'd save more than enough money on gas to pay for it — and save wear and tear on our van.

As we turned onto Pickering Road from Route 3, I saw a white SUV behind us and it followed us right into Noah and Natasha's driveway, Natasha, Morgan, and Opal returning from school. The kids helped carry in our suitcases and their presents and were soon running all over the yard in the afternoon sunshine, chasing and being chased by their dog, Sugar, who likes to

Two-hundred-eleven: To Harstine Island

play ball but not share. Later Morgan demonstrated his increasing skill on his skateboard and Opal rode up and down the driveway on her big-girl bike sans training wheels. Noah was home about a hour later and he and I took Sugar and McKinley for a walk almost to the entrance of the state park. His teaching job situation had clarified: he'd have a job next year but it would change — and he'd be driving to other schools to meet with students enrolled in the hybrid on-line classes he taught. Sadly, his colleague, Eric would suffer an involuntary transfer and Noah wasn't sure why since Eric was skilled and reliable. On the back deck, facing Pickering Passage, we sat in the sun, this time of year in the northwest late in the day, while the kids played on the slide and swing set Noah had built, Opal doing tricks on the slide and Morgan showing how he could swing and then jump. Corrina introduced a word game and it took a while to guess how it worked — and then we couldn't stop. Example: the wee people like Mommy and Daddy but not Mom and Dad. The little people like jelly but not peanut butter. The little people like Yvonne but not John.

After dinner, in the lingering light, Corrina found that her car wouldn't start, the battery severely depleted after sitting in the driveway since last November when Corrina left it there, in storage while she went to India. Noah had cleaned the Corolla and jump started it and had let it run but the charge hadn't stuck. Another jump start this evening and Corrina took off — after Noah and I advised her that she might not be able to start the car the next morning after parking it overnight in Seattle and she might need to replace the battery before she left for Philadelphia in a few weeks to start her MFA program. Natasha printed out driving instructions for getting back to Seattle via Olympia and Corrina was off in the dusk. The kids had a hard time getting in bed since the sky was light now until nearly 10:00. The adults sat in the living room visiting and trying to stay awake.

It had been a good day. About noon when Yvonne was shopping at the Columbia outlet store for a jacket for Eric, I was sitting in the car checking my email with the iPad — finding, happily, that the retired professor I'd contacted about using his translation of Kafka's *The Metamorphosis* had granted us permission so I wrote Jens — who had found the source for the images we wanted to use and their tariff was acceptable. We could create an edition that was unproblematic and I'd work on the changes once we returned from California.

Two-hundred-eleven: To Harstine Island

211B: Noah and Morgan after school

Two-hundred-twelve: On the Road Again

"How lucky I am to have something that makes saying goodbye so hard." - A.A. Milne, *Winnie-the-Pooh*

Awake before 5:00, I was at work downstairs by 5:30 catching up on email and sending Jens the image and text files he'd asked for, the first relating to acquiring necessary permissions from Wagenbach Verlag and the latter to use as source material for *The Penal Colony*, his new project. Natasha was soon up and walked the dogs and then began making pancakes and chicken sausage for the waking group. She told me she'd gone to a job interview on Monday for a small patient information system company created by a local doctor that was trying to grow but the woman she would work with talked about how the job required a life commitment — it seemed to Natasha — that would exclude life with her family — and therefore out of balance — so when she got home she'd sent her regrets. Natasha had become less inclined to go to graduate school — for a teaching degree, since that looked increasingly unpromising — or for an MBA, which would be expensive in time and money and wouldn't guarantee a job she'd enjoy.

Yvonne and I were on the road by 7:45, ahead of Noah and the kids also on their way south. Just after 9:00 we pulled up in front of the house where Gina, Yvonne's niece, was now living in Centralia. Knowing that we would stop, she had gone to Ephrata in Eastern Washington the day before to pick up her daughter Maria and her new baby, Cresi, named after her sister. We hadn't seen Gina in about 18 months — after she dropped out of sight and didn't answer emails. Recently Yvonne found her on FaceBook and she seemed ready for new contact. We'd heard that she'd been sick and today though her color was good she was puffy probably from her medications, though we didn't ask. Yvonne had met Maria before but I hadn't and neither of us her new baby, now about six weeks old.

Maria was clearly very happy being a mother and had a palpable physical and emotional intimacy with her new daughter that glowed, both buoyed by some invisible goddess of mothers and babies — new life in the human family. Yvonne had told me that Maria was happy-go-lucky and her unproblematic enthusiasm and joy infected the rest of us I think — even knowing all the difficulties she faced.

Yvonne, Maria holding Cresi, and Gina

Gina, living with Mark, who we didn't meet and who travelled to Redmond to work, was short of breath and said several times that overall she felt weak though right now better than she had. So she stayed close to home, rarely going out and filled her days with reading — now using a Kindle, having recently discovered how to download free books. I showed her the Barnes & Noble website and installed the Nook PC reader on her notebook computer. Gina responded enthusiastically to Yvonne's offer to send her boxes of books regularly — and now we had a purpose for the hundreds of good paperbacks that collected dust on our shelves. Perhaps Gina would be interested in our eNotated Classics books. I'd give that a try later on.

And then we were off — heading south on "The Five," through Vancouver, Washington, then across the Columbia, and Portland, Salem, Eugene, and points south — a beautiful sunny, intensely green day in all directions but the blue of up — but we barely noticed because we were listening to Timothy Egan's *Big Burn*, the story of the massive 1910 wildfire in the northern Rockies, a coming of age for the newly-formed Forest Service and the confirmation of the conservation agenda for America that though challenged in spots remains a defining value for our country. Yvonne and I were both very impressed with Egan's writing and the story he told — about Teddy Roosevelt and his good friend Gifford Pinchot, the Progressives and the Conservation agenda and the economic and political forces that opposed it and the idealistic Forest Rangers who defended and died in the firestorm that leveled more than 3 million acres of forest and the towns within. Like the northern Rockies, the San Juan islands are tinder-dry in the summer, with islands like Orcas and Crane covered mostly with thick forest perhaps even more susceptible to out of control wild-fires because the undergrowth is thicker, growing rapidly in the rainy season. And like the mountains of Idaho and Montana, much of the forest on the islands is essentially inaccessible. Egan's account of the Big Burn was sobering about the danger we live amongst and the overriding need to educate our residents, protect our island from irresponsible outsiders (the unattended burn pile in late March), the need for equipment, training, and coordination with Orcas firefighters, and the importance of "Fire Wise" practices — especially the clearing of brush and combustibles from around dwellings.

About 7:00 we pulled into Chico, California, having driven about 600 miles and the confinement in the car had made me feel groggy. We made our way to Tres Hombres, near the campus, and joined what seemed like thousands of other diners, many collected at long tables celebrating birthday parties, "Happy Birthday," starting up again and again here and there in the very noisy space. I was struck by how all the young women college students looked exactly the same — clothes, hair, body shape, behavior — and it reminded me of the day we brought James to Forbes College at Princeton his freshman year — and I thought I saw the same pattern. I was tired — too much sitting — and ready to go to bed — and we did after indulging a little computer time after our late dinner .

Two-hundred-thirteen: Los Osos

"Progress is impossible without change, and those who cannot change their minds cannot change anything." - George Bernard Shaw

Waking up about 5:30, I was in the motel breakfast room when it opened, making myself a waffle and putting it on a plate with a hardboiled egg and two sausages — with a cup of hot tea and caffeine to wake me up a bit. I responded to some email threads and initiated some others and then did some writing, Yvonne appearing about 8:00 and we were soon on our way south again, picking up *The Big Burn: Teddy Roosevelt and the Fire that Saved America* by Timothy Egan where we'd left off the evening before, now hearing about the aftermath of the fire — the stories of those like Pulaski who had lost so much and who had been so disappointed at the failure of the Federal Government to pay for the medical care of the injured firefighters or even to express any appreciation — and the athletic response of Roosevelt who could no longer contain his criticism of his protegee-turned-nemesis, Taft. Not surprising really except in its specificity, the struggle between instant gratification and sustainable practices, including setting aside land for recreational and even wilderness areas — the conflict played out all through the west over the last century — even on Orcas and Crane — where over-fishing depleted salmon and other stocks that have yet to recover, where forests were cleared to feed furnaces to make cement, where fruit farming bubbles popped and island populations declined, and where tourism, real estate, and building created another kind of economy, another bubble, but where some elements of the population are determined to create a sustainable community while others fight the mere idea tooth and nail because it interferes with the right of each property owner to plunder as he or she sees fit. A century from now the same struggles will continue in the Islands and the West and I suppose on the planet.

Two-hundred-thirteen: Los Osos

South and south, skirting the Bay Area to the west, past Silicon Valley, past the garlic fields, past Monterey and Carmel, Steinbeck country, his threatening eastern mountains on the left and beneficent western mountains on the right and the irrigated, prolific, agribusiness farms in between, past missions we'd visited on the Camino Real, the King's Highway, flat land becoming rolling, oak scattered hillsides, and then the descent from the hills to Morro Bay and then Los Osos, the warm sun now hidden by fog born on the cool waters of the Pacific, the same water that in a briny form that the tides slosh in and out of the Salish Sea through the Straight of Juan de Fuca. No Douglas firs here. No western cedars. No salal in this desert by the sea.

We let ourselves into the house and soon heard the voices of grandchildren Jackson and Maddie and then Kristin, she having picked them up after his kindergarten and day care and her pre-school. Both were especially interested in the coloring books Grandma Bon had brought for them and they were soon at work — looking forward to the spin painting and tee-shirt projects scheduled for Friday afternoon. The big news was that the Chamber Board had chosen Dave's successor, a dynamic young woman that Kristin worked well with — and the success of yesterday's Chamber local trade show — 150 businesses serving businesses attended by more than 6000 — one of Kristin's membership services projects. Then we crowded into the rented Impala and drove the ten miles to the CalPoly campus where the Aerospace Engineering department was hosting its 18th Annual Industrial Design Symposium, an opportunity for graduating seniors to show off their projects to faculty, parents, and most notably to industry representatives who might hire them. According to our son Eric most of their graduates were employed within three months of graduation — a remarkable statistic when so many young people are looking for work. The reception room was filled with table top folding illustrated cards, scale models, and computer simulations and I interviewed three of the students, looking both good and uncomfortable in suits and ties, about their asteroid material collection, electric powered airplane, and ultra heavy-lift massive hybrid air vehicles (a heavier than air blimp — with lifting surfaces) projects — all fascinating and indicative of what the government and the aerospace industries considered feasible and short-term priorities. Eric said CalPoly regularly won the national competitions these projects were in part created for.

Maddie, Jackson, and Kristin with the Balloon Man

Thursday evening is Farmer's Market time in San Luis Obispo and we made our way through the crowds to Mother's Tavern, where the kids continued their coloring book projects and Kristin soon joined us having attended the "Toast" to the incoming Chamber director. Then the kids stood in line for the Balloon Man, whose talented hands created a pink lady-bug to be worn on her wrist for Maddie and a green sword for Jackson. Home again, the kids in bed, Kristin wanted to know about eNotated Classics and then once she faded after having spent several long intense days with Chamber projects Eric and I — with Yvonne mostly listening — talked about the multi-verse and the projection of mind — Eric seeing connection with the "transcendence" theme talk he'd have to give, as department chair, to the graduating seniors. And then we were too tired to think about anything except bed.

Two-hundred-fourteen: Projects

"Let him be himself." - Maria Montessori

Eric was busy cleaning out Jackson's frog terrarium, and the three frogs made continual efforts to escape the plastic container he'd temporarily stored them in. Why, now, at breakfast time and with Jackson needing to get ready for school? Ah. Since Friday is show and tell at Jackson's Kindergarten class, it was an opportunity for Jackson to show off the three small frogs, two, dad and son discovered in and making their home in their unused hot tub and one that mysteriously appeared in Kristin's Chamber office on the second floor of a building in downtown SLO. How did that happen? Jackson had several tadpoles as well, one or two that were growing legs but they were kept in their own aquarium. Originally they'd come from Del Mar Park on Morro Bay. When Kristin brought the frogs home in their aquarium about an hour later she reported that the presentation had been a big success.

Yvonne's plan was to take Maddie shopping with her, their special destination, Trio in SLO, a boutique Yvonne especially liked but when she arrived at about 10:15 the sign in the window said the store wouldn't open until 11:00 and she was due to pick Jackson up from Kindergarten at noon and would need to stop at Trader Joe's on the way. To fill the waiting time Yvonne and Maddie walked to Ross and found a pair of pink sandals both girls liked, in design something like my Keen's. When they returned to Trio at 11:00 it was still closed and didn't open for another fifteen minutes, poor form for a retailer Yvonne thought. Yvonne found a top on the half-price rack but not before Maddie needed attendance in the restroom, the whole time Yvonne was worried about being late to pick up Jackson — and she couldn't call me to walk over to the school because I don't have a cell phone and Eric and Kristin, like an increasing number of households, don't have a land line. After super-shopping Trio the pair drove to Trader Joe's where Yvonne was delighted to find the chain now carried Three Buck Chuck Sauvignon Blanc, drier and more satisfying than the Chardonnay she usually bought there.

214: Spin painting wonders

We had two kid projects to do: tie-dyed scarfs and spin painting and we got started right after lunch. First up, the Alex Toys Tie Dye Partners scarf project — one for Jackson and one for Maddie May. The kit came with three dye colors: red, blue, and yellow — plus two pairs of gloves and some spacers, ties, and rubber bands — but no directions — unless they had somehow disappeared from the box after it got home. I looked online, first at alex.com, an adult site — that wouldn't work — and then alextoys.com — that hosted a step-by-step video we all watched in stages to understand the process —

which, for our purposes, wasn't very complicated. We folded the cotton scarves in half, then bunched one end, putting in spacers that stuck out past the sides of the fabric and tied them together with rubber bands. We then used ties to gather middle sections of the fabric and then what the directions called explosive bolts to create what would appear to be targets. More of less following directions the kids then applied dye from spouted plastic bottles, while wearing gloves and empty garbage bags Yvonne had cut holes in for head and arms. No dye stains on the kids or the table — but plenty on the adults hands. Each scarf was then put in a plastic bag and placed in the refrigerator for an overnight dye soak session.

Jackson relaxed by watching Disney cartoons — and I was struck by how ugly they were — the animated figures, their gestures, the nature of the stories — really awful but Jackson seemed to enjoy them and then I couldn't stay awake and took a little nap while Yvonne made dinner preparations. When Maddie hadn't woken from her nap by 4:00 Jackson politely woke her so we could work on the spin paintings. The Spin 'n Spin Art kit included a spinner, four tubes of paint, and two dozen cardboard squares. The project was a big success, each child creating three paintings — all quite different from one another — and when they were done we put them on newspaper to dry overnight.

After work Eric and Kristin stayed in town briefly, hoping for time to enjoy a drink and conversation together but instead they were drawn into a Chamber activity, arriving home just after six to Yvonne's risotto, broccoli, and salad dinner — very good. Eric and Kristin were now using a new Kodak still and video camera and took us through recent events — such as Jackson's birthday party — which we had missed. A busy day, cool and windy outside, and I'd spent virtually the whole time inside. Tomorrow we'd have a picnic — but away from the ocean where the temperature was expected to hit 75.

Two-hundred-fifteen: First Birthday Party

"The world is a book and those who do not travel read only one page." - Saint Augustine

Son Eric was hand-crafting pancakes — more or less round — and two with Star War themes — one resembling Darth Vadar and another Yoda. As I cleaned up the breakfast dishes I could see how Eric did his trick. We took our time but we did have a deadline: we'd needed to leave by about 10:30 to meet son, James and his partner, Keith and bonus-daughter, Corrina and her friend, Dave (who had attended a Kylie Minogue Aphrodite concert Friday evening — having flown from Seattle for the occasion and staying with James and Keith over the weekend). The morning was cool and windy so meeting in Santa Barbara seemed less desirable than being warmer inland where the temperature was to be 75 and the sky sunny. James told us that Google driving directions predicted a two hour drive from Los Angeles to Solvang; it would be less for us. We were on the road by 10:30, driving south and east from Los Osos.

We'd visited Solvang years before when Eric was a student at UC Santa Barbara and frequently rode his bicycle over San Marco Pass to Santa Ynez and Solvang and later when we visited the Santa Ynez Mission and then the Gainey Vineyard when grandson, Jackson, was just a baby. Yvonne sat in the Pilot way-back, daughter-in-law, Kristin between the kids and Eric and I in the front, talking most of the way about life-time financial planning — our situation, hammered by both falling real estate values and very low CD and bond rates — and his situation — a lower interest mortgage and a defined benefit California pension, unless something got in its way in the future.

At the vineyard, on this beautiful day, we gathered three wrought-iron tables together, putting ten chairs around the periphery, and brought the sandwiches and other food from the car — and there was James and company — with potato salad and a carrot cake for Eric's birthday. While the rest of us arranged the table Eric brought out two bottles of wine and glasses and we got down to the important business of lunch. We talked with James and Keith about their upcoming Europe trip, especially concerning the relatives he'd see in Sweden. They'd planned their whole trip day by day, knew where they'd be staying, and had their Eurail passes. In Los Angeles they'd hosted visitors from abroad in their apartment and expected to enjoy the other side of the transaction in Europe, intending to stay for free wherever they went. Certainly their week in Sweden would cost next to nothing. By staying with private parties elsewhere they hoped to stay for free and be connected into the local environment.

Dave, especially, and Corrina (mostly along for the ride) had enjoyed the Australian singers concert, even with the expense and time of having come from Seattle and they had appreciated its art deco theme. Dave, a graphics art major, was a Panera store manager in Seattle and liked it better than his native Pittsburgh.

Corrina brought out the cake but couldn't light the candles in the light wind but that didn't matter. We finished with Ja, må han leva and Eric opened this batch of presents, appreciating the Columbia jacket Yvonne had picked up en route to Los Osos. Kristin played hide and seek with the kids on the circle lawn at the entrance to the wine tasting area while the others imbibed, finding they liked the wines enough to buy a few bottles, benefiting from the discount Eric and Kristin could apply.

Los Olivos is close to Santa Ynez and the Gainey Winery (and Solvang) with the ambience of a small, historic, viniculture town. Yvonne encouraged James to buy presents for the Swedes and he found some lavender soap and cast iron mice holding votive candles. A small classic auto show was in town and one shop had hired a band, its grassy yard filled with couples, families, locals, and old timers enjoying the outdoor rock music concert. Lots of wine tasting parlors, olive oil vendors, souvenirs, galleries, and a few restaurants — all on a very small scale and with some sense of authenticity.

Both Lopez and San Juan Islands, in our neighborhood, had vineyards, and wine tasting, though extremely modest in comparison to what California had to offer. Late in the summer, in order to compensate and to fund raise, the Deer Harbor Community Club would sponsor a wine tasting event — but probably not with local or even domestic wines. About 4:30 James and crew headed south to Los Angeles and an evening of club crawling while we cruised north to SLO and Los Osos, Maddie falling deeply asleep on the drive back. A dinner of leftovers — from lunch and the day before — and once the kids were in bed we could barely sit up, soon retiring from a busy day, spent mostly outside, enjoyable to the kids, an opportunity for conservation, and for those so inclined a chance to taste new wines and maybe get a little buzz. California....

215: Gainey Winery - James, Eric, Yvonne, Keith - Kristin taking a picture

Two-hundred-sixteen: Elfin Forest

"Call it a clan, call it a network, call it a tribe, call it a family. Whatever you call it, whoever you are, you need one." - Jane Howard

Kristin had made coffee cake with the kids the night before so I made myself a cup of tea and cut myself a piece, joining the kids at the kitchen table. And then I cut a smaller piece. Eric went outside to pick up the Sunday paper and we each picked a section to read. Then Kristin sat down and soon Yvonne appeared and asked who wanted a fried egg. I did — but then I was too full. No stories in the local paper about the forever-in-process Los Osos sewer system project but binge drinking on the CalPoly campus was covered in excruciating detail — including the fact that the percentage of students practicing it had remained about the same over the years no matter the programs applied to combat it. Not much followup on the failure of the Rapture to appear — interest having faded rapidly.

On Crane I walk the island every other day and had had little exercise for five days. Did Yvonne want to go out with me? We could take the kids. As it turned out Eric wanted Jackson to accompany him to the nearby hardware/lumber store to pick up materials for the fort Eric was building for Jackson so Yvonne and I took Maddie while Kristin did the wash. We'd been to the Elfin Forest many times, first with Jackson and then both kids, and the last few times with just Maddie. The 90 acre site above a tidal area contains a surprising number of dune and desert type bushes and trees, century old live oak much smaller than elsewhere because of the winds and dryness of the location, the path through the park on a raised boardwalk installed in 1999. Out of the wind the sun was warm and as usual we read the placards about the Chumash Indians who had left middens on the site and the Brant geese who winter here after making non-stop flights from Alaska. The cormorants, Canada geese, Blue Herons and many other birds were common to the San Juans as well — but not the pelicans — so common along the California coast.

Here rain was rare most of year and flora struggled to survive. On our island, the good rain fell often and it was a struggle to keep the flora from overwhelming signs of humanity.

216A: Eric at work on Jackson's fort

Eric had begun work on Jackson's fort and Jackson and Bennett were helping by creating mud wherever they could. Though I wasn't much help I spent the next hour or so holding 2 x 4s or OSB panels while Eric made cuts or did nailing and we went to get more lumber and nails to move the project along. And then I wasn't much help again and went inside to catch up on my writing while Eric worked on moving the electrical wiring for his spa, a necessity since he pulled the circuit box out of the wall where he installed two bookcases on either side of what would be a Murphy bed frame — part of a project to make the enclosed back deck into a year-round guest room/home office. I told him how when we first moved into the Crane house I replaced the spa/hot tub pump, heater, blower, and switches with a kit I'd gotten from Spa-Guts. I'd enjoyed removing the old system and installing the new one — which required quite a bit of PVC plumbing and having made lots of mistakes in the process could probably do it much better now but likely wouldn't have (or want) another chance. And I'd converted space from one purpose to another — from garage to studio — with pantry, guest room, and loft on a cantilevered balcony that overhung the studio portion of the space — a project of the first three or so months after moving to Crane.

Kristin's parents, Bob and Diane, arrived about 5:30 while Eric was cooking a halibut dinner with fresh fish he'd picked up earlier in the day at Giovanni's in Morro Bay when we all went there for lunch on the deck above the Bay, sea lions on a float mid bay and the light soft because of the moisture in the air — moisture that had been and would again be fog and low clouds as the sun-warmed air cooled that evening. The fish, with a grapefruit remoulade was delicious — served with 18-hour no-knead bread Kristin had baked, a green salad Diane brought from SLO and a pasta salad Yvonne had made. I cleaned up the dishes.

Word from Diane was that daughter Lauren and her fiancé Dave had decided they did not need to be married in the Huntington Beach Ritz Carlton — but hadn't decided on another venue or date for their wedding. I asked Bob how he was adjusting to retirement and SLO and he replied that he wasn't quite retired — he continued to have small projects from time to time in San Diego. So far he was disappointed in SLO. He'd played an executive role in a number of start-ups and wanted to share what he'd learned with new businesses on the Central Coast but SLO seemed unresponsive — so he was unwilling to invest much attention in the university town — in SLO to be with the grandchildren but ready to return to La Jolla if and when Jackson and Maddie were more independent and perhaps less interested in grandparents.

Bob had been disappointed in the SLO country club as a place to meet people. This evening he asked about our volunteer experience on Orcas and Yvonne and I went into considerable detail — though Maddie's climbing on Bob brought an end to that discussion before we could finish.

216B: Bob, Kristin, and Diane

Finally I suggested to Bob that he look into the CalPoly business incubator — since presumably they would be happy to have knowledgeable business start-up help. You're looking to be an elder in a way, right? Right.

Two-hundred-seventeen: On the Road Yet Again

"Heaven goes by favor. If it went by merit, you would stay out and your dog would go in." - Mark Twain

Yvonne woke early and after hugs and thank-yous we were on our way north again, planning to stay in Roseburg, Oregon for the night, a drive of about 600 miles. Yvonne loaded the first disc of Bill Bryson's *At Home: A Short History of Private Life* and we happily followed his voyage around his Victorian house, with long side trips all over the planet and backward in time, coming to think about our home on Crane Island in a new way, more aware of the long social and technical history behind what we take as obvious — if we notice it at all. I've thought for some time that what I especially appreciate is hot and cold running water, showers and toilets, clean, efficient heat, artificial light, and ways to store and cook food, wash and dry clothes, and the telephone — all available, even common in the US even a century ago but rare or non-existent before then. It's not at all clear to me that what's happened since the late Victorian period is a significant improvement — and perhaps is quite the opposite — making private life not more satisfying but less.

We'd stayed in Roseburg many times in the past — usually with our little black mutt Samantha, or as Opal named her five years ago 'Mantha Moo Moo — the last time a year ago when we spent an hour in the evening walking along the Umpqua River at the park off Centennial Drive. She and Yvonne chased each other across the green green fields. Evening walkers passed us going in both directions along the river savoring the still warm sun that would soon slip behind the forested hills to the west. Three teenage boys waded in the river, involved in some project I couldn't decipher, the river bottom in places green with water plants and still pretty clear probably not experiencing much agricultural run-off.

Two-hundred-seventeen: On the Road Yet Again

217: 'Mantha Moo Moo - world's best dog (July 2008)

Samantha, rescued from the Boulder Humane Society years ago, was about twelve and with graying muzzle was less active than in previous years — but always a patient traveler, taking her place on a towel on a back seat and more or less not moving for the hours it took between the infrequent stops we made when traveling between Washington and Colorado or California. She didn't like traveling but she liked staying in a kennel much less — a last resort alternative when we flew.

Now she was buried in a hole I dug near the compost bins in our yard on Crane. Yvonne had lain rocks in an oval around the site and created a rocky "S" and planned to create a concrete "grotto" at some point over the grave. When Samantha had suddenly become weak and could barely stand we took her to a vet on Orcas who said she was bleeding internally from a tumor on her spleen and though she might recover probably wouldn't before she bled to death — and there wasn't anything he could do to help. We couldn't bear the thought of leaving her at the vet's or euthanizing her so we brought her home to Crane and she died that evening.

Samantha loved Orcas Island and especially Crane and was free to come and go as the urge moved her, never going far from home and never causing any trouble except when defending her home against other dogs — when she could be surprisingly hostile. She hated thunder and fireworks and the sound of a pneumatic stapler, disappearing one day when I was especially busy with one. Yvonne finally found her in the cockpit of the *Huginn*. 'Mantha Moo Moo had walked to the community dock and leapt into the boat — feeling safer there — where she was usually very anxious — than being at home and subjected to the sound of stapling.

It took me at least a hour to dig her grave through the island clay and rocks and Yvonne, Margaret, from next door, and I cried when I laid her in it. I felt bereft in a very simple, unproblematic way, frustrated at having to accept the inevitable, but without the complex of thoughts I would have were she human. But the experience was visceral, elemental, direct — giving her back to the soil from whence she and all of us ultimately come — very different from the experience of losing a human family member — with its primacy of ideas over the physicality of the experience. Those experiences perhaps seemed less real.

Two-hundred-eighteen: Jiggety Jog

"There is no place like home." - L. Frank Baum, *The Wonderful Wizard of Oz*

Dropping off the rental Impala in Olympia I calculated that it had delivered 30 mpg over 2125 miles. At $4.00 per gallon we'd saved about $140m over what gas for our van would have cost — roughly the cost of the rental — and we'd saved wear and tear on the van. The experiment was a success. In Oregon, a highway sign warned of a severe traffic slowdown south of Salem. Yvonne checked Google Maps on the iPad, saw the red section of I-5 and then directed me on a detour around the problem. Driving through residential areas we were struck at how luxuriously the Rhododendrons were flowering and talked about how plant life is happy in Washington but blissful in Oregon. Stops at Costco, Famous Footwear, and Home Depot in Burlington and we were soon parked in the ferry line at the Anacortes terminal where I could devour my Costco pizza slice and Yvonne her salad.

While Yvonne relaxed in the van on board the *Chelan* I climbed to the passenger deck and began to write, sunshine streaming through the big windows. And then I saw Ruthie sitting a few rows ahead. She came over, sat down and told me that she had just fallen in the restroom and both her hip and elbow hurt a good deal though she was certain she hadn't broken anything. She was returning from Boston where her granddaughter had just graduated from Tufts, her travel complicated by American canceling the flight her son was depending on to meet her at Logan Airport in Boston. The pain got worse. I walked with her down to the lower car deck and helped her get into her Subaru and by the look on her face I could tell the process was very painful. I encouraged her to call her doctor David Shinstrom and she left a message and then called Andrea who would go to Ruthie's house to meet her when she got home. Later Yvonne called Ruthie to follow up and the report was positive: she'd taken some ibuprofen.

Two-hundred-eighteen: Jiggety Jog

218: Chelan docks at Orcas Landing

Nancy was parked on the ferry near Ruthie and I said hello but couldn't talk to her because of my focus on Ruthie but Yvonne and I met her in the Crane Island parking lot on Orcas and she rushed off with Jim, anxious to get home to watch the final installment of American Idol, a television show Yvonne and I had heard of but never watched. We loaded the dock cart, leaving non-rush items for the next day. The water was calm and the sun warm and bright at 7:45 in the evening, sunset in the summer because of the oblique path the sun takes lasting for a hour or more. Driving from the ferry we could see that the willows, ocean spray, and maples were fully leafed out, the sun shinning around and through the green Pacific Northwest jungle. Leaving the Orcas dock, the water was very calm and few boats remained in the marina except the blue-hulled sailboat that had been moored in the 48 hour zone for the last four weeks. I was considering moving it myself but would first contact its owner. The Pronto rowboat had little water on its floor, probably because there'd been little rain while we were gone.

We could barely see two kayaks paddle through Pole Pass because of the reflection of the sinking sun on the water but caught up to them at the dock on Crane as they were pulling their kayaks out. Cabot and Cynthia were returning from an evening paddle to nearby Shaw Island, Cynthia now furiously texting on her cell phone, so we didn't stay to chat up this Anchorage couple. After I turned on the water at home, I joined Yvonne next door at Margaret's, newly returned from teaching at Ohio State and found her on the phone making arrangements with Rachel and Marilyn, former Crainians, to get together the following week. She'd come over for dinner Friday night, before our weekend guests arrived on Saturday. Margaret reported she'd been struggling with CenturyLink to provide her with DSL, important because she needed the internet for research. The phone company told her it would be two weeks before they could come to Crane and tried to stonewall her even after she explained that they didn't need to come to Crane — they could do their magic by changing some setting on her record in their computer. I'd set the hot tub to 79 before we left home so it wouldn't be ready this evening but the house was warm because the day had been mild and sunny. We were happy to be home.

Two-hundred-nineteen: Making Choices

"Have nothing in your house that you do not know to be useful, or believe to be beautiful." - William Morris

Though rain was predicted and the sky gray, Yvonne was determined to begin the process of sorting through our plethora of stuff, choosing what should stay and what should go. The immediate motivation was the upcoming Deer Harbor Community Club bi-annual yard sale for which she was the organizer. The underlying reason was to begin to get rid of everything we really didn't need since if we didn't take care of that now, we, or someone else, would have to take care of it later. Over the last 15 years we'd accumulated an inventory of objects, many at Orcas garage sales, that at the time seemed important or might be important for some project or other in the future. Over the last four years on Crane we'd completed many projects, had a short list of more we wanted to do, but had become less ambitious to do things with marginal value.

Yvonne first attacked the small attic accessed by a fold-down ladder in the master bedroom closet. I stood at the bottom of the ladder receiving what Yvonne handed down — a CD player and a VHS tape player we hadn't used in years, the former because the iPod had replaced our audio system and the latter because DVD had replaced VHS. Would anyone actually buy these obsolete electronic systems? And she found a pair of audio speakers, enclosed in hardwood and very attractive, that we'd used for years but replaced with very small, powered speakers, including a woofer, that were driven by the iPod. Use of these big speakers required an amplifier and when ours burned out we couldn't find another — they'd disappeared from the electronics store. The attic also yielded unneeded lamps and baby toys we no longer needed for our grandchildren's visits. And there were generic pictures Yvonne had removed from frames she'd bought and which had no meaning for us. We'd bought a deluxe German gas lantern ten years ago at a garage sale but hadn't used it because it required a part not available in the US. Out it went.

219: A little tree frog can make a big noise

Moving next to her shop, Yvonne pulled out planting pots, metal candle lanterns, baking pans, clay masks, canning jars, baskets, a faucet, outdoor light globes, flatware trays, a watering can, buckets, pot stands, burlap bags — and more — moving it all to the covered walkway leading to our front door — as a staging area to eventually move it Orcas.

I had a more complicated task: I needed to sort through the contents of my shop, toss into the garbage what was, pull out what I didn't need but someone might, while emptying the current shelves and cabinets, hauling them out of the shop and then moving in the cabinets we'd removed from the kitchen and stored in the rain shelter. It was mind boggling and so I asked Yvonne for some advice since she had an expert sense of organization I seemed to lack.

I took a big tarp covering the wood waiting to be split outside the fence in the front yard and laid it on the ground intending to put there everything I wanted to donate to the yard sale. But I couldn't get started because I couldn't get into my shop — even with the two four foot wide hanging doors fully opened. I'd failed to put away tools I'd used over the last six months. Further, I'd stored wood saved from the kitchen remodel effort I thought I might use sometime. So I spent the next hour making the shop accessible. And then the threatened rain began — a drop or two at a time. I was ready to quit for the day, having accomplished almost nothing, but Yvonne pointed out that I could temporarily store electrical related items under a copse of trees so that I could empty the cabinet I'd stored them in and replace it with former kitchen cabinets. So I did, putting everything electrical outside, some in the save pile and some in the to go pile and then dragged the cupboard out, putting substitute cabinets in, and loading them with what made sense to keep — though I could see I was keeping too much. What would I ever do with 30 outlet and switch cover plates? Or ten circuit box breakers? I had let go of coils of insulated wiring — though kept enough for possible vague needs. I'd also put out the garbage disposal I'd taken out of the kitchen and the instant hot water maker — and I'd put out the stainless steel kitchen sink — even the kitchen sink — so maybe I was making progress. But then the rain started in earnest and I covered what I couldn't easily put back in the shop. I'd managed to clean out one corner of my shop — maybe 10% of the effort I'd need to make. This wasn't going to be so simple.

Two-hundred-twenty: A Kind of Life

"A friend is one that knows you as you are, understands where you have been, accepts what you have become, and still, gently allows you to grow." - William Shakespeare

The San Juan Islands are rocky with few beaches, in some places cliffs rising straight out of the water hundreds of feet, or as on Crane where rocky bluffs rise about 20 feet above the high tide mark, a very clear line that circles the island, below which its basalt foundation is sometimes concave, hollowed out by waves hitting it time out of mind. Crane Island has another waistline that became obvious to me this morning: the one created by the island's black tail deer. With thoroughly wet soil and warming days, the salal along Circle Road was sprouting new leaves, smaller and a lighter green than the older leaves on this evergreen bush pervasive in the Pacific Northwest. But the new leaves weren't everywhere; they were only evident higher in the salal or away from the road. I could see clearly where the deer had nibbled the new growth and the effect of this selective browsing was to keep the salal from growing into the road and in this way the deer were inadvertently creating salal hedges. Along the north end of the air strip deer had nibbled the new growth on Douglas firs transforming what would normally be fast-growing single-trunked trees into low to the ground bushes — except for three the deer hadn't totaling crippled where the trunk rising out of the bush was topped by growth too high for the deer to reach. Skip's landscaping, 30 or 40 specially planted pines had all acquired diamond shapes, the widest part of the trees just above deer head height. As I walked across the meadow north of the house to pass through the ring of trees and bushes that shield it from view I could see that browsing deer had been busy along this tree line as well, their munching keeping the lower level of this green wall from further invading the meadow and that the firs coming up in the meadow — that hadn't been mown in many years — had become bushes rather than trees.

Just before 9:00 I docked the *Huginn* in an empty slip on the east side of the Cayou Quay Marina that Howard had told me would be available, tied up and waited not more than a minute for my passengers — today Howard and David. Chris was sick again (Lynn was recovering from pneumonia) and Brian had called Howard at 6:30 a.m. to tell Howard he had been awake all night — presumably a side-effect of his numerous medications — and wouldn't be coming. This morning's Kenmore floatplane flight from Seattle had landed well south of the Deer Harbor Marina, the second marina in the harbor and close to Cayou Quay, and had followed me in, docking at the northeast end of the marina to board two outgoing passengers as we cruised slowly by. Once away from the marina and the few boats tied to mooring buoys south of the two marinas I took the *Huginn* up on plane and we rushed past Fawn Island guarding the west entrance to the harbor heading south toward the west side of Crane Island. We were on our way to Friday Harbor on San Juan Island to visit Bob, emeritus member of our Greybeards group — or as Howard has come to describe it, the Grebs.

The waves in San Juan Channel were high enough to make the ride bumpy and Howard and David hung on, Howard choosing to stand rather than sit. I found myself regularly adjusting the trim to even the keel. In twenty minutes we were tying up just in front of the Sheriff's boat near the fuel dock. Walking up Spring Street in Friday Harbor we were soon at the Islands Convalescent Center, where Bob was now living. He needed that level of care and no comparable facility was available on Orcas, where Megan now lived by herself. Though Friday Harbor was only six miles from Deer Harbor — a bit less from Crane — getting there and back was time consuming, since for most people it meant taking the Interisland Ferry both ways and given its schedule the round trip — with some time on San Juan Island — could take much of the day.

Bob was waiting for us in a wheel chair in his room and after bundling him into a warm coat (the sun was trying to break through the clouds but with wind it was cool) and pushed him across Spring Street to Friday Harbor Expresso where Bob was greeted by a staff that saw him regularly. With Bob at the head of a table pushed against the wall, we nursed our coffees (me my tea) and enjoyed one another's company. Howard had spoken to the Unitarian group on humor the Sunday before (when Yvonne and I were in California) and had been well-received — the largest crowd of the year — and clearly more enjoyable than my ruminations on bleak philosophical topics. I wanted to hear about his talk and it seemed a better focus than Bob's frustrations at his new living arrangements.

220: Doe strolls a Crane beach

Both Howard and David were experts at remembering jokes; I can't remember any so we spent more than an hour chuckling and smiling. By 11:30, after Howard stopped at a jewelers to get a new battery for a pocket watch and David had stopped at the County Courthouse to do a filing connected with his homeowners association we were on our way back to Deer Harbor. We'd do this again. Yvonne would need to leave for Eastsound before 1:00 for a Master Gardeners meeting and Rock on the Rock Choir practice. I tied up at the Crane Island Association dock with plenty of time to spare.

Two-hundred-twenty-one: Two Steps Forward

"Community is much more than belonging to something; it's about doing something together that makes belonging matter." - Brian Solis

I was out of bed before 4:00 a.m., sitting at my desk looking at my MacBook Pro screen trying to understand a problem Jens had alerted me to in an email I received the night before — just as Yvonne arrived home from choir practice: he reported that the new version of *The eNotated Metamorphosis* was defective in a serious way. The return links in the second and third parts of the book returned — not to the passage they illuminated — but apparently arbitrary areas in Kafka's translated text. That made no sense and I fell into a blue funk that spoiled my evening and then Yvonne's when she got home from choir practice about 8:00. This morning once I could look at the HTML code that was causing the goofy linking I immediately saw the cause of the problem — ambiguity in the naming of the links — fixed with two lines of code. The bug had been there all the time but hadn't shown up until this new version of *Metamorphosis*. A big relief. The day looked bright. I met Jens in Eastsound at Enzo's — surprisingly busy with people coming in for mid-morning coffee — and I reviewed with Jens how to load a book into the Kindle iPad app from a Mac running iTunes. Soon I would upload the book to Amazon and re-initiate the publication process.

On my way into Eastsound, I stopped at Key Bank and deposited donations to the No Wake Zone committee. While Yvonne and I were in California, Jim had worked with Baja Boats to install three new buoys, one on the west side of Pole Pass, south of Cal's, one between Bell Island and the southeast corner of Crane and Wasp Passage and one on the east side of Pole Pass south of Hobie's dock. It was hard to know how much good the buoys would do — many boaters would ignore them — but some would pay attention and slow down. Donations had exceeded our expenses thus far, leaving a reserve cushion or the ability to buy another buoy. I was pleased that we were restoring the buoy arrangement to what it had been when I'd fist noticed it twelve years before when cruising through Pole Pass. At that time I didn't know who had placed the buoys or how. Now I did.

Right after lunch, Yvonne and I drove separately to the Deer Harbor Community Club, set up tables and emptied the van we'd filled the day before, moving discards from Crane to Orcas. Home again I spent the next hour and a half loading the *Huginn* with the remaining items Yvonne had staged on the front walkway and by the time I got back to Orcas she was already there and we quickly filled the van and most of the pickup — putting a tarp over the pickup bed and then headed home. We'd take the the van and truck to the Community Club in the morning.

Margaret was at the back door at 6:02 and Yvonne was nearly ready with the Thai chicken soup she was making for dinner. It was delicious. We hadn't seen Margaret, our next door neighbor, since the previous August and we had lots to talk about. Her retirement plans had firmed up. She'd spend one more school year teaching at Ohio State and then live full time on Crane. Yvonne and I looked forward to it. By July, she was certain, she would have all the windows in her house replaced with double-glazed models, one step in making her house more comfortable in the winter. I told her about the ductless heat pump systems OPALCO was promoting as a way to make her house warm without an exorbitant electrical bill. She had just about finished making improvements to her farmhouse near Columbus so that she could put it up for sale. And then we brought her up to date on Crane and Pole Pass people and doings, some she already knew because of emails or from having talked to Rachel and Marilyn, who although then hadn't lived on Crane for nine years seemed to know everything anyway. We talked for quite a while about Tom, his care and contributions to Crane and his near-paranoid behavior, Jim and Nancy, Blair and Molly, on Orcas Steve and Pam, Mick and Marion, her brother's fatal heart attach, her 91 year old aunt's recovery from cancer surgery, our travels, kids, and grandkids — and we just scratched the surface. She talked about how happy she was to have us as neighbors and we felt the same. And I saw clearly how Yvonne and I had, over the years, gone from being new to being established — not old timers — but imbedded in the life of the community.

Two-hundred-twenty-one: Two Steps Forward

221: Front walk

We knew and knew about many of the people on Crane and on Deer Harbor Road across Pole Pass — and Deer Harbor — and Orcas and its institutions like the Library where Margaret had volunteered the previous summer and would be happy to serve on its Board as I had. She also looked forward to serving on the Crane Island Association Board and as Water System Chair. From her point of view the Board was too much of a boys club and she was eager to change that — not just in having women on the Board but that the condescension she sometimes felt toward women be eliminated. About 8:00 she made her way home and to Moonie, her tom cat who had almost died in December and looked pale to Yvonne and to me — though that made no sense because he was covered in fur.

Two-hundred-twenty-two: Short Cut

"Life is what happens when you're busy making other plans." - John Lennon

At 9:30 Yvonne and I left the house, me pushing our dock cart, filled with items I'd taken out of my shop/shed and was donating to the Community Club yard sale effort. With these new treasures both our F-150 pickup and Freestar van were filed to capacity after receiving loads the day before. At the Community Club building we began to unload the vehicles from the lot behind the building and soon Howard and Sheila were parked along side bringing in their donations — including two bags of sails — sails for boats long gone. All four of us agreed that our transporting of physical objects would be one way only — out of the house to the yard sale. Then I showed Howard the speakers I was donating and he tip-toed out of the building and put the speakers into his Fit. Then I tried to interest him in a classy German lantern I bought at a yard sale ten years before but never used but he demurred. By the time we'd unloaded everything we had almost enough to conduct a respectable sale — from only two sources — and much more would be coming — from us and others over the next week.

Daughter Jeni had called from Seattle about 8:00; the *Victoria Clipper*, the boat she and Matt, Kay, and baby Samuel, would be taking to Friday Harbor was delayed because the crew couldn't start one of the engines. At 8:38 she called to say they were underway but because they were an hour late would miss their inter-island ferry connection in Friday Harbor, with a departure time of 11:30. The next ferry wasn't until after 3:00 so I would need to pick them up. And, in another call Corrina explained she wouldn't be coming up today because friends were arriving from California. She would come up Sunday — and wanted her friends to come as well. Was that OK? Of course. At 11:15 Jeni called again; the *Victoria Clipper* was pulling up to the Spring Street dock in Friday Harbor and the *Sealth*, not scheduled for departure until

11:30 was still in its slip. They would make the inter-island ferry after all; I didn't need to come pick them up in Friday Harbor. I could meet them at the much closer Orcas ferry landing.

I left the Crane dock in the *Huginn* about 11:50 and saw that Hans and Ute, and family were approaching the Crane dock in their SeaSport. Their eight-year old grandson waved wildly from the dock as I pulled out and ran all the way to the end as I glided the *Huginn* past. He was very happy and excited to be on Crane. I was tempted to stop and ask them when they intended to move their sailboat from the 48 hour parking zone on the Orcas dock, where it had been for the last 6 weeks, but I held my tongue thinking that they would take care of it now that they were back.

Yvonne came down the ramp on the Orcas dock and we were soon on our way to the ferry landing. Sail and power boats were now abundant on the water and would continue to be through Labor Day, two coming toward us from the east and I had to steer south to go around them and we cruised to the county dock, the inter-island ferry standing off from the *Elwah* soon to depart Orcas for Shaw, Lopez and then Anacortes. Bright sun, two big green and white Washington State ferries, the Shaw Island landing across Harney Channel, an abundance of tourists, happy to be in the islands, a south breeze strong enough to move the nearby sailboats along smartly, a man on a high ladder hanging a new sign, the landing market new space on the first floor now integrated with the rest of the store, giving it a spacious feeling.

Yvonne walked up the ramp to the driveway and walked across the road to the public restroom next to the ferry system office and waiting room and then visited the market to look for dinner fixings. Dan, captain of the *Orcas Express* whale watching boat moored on the other side of the county dock told me they had strong reservations for the weekend. A sheriff's deputy walked down the ramp to the sheriff's boat and prepared to castoff. The little Waldron Island ferry collected its six passengers and then left on its ten mile trip around the west side of Orcas to the island just northwest.

The *Sealth* pulled in between the guide structures, the stern of the big boat carried west on the tide so that it docked an an angle rather than perpendicular to the shore — and then there was Jeni and friends striding up the ferry ramp, Samuel wrapped to Kay, turning his head to see who she was talking to.

Two-hundred-twenty-two: Short Cut

222: Jeni, Yvonne, and Kay making dinner

Kay had brought along a whole salmon and began to fillet it and make other preparations for dinner once we got home. Yvonne and I walked out to my shop and began moving material from it and then bringing in floor and wall cabinets we'd removed from the kitchen during the remodel process as part of a transformation of the space that would make it more useful, get rid of items we really didn't need, and empty the tarp swaddled rain shelter so we could put up the tent that served as summer overflow housing.

The blackened salmon dinner was delicious — with plenty left over for another meal, perhaps of salmon patties. By 10:30, our eyelids hanging low, we called it a night.

Two-hundred-twenty-three: Guests

*"I could weep and I could laugh, I am light and heavy. Welcome. –
William Shakespeare*

Matt was up early with baby Samuel while Kay tried to get a bit more sleep and they played together while I finished my oatmeal and read the *New York Times* online. Yvonne, soon up, made drop biscuits and we all sat around the dining room table, sun streaming in, from the sky above and the water below, feeling no rush to do anything in particular.

Corrina called from Friday Harbor; the *Victoria Clipper* had arrived on time and she was on her way walking over to the inter-island ferry. She'd be at Orcas Landing about 12:15 so Jen, Matt, and I cruised the two miles and parked against the inside of the county dock and walked up to the Market. I saw Ron, Village Market shopkeeper, busy unpacking a box, and asked him what his plans were for the second story, all windows and what looked to me like a nice area for a coffee shop. He said they didn't have adequate parking to use the space that way, that it would be office and storage for now. He went on to say that they had slowed down their building expansion and wouldn't do anything else until they saw how the summer went. I wasn't surprised. The building addition project started a year ago had slowed to a crawl and I assumed business reasons lay behind it. With Corrina aboard we dashed back to Crane for lunch — though I had already eaten and went outside to my shop to continue the rearrangement and sorting for donation to the Deer Harbor Community Club yard sale or disposal.

By mid afternoon it was finally certain that Corrina's friends, Clint and Bun, driving up the West Coast, would be coming to Crane and late in the afternoon I returned to Orcas Landing with Corrina to pick them up. They'd parked their car at the Anacortes ferry landing and walked aboard. On the way back we saw the Sheriff's boat near Pole Pass and a deputy citing a dad, with his son, in a small boat. I was happy that the County was enforcing the

Two-hundred-twenty-three: Guests

No Wake Zone ordinance for Pole Pass. Then a larger boat came through Pole Pass going west at about 30 mph, very dangerous, and the deputy rushed to finish his process then turned on his siren and caught the malefactor two miles east at the Ferry Landing. Good! Four young kids were walking on the beach at the Crane Community dock, watched by their two moms — connected with Brooks I think, though it was hard to remember people I saw very briefly only once a year, if that. Later I talked with Mike and Cindy coming through our yard on the outer path, walking to their house and we talked about the ticketing with satisfaction. Mike, having been in Eastsound the day before, said he was surprised to hear about how many business had closed and we talked about the future of the economy — none of the three of us optimistic. Hearing about the upcoming yard sale they later volunteered to donate unneeded stuff they were clearing out and left it under our yard rain shelter.

Bun is a chef in a New York restaurant in the West Village, Bleaker and Seventh, and was interested in cooking since childhood — spent watching cooking shows. Rather than pursue music, another interest, after high school he attended a culinary school in Baltimore and after some years back in Harrisburg he went off to New York to seek his fortune. Yvonne had planned for risotto and had all the ingredients on hand. Bun volunteered to prepare the meal and did in short order — and the risotto was delicious. His parents somehow had survived Khmer Rouge and his background is Buddhist so he and I talked about his impression of religion in America.

Clint is a musician who left Harrisburg for California a few years ago and now lives in Santa Cruz, working odd jobs to make ends meet while he pursue his music and tries to get bookings — which are few and far between. In the afternoon, with Hall and Oates playing on the iPod he expressed his admiration for this Philadelphia duo, popular before he was born, that I too liked.

We all sat in the living room area enjoying the chocolate mousse on white cake desserts Kay had made, partly because I had asked whether she was going to make something chocolaty several times during the day and sipping (except for me) a Santa Cruz porto Clint had carried north in his drive with Bun to see Corrina and the Pacific Northwest when Corrina suggested that we all play Celebrity, men against women, and the game was on. Looking at the clock and knowing that we were eight I suggested we limit the number of

Two-hundred-twenty-three: Guests

names submitted per person to three — or it might be very late before we finished.

223: Bun, Clint, Matt, and Kay

I couldn't recall how Celebrity entered our family but Yvonne knew — from our friend Tessa, in Boulder. Each person writes down names on slips of paper, folds them, and drops them into a bowl. The names should refer to generally known living, dead, or fictional persons (or characters). Then play proceeds in three stages: descriptions, charades, and a single word. In the first stage one can describe the person using any words except the name. In the second stage no words are allowed. In the third third stage only one word can be provided as a clue. The players are divided into two teams and the time

Two-hundred-twenty-three: Guests

allowed for each turn agreed on (for us this evening 45 seconds). A timer and a scorer are assigned. The first player on the first team draws a name out of the bowl and his/her teammates guess until they're correct and then the player draws another name and so on until either all the names are gone or time has elapsed. Then the first player from the second team takes a turn and so on until all the names have been guessed in the first stage. Play starts over with the second stage and then the third. The team with the most correct answers wins. This evening it was the women — which it is often though not always. Yvonne and I withdrew to our room and the group carried on outside in the hot tub. We couldn't hear a thing — because we were asleep.

Two-hundred-twenty-four: Memorable Day

"Life is like a box of chocolates. You never know what you're gonna get." - Forrest Gump

Jeni, Matt, and Kay all said they'd eat some oatmeal if I made it so I put a big pot on. Yvonne had put together a baked French toast casserole the evening before, storing it in the refrigerator overnight, and put it in the oven while the rest of us — who were up — ate oatmeal. Yvonne heated maple syrup and peach juice (she put peaches into the french toast) and soon we were at the dining room table enjoying the rich baked french toast and watermelon Kay had cut up. Clint straggled in from the studio, having shared the loft with Bun, and then Corrina and then Bun appeared and the eight of us sat at the table — with baby Samuel down for his morning nap in the guest bedroom in the studio.

Then Jen was on the phone to see whether she could book a seat on the afternoon's *Clipper* back to Seattle. and managed to use her half-price discount letter, given to her when the *Clipper* was late leaving Seattle on Saturday for this return reservation. Corrina and her two friends hadn't made up their minds about when they would leave Crane — but Bun had to be in San Francisco Wednesday afternoon for his flight back to New York and the travel from Crane would require at least 16 hours.

Though Yvonne and I like company, especially family, young people, and old friends, it's taxing and by late morning the two of us left the house to the guests and headed out to Circle Road for a walk around the island. At Dan's driveway, looking up at the osprey nest we could see two adults floating above it, one 20 and another 50 feet above it. I assumed they were guarding the nest from predators. The lower bird called with a sound like whistling through one's teeth. A larger bird appeared briefly and then was chased off, the lower bird then landing in the nest and calling with a chirping sound. Yvonne read later that ospreys mate for life, nesting when they're five to seven years old and can find a suitable nest or spot to build one, and that though three eggs are laid typically, they're hatched at different times so that feeding can be more successful. That would explain why we saw a chick two months earlier and there was still a chick (a different one) in the nest. I was especially interested in seeing how the osprey soared — sometimes folding their wings into a "W" shape to lose lift I suppose and sometimes closing them entirely to quickly lose altitude; wonderful flyers.

I'd brought along two Crane Island Association checks that needed a second signature before I could send them out so Yvonne and I walked down to Jason and Theresa's driveway when we got to the north side of the island. Their daughter, son, and young golden lab were playing outside in front of the cabin, a camp fire still burning. Jason said he needed to talk with me and Yvonne, who, sensing a potentially interminable delay, said goodbye and walked out to Circle Road and continued home. Jason had some news about Tom. He had found out yesterday that Tom had installed a camera in the members' storage shed in the parking lot above the Orcas dock to spy on the people in the parking lot. What? Martha had advised Jason to seek legal recourse. I suggested that we see Tom immediately and ask him to remove the camera before the incident became public and he embarrassed. Jason and I took his Gator out on Circle Road and drove noisily to the other corner of the island, parked in Tom's driveway and walked to the house.

Tom must have seen us walking toward the house because when we neared the back deck he opened the door and came out. We spent the next hour and a half listening to his complaints about his neighbor — who he was certain was putting nails, screws, and staples into his truck tires to get back at him for notifying the Board that a portable shed was too close to the lot line of their shared neighbor. Jason and I had heard all these complaints many times before — including the claim that Jim had stolen rocks from the common area and was unrepentant about it, the only accusation for which he could muster any evidence — but now he was talking about getting a license to carry a gun, that he would get a gun to protect himself from Jim who he was convinced wanted to kill him — because he said, two people had told him Jim was out to get him, to tie him in chains connected to a block of cement and dump him in the water. Jason and I were both alarmed and at a loss to know what to do. I repeated my offer to bring a retired judge into the situation who would take testimony, sift through the evidence, and then make a finding — which Tom would have to abide by. Tom replied that his lawyer advised him not to participate in such a procedure because it might interfere with his ability to bring suit for damages later on. Jason got Tom to agree to let him know by the end of the week whether he would agree to the process — explaining that we wanted to help but had no standing or competency to do so. Tom agreed to remove the camera and not install another one — saying that he couldn't understand why we worried about it because it couldn't take pictures anyway — and that it was unobtrusive — no one would notice it.

224: Yvonne holds baby Samuel

That made no sense to me. I was upset about the camera and Tom's high-handed way of dealing with the Crane community and told him so. I didn't want to be condescending and I had no training for or idea about how to be deal with what seemed like paranoid behavior but I also didn't want him to think he could do as he pleased so I told him the truth as I saw it. He seemed unfazed and came back again and again to his list of grievances against Jim. We left and Jason drove me to the head of Eagle Lane, but not before we saw our six guests walking along Circle Road, while Yvonne watched the sleeping baby.

At 3:00 Jeni, Matt, Kay, baby Samuel and I dashed over to Friday Harbor where I dropped them at the Spring Street dock to pick up the *Clipper* return trip to Seattle. At 4:30, Corrina, Clint, Bun, and I left the Crane dock for the Orcas Ferry Landing — and the *Huginn's* engine stopped and wouldn't restart. We were 50 feet from the end of the dock, near where the tides would pour back and forth through Pole Pass — but the tide was slack and the wind calm. Clint and I were able to paddle back to the dock while Corrina called Yvonne — who came running with the key to Margaret's boat — we transferred luggage — and were off again — tying up just as the *Elwah* docked. They'd make the ferry. No problem. Back at the Crane dock I took the air filter off the *Huginn's* engine and tried to start it again. It cranked. The gas gauge read a quarter tank. Everything else I could think of to check seemed to be in order. Ugh! Our house was quiet again and we dined on the leftover risotto. Time for a Netflix. Tomorrow would be another day.

Two-hundred-twenty-five: Customer Service

"Problems are not stop signs, they are guidelines." - Robert H. Schuller

Not long after breakfast Yvonne began to pester me about the *Huginn*. Wasn't I going to call West Sound Marina. Yes but they wouldn't open until 9:00 and then I would call Ian for advice. But I'm worried, she said. I have to go to Orcas this morning. But Margaret said you could use her boat, I said. Well, I'm worried about our boat situation. OK. I walked down to the dock and tried to start the *Huginn*. Same as yesterday afternoon when it died leaving the dock and wouldn't start again. Then we had to paddle back to the dock and then borrow Margaret's boat to take our guests to the ferry landing.

Yvonne, sitting at the kitchen counter viewing Facebook exclaimed, "She had her baby!!" The first reports were coming in. Kelly had delivered at about 8:30 this morning. Everything had gone well. Her mother had arrived the night before. We'd followed Kelly and Tim's relationship for about five years and had played minor roles now and again — for instance at their wedding the previous July at the Orcas Hotel — when I officiated and we hosted a dozen attendees. We'd know more later.

I took Yvonne over to Orcas, came back and then called West Sound Marina. Ian driving the lift — so I talked to Betsy and described the problem. She said she didn't have an answer but would have Ian call me later. I called back in half an hour and Jan told me Ian had been called out to a fire. I told her I would be available at noon and that Ian could call me or I him. Then I spent about 90 minutes working in my shop installing shelves into what had been the pantry unit we'd had in the kitchen and began to put away hardware of various kinds. Then I sorted all the paint cans I put outside, choosing what to keep, donate to the Deer Harbor Community Club yard sale effort, or dispose of and then did the same for plumbing supplies. I was determined to un-

Two-hundred-twenty-five: Customer Service

crowd my shop and make it more useful and accessible but didn't finish before breaking for lunch.

Ian had left a message so I called back and he was gone for lunch. So I made myself my favorite lunch — PB&J with cheese on toast. Yum! And then Ian called. I went through the symptoms: it started, quit, started, quit, then wouldn't start. Quarter tank of gas. Batteries fully charged, cranking well. Man overboard pull switch as it should be — with half-ring underneath holding it up from the dash. Ian's telephone diagnosis — a bad fuel pump. Before I could ask he volunteered to come to the Crane dock to see what he could do. Wonderful. Much appreciated. But he needed to finish a haul out. It would probably be an hour before he could make it. I'd watch for his SeaSport coming around Caldwell Point from the living room and then walk to the Crane dock. And then I turned my attention to finishing edits to Ian Johnston translation of *The Metamorphosis* that Jens and I had been working on.

As far as I could tell I was just about finished — and only needed to write some code to handle the images a bit differently. By the time I saw Ian's boat I was just about done. I could see publication only a day or two away.

Maybe for the first time this spring it was shirt-sleeve weather, a beautiful day, sunny, with a light breeze out of the west. The predicted rain hadn't materialized. Ian was wearing shorts and a tee-shirt while I sported torn Levis and a hoodie, always happier to be a little too warm than cold. Ian asked me to turn on the ignition switch but not start the engine — and I heard the same whirring sound I'd heard the day before — but couldn't identify. Ian explained it was the fuel pump — but that it should stop after a few seconds — but that wasn't the reason the engine wouldn't start. The problem was ignition not fuel. In a few minutes Ian determined that the coil wasn't delivering power to the distributor, something he said was very unusual but not unprecedented; he'd seen three or four bad coils in his years servicing boat engines. Then he was on his way back to his shop to pick up a coil and was back in about an hour. A few minutes to install the new coil and the engine started without a hitch. Ian then worked on the fuel pump issue, mentioning that when his employee Kelly had installed our rebuilt engine he hadn't wired the pump correctly. It wouldn't cause us problems but the next time we brought it in he'd fix it. Then before leaving he topped up the hydraulic trim tab reservoir that I had pointed out was a bit low before he left the first time. While Ian worked on the fuel pump wiring we talked a bit — about one Crane resident he said was very difficult, about his experience with the new Orcas fire engines, which, because they were lengthened to accommodate a passenger cab get hung up on road crests.

225: Boats moored at Orcas on the north side of Pole Pass

That led to a discussion of the Chief, who I talked to a number of times and was friendly enough, but I thought had shown poor judgment failing to take seriously Deer Harbor resident objections to the design of the fire station he wanted to build — until forced to — leaving a bad taste in the collective mouth of the hamlet.

I picked up Yvonne just before 6:00 on her way back from her book group and she was pleased to see that the *Huginn* was back in service. Tim had sent

Two-hundred-twenty-five: Customer Service

out an email from the hospital with pictures of baby Noah (Noah — our oldest son's name), Kelly, and Tim. Yvonne called Tim, expressed our joy, was tearing up and eager to talk with Kelly about her labor. I was tired — even though I hadn't done heavy work. A broken boat, a boat one depends on, carries with it no small amount of stress, I suppose. Because she had some unidentified bug bites, Yvonne passed on the hot tub but I sat out in the twilight noticing that at the end of May the remains of the day last almost to 10:00. And then some reading about ravens and then goodnight.

Two-hundred-twenty-six: More Boat Troubles

"Life is a series of natural and spontaneous changes. Don't resist them; that only creates sorrow. Let reality be reality. Let things flow naturally forward in whatever way they like." - Lao Tzu

Our eleven-year old Ariens string mower was covered with dried grass and exuded oil here and there and what sloughed off added to the mess accumulating in the *Huginn*'s cockpit. I would be mowing the community club lawn later in the day and needed the mower. On the other hand since Yvonne and I would be moving another batch of yard sale donations to Orcas later in the morning, it made sense to have the mower moved out of the way.

I followed Brian up Howard's driveway. Chris and Howard were already sipping tea in the honeymoon cottage (the Grebe's - graybeard's - clubhouse) and seeing me coming Howard had already poured me a cup and it sat waiting on the wooden arm of the couch. We talked about last week's visit to Bob in Friday Harbor and Jim, with MS, in Deer Harbor — how they were both running out of money — and how perhaps they could benefit by sharing a house and care together — but we didn't see any way to help that happen or even whether the plan would work. I then described the escalating Crane Tom-Jim situation (changing the names and swearing the group to secrecy) and asked for advice. All agreed it made no sense to become directly involved or to try to fix it — I had no relevant training and could even create some kind of liability. All agreed that I should talk to the Sheriff's department — not to ask them to do anything — but to provide them more information to add to their files. That made sense but only with someone else from the Crane Board — preferably Jason because Tom had tried to pull both of us in for more than a year.

Back on Crane Yvonne and I loaded two dock carts (I'd brought one to the house from the community dock) with donations we'd stored under the

Two-hundred-twenty-six: More Boat Troubles

rain shelter and that Mike and his family had deposited there — shop lights, boat power cables, a boat diesel heater, a boat propane grill, an IKEA shelf unit on wheels, a folding table, plumbing supplies, boat hull repair supplies, tongue-in-groove cedar closet paneling, a vacuum cleaner, and more — so much more — and pushed them to the dock. Gary was on the dock on his way to Jones Island where he was responsible for the State Park's water system and Wilma was reading meters. He and I talked for a few minutes about the heavy use of water over the weekend, the budget for the coming fiscal year, the need to complete several unfinished projects before the Annual Meeting in August, and the cross connect survey and then he took off for Jones and would return later to pick up Wilma.

The tide was very low and the ramp steep so Yvonne let me take the carts down the ramp to the *Huginn* for transfer to the boat — though one was so heavy I asked her to help. This would be our fourth boat trip and we had at least one more to go in the few days remaining before the yard sale. At the Orcas side Yvonne rushed up the ramp to get to the Community Club before her staff of volunteers and others with donations showed up. Kerry came into the marina just after we did to pick up a housekeeper to clean Tom H's two houses on Crane and he generously helped me move the contents of the *Huginn* to the parking lot. He reported that Tom and Jessica's baby, born prematurely and after they'd lost their first, was doing well but that the couple I'd married (officiated) last August had lost their baby. Very sad. His analysis was that these two athletic women were too thin and too active. I filled the bed of the F-150, adding to the string mower I put there a few hours earlier and drove to the Community Club. The back parking lot was full and the building was filled with women sorting donations to the sale sections Yvonne had laid out. After emptying the pickup and then the few things Yvonne had carried in the van, I turned my attention to the big grassy area between Deer Harbor Road and the Community Club building, a pleasing white school house structure built in 1905, noting that the grass was at least a foot high and covered with grass cuttings from the last mowing — Taylor had done perhaps six weeks before. I'd brought a roll of .155" string with me and replaced the two damaged strings, put on my blue reflecting sun/safety glasses and began to mow. Slow going and I had to replace each of the two sets of strings after a while. Then I moved to the north, east (back), and south sides on the building trimming the grass around plantings. A ramp connects the back door, into the kitchen we'd built five years before, with the parking lot, a ramp Jim's caretakers use to bring him to potlucks. Gene had installed low voltage lighting under the railing and somehow the mower caught wiring under the ramp and rolled it onto the axel that spins the strings. Uh, oh. I'd have to fix that later.

226: A minus low tide means steep ramps

The process had taken so long that by the time I was done Yvonne was ready to leave and we did. I left the mower in the bed of the pickup in the upper lot for use on the Crane Association property on Orcas and we went home. James called to talk about his prothesis repair project and travel plans. After concluding the call Yvonne noticed that someone had left a message; it

Two-hundred-twenty-six: More Boat Troubles

was a boater who had found Margaret adrift in San Juan Channel hoping we could come tow her back to Crane. I rushed out the door but the phone rang and it was Margaret calling from the Crane dock where she'd been towed by Vessel Assist — to the tune of $300. She had no boat or towing insurance. She'd run out of gas — and the engine sputtered as that happened. When she connected the spare tank the fairly new Yamaha just continued to sputter. She thought because she had totally drained the first tank she might have picked up some water or grunge in the bottom of the tank. I offered to go get new gas — but she had two more spare tanks freshly filled and stabilized. I offered to bring her the gas drying additive I had just had my hands on when cleaning up my shop but she said she'd wait for Mike's diagnosis expected the next day. Yvonne and I were sorry we hadn't been able to receive the rescue call when it came in and I was concerned that I'd done something wrong with the gas in her tanks — that I'd filled over the months she was gone and we'd used the boat from time to time — but we'd used the boat with no problems.

While I was cleaning up the dinner dishes, Yvonne moved our Windows notebook computer from the dining room table to the kitchen counter where we each do web surfing and email — and then crash — it was on the floor — having slipped through her arthritic hands. It was six or seven years old and had survived one serious fall already when I missed a step in our Deer Harbor house and fallen — intentionally turning to keep the notebook from hitting the floor by taking the shock with my right shoulder — and did that hurt! The Averatec had survived that fall but tonight the screen was damaged — only the top left acting as it ought. Ninety percent of the screen was plaid. It didn't matter — except that the Kindle MOBI bookmaking software required Windows and our two remaining computers were Macs. Since I was in the middle of trying to publish our new version of *The Metamorphosis* I'd need access to a Windows machine or a monitor or the right kind of cable to connect the Averatec to our television. A task for tomorrow.

Two-hundred-twenty-seven: Try, Try Again

"The mind is not a vessel to be filled, but a fire to be kindled." - Plutarch

Rain was predicted and I was a bit concerned about the string mower I'd left in the bed of my pickup uncovered in the upper Crane lot on Orcas. By the time we tied up at the dock drops were puckering the water in the marina and I hurried up the ramp after Yvonne, who would be taking the van to the Deer Harbor Community Club to meet her yard sale crew while I took the F-150 to Eastsound for meetings and errands. After covering the mower with a tarp we carry under the jump seat and then securing it with a bungee cord web (the rain never materialized), I drove north past the post office and near where upper Deer Harbor Road cuts off to dead end a quarter mile south to provide for Waldron Islanders who leave a car on Orcas so they can take the ferry to the mainland (their island a mile northwest of Orcas and served by a small taxi boat but no ferry), I saw a hitchhiker and stopped to pick him up. Where are you going? To Eastsound. I'm going there too. Hop in. Thanks. Probably in his mid to late 30s, bald, cleanly dressed, earning some money as a carpenter, just finishing a basement and soon to work on the deck of a Deer Harbor house.

Then he started to tell me about a system for generating power he was working on that seemed preposterous but the more I heard sounded at least interesting. He said he had studied power systems while in the military as well as Tesla and a recent inventor who could charge a capacitor with ambient electricity and use it to power three lightbulbs. My father had had a perennial interest in the unconventional Tesla, who had spent time in Colorado Springs, where my father was born, and who had created electrical phenomenon no one had been able to duplicate, who had favored alternating current for transmission over Edison's direct current and who had been destroyed by Edison, like many other inventors.

Two-hundred-twenty-seven: Try, Try Again

My passenger said he had spent the last three years working on a power generator prototype and having already invested $60,000 was about half done and was in the process of raising more capital. The device, less that three feet on a side, would generate a steady 25kw, enough to power a house, maybe two, and require no input other than the electrical differential already available in the air, using magnets to leverage the ambient power. As we neared Eastsound I told him I was skeptical but wished him good luck. Though I didn't say so his project smacked of perpetual motion machines — except of course it wasn't really — because he'd get power from the atmosphere. But could he really use magnets to magnify that power, to amplify it, without some other power input? Why hadn't someone else done this? What about friction? My reaction was to assume he had left out some important variable from his calculations; that he was trying to get something from nothing — or not much — and that was impossible. I'd send Chris a note. Maybe OPALCO would be interested.

Arriving at Enzo's just at 10:00 I set my backpack on the large table that backs up to the window seat and got a cup of tea. Susan K walked in the front door as I waited to pick up my tea and I ordered her a cup of coffee and we sat side by side, each with our MacBook Pros open (hers very new, my five years old) and looked at the eNotated Classics website. She showed me the HTML source code for the Home page and pointed out how verbose it was, containing style specifications that weren't even used on the page. I explained that I'd put the site together quickly with Apple's iWeb and that Chris had done more with iWeb and that I considered it a placeholder for something better — though Chris seemed to think it was fine as is. The real problems weren't under the hood though, they were in plain view — confusing, inconsistent organization, black-screen videos, out of focus images, diagrams that didn't explain, menu items that didn't match the content they pointed to, and on and on. She clearly knew what she was talking about and her help would be valuable — but Chris at least didn't think it was necessary and it would cost money we didn't have.

I'd scheduled Susan M for 11:00 and though I wasn't really sure what she looked like recognized her when she came in because she resembled my sister Marcy, Yvonne had said, and yes somehow she did. Susan K was collecting her belongings and I introduced the two women to each other. Jens and Susan K had invited Yvonne and me to dinner Monday so I'd see her again so I thought perhaps we could carry on our discussion then — provided that didn't interfere with the social aspect of the occasion. Susan M, newly retired from California with her husband and living in Eagle Lakes at the other end of Orcas, a 30 mile drive at least from the Orcas parking lot, was looking for volunteer projects and wanted to take on the UU website, which I'd done for years but let languish for the last 18 months. I explained that I had been using obsolete software and that the UU site was hosted on our family server. For those two reasons I had encouraged her to look at WordPress, a free template-based hosting service the Deer Harbor Community Club was using for its new site. By 11:45 we'd finished and she had a homework assignment: do a single page site with WordPress.

    I drove to the Library to make copies of the Cross Connect Survey pages I'd gotten back from Crane owners and would need to forward to Gary, eating part of a sandwich in the pickup, but the feed on the copy machine was acting up so I drove to the Office Cupboard and made the copies there — 53 — went on to Ace Hardware to buy shock and chlorine treatments for our hot tub, found out from Harold that Eastsound Electronics had opened in the space Ken and Kate had vacated when they closed their real estate office, walked across North Beach Road, and with the help of the new proprietor, bought a male-to-male monitor cable I hoped would make my Averatec notebook usable again after the screen was damaged in a fall from the kitchen counter to floor. I told the new owner how happy I was that he'd opened his store — with the loss of Radio Shack — and he agreed because that's where he had been working. Then to Keybank to deposit the Rankin's contribution to the No Wake Zone committee. By about 1:25 I was at work mowing grass in the Crane lot above Deer Harbor Road, getting as far as I could underneath the trailers parked there in perpetuity and cutting back the thriving blackberry bushes as far as I could. I arrived at the Deer Harbor Community Club just before 2:00 when Yvonne and her crew were breaking up for the day. They'd had few donations on the second day of receiving and hoped Friday would bring a flood. Yvonne had picked out a kitchen pots and pans set she'd get for Natasha.

    Back on the Crane dock I talked with Margaret for a while. She had been able to start her Yamaha outboard and didn't know why she hadn't been able to the day before. I had become annoyed that Ochs had left their small, decrepit Whaler moored in the center of the dock I use and Margaret and I moved it to the bottom of the V where it would be out of the way. Mike was coming over to replace a fuel line and I could see his boat a few hundred yards northeast of the Crane dock headed in.

227: Crane power comes from Shaw Island under Wasp Passage

Using the new cable I'd bought I was able to use our TV as a monitor for my Averatec notebook and so could use Kindlegen, the Amazon Windows software for creating MOBI format ebooks, and it worked! In a few minutes I'd uploaded our new *The eNotated Metamorphosis*, with the Ian Johnston translation, to Amazon, and let Jens, David, Chris, and Natasha know that we were back in the game. A new email, from Marcy, described how Corey, Paul's estranged son, was back in their lives, having left California in despair, sick, penniless, friendless, and probably addicted to alcohol. The opportunity for reconciliation was great but his condition troubling. We'd hear more later.

And James sent us a publication draft of his latest research article, very official looking, and only partially comprehensible to me. He'd reported earlier that he was very happy at having received high marks from the students he'd taught/assisted as a TA for an introductory neuroscience course at UCLA. Along the way he'd told us how the professor's lecture style was obscure at best and more often otiose so his goal was to explain what the professor had said, making it clear to these undergraduates — and apparently they'd appreciated his effort.

After Yvonne finished her evening Facebook session we turned up the tension by watching *The Fighter*, a gripping portrait of an American family, an expertly rendered vision of pain, love, reconciliation, and transformation. Wow!

Two-hundred-twenty-eight: Ripening

"We cannot live only for ourselves. A thousand fibers connect us with our fellow men." - Herman Melville

Yvonne's crew would be arriving by 10:00 so we left the house about 9:20. I'd already loaded the two rain barrels that Mike had donated as well as four brown tarps, one blue tarp, eight fluorescent tube lights, and a big red shop vac Dean and Iris left us when we bought their house. Yvonne went ahead in the van and I loaded the pickup — which still had the string mower in the bed — which I thought I might use to trim the grass near the road and in the ditch I'd skipped on Wednesday. Pam and Steve came down to the Crane Association parking lot from their house above it intending to help Yvonne unload the cart. As it turned out I took the pickup to their house and we loaded the donations they hadn't been able to fit into their Volvo wagon and then met at the Community Club.

My immediate task was to rake the grass in the area I had cut — which now looked like mown hay. I used a leaf rake to create strips of cut grass and then moved the concentrated grass to a blue tarp. Once the pile on the tarp was about 4 feet high, I closed the tarp around the grass and dragged it to the back parking lot and dumped it in a corner near a pile of branches. After a while Steve joined the cut grass cleanup project and the front yard was soon ready for the laying of the tarps to display rummage sale items. Steve and Pam and I opened up the tarps (two were 24' x 20') and lay down three, holding aside the biggest ones since they were to serve as covers to keep off the dew and prying eyes. We moved all the tools, construction items, boat stuff and garden treasures to the tarps, sorting them by general category. Deer Harbor Community Club members and others continued to bring more items during the day and by 2:00 most everything had been sorted and priced.

Two-hundred-twenty-eight: Ripening

227A: Sorting and pricing

At noon I went home for lunch and then returning to Orcas brought over a few more items: two gallons of blue windshield washer fluid and two gallons of pink toilet antifreeze. At 2:00 Yvonne dismissed the crew, telling them to report back for duty Saturday morning, the next day, by 8:30. Before we left, concerned about the wind blowing the top tarps off, we tied ropes and electric lines across the two big tarps and laid free weights on the corners. During the short cruise back to Crane Island the *Huginn*'s engine stopped unexpectedly and ominously but I was able to restart it and we were soon back on Cane.

I had several emails from Jens — with good news — our book was now listed in the Amazon Kindle catalog — there had been no challenge like last time — and with bad news — his name was spelled wrong in the catalog, and I suspected immediately that I must have typed it into the Kindle on-line form incorrectly. I was embarrassed. Amazon had locked the book when I submitted it and it was still locked so I couldn't make the correction and called Jens to explain and apologize. He was understanding — but we wouldn't be able to activate our marketing machine until the catalog was correct. Then each of us fell asleep — Yvonne on the couch and me on the love seat.

Yvonne was already baking the bread she'd take to Margaret's where we were invited for dinner, a loaf of 18-hour no-knead bread, an artisan bread in a wide oval loaf with a chewy crust and light interior, a bit like sourdough but not.

228B: Yvonne, Marilyn, Rachel, Lou, Iris, Deedee, and Margaret

We walked next door about 5:30 — after I put a manila envelope with cross connect surveys for Gary inside the glass doors of the island's bulletin

Two-hundred-twenty-eight: Ripening

board and at the dock met Lou who was on his way to Margaret's as well — and were greeted by Margaret, Lou, Rachel and Marilyn, Deedee, and Iris — and Iris' Papillon Coda (because she would be Iris' last dog and was some compensation for the loss of Dean, only months after they sold us their house and retired from Crane to Bellingham). Iris, 85 and a flautist, played with seven different groups in Bellingham and had recently joined Facebook and looked forward to connecting up with friends and she encouraged us to attend the UU church in Bellingham, with a minister and congregation she liked a lot.

I had taken our iPad next door and couldn't help doing a brief dog and pony show about *The eNotated Metamorphosis* to what turned out to be an appreciative audience. Understanding that we were publishing classics and after I had talked about Mary Shelley's *Frankenstein*, Marilyn mentioned Mary Wollstonecraft and was delighted that Yvonne and I knew her work and significance.

Then Margaret called us to the table — with two kinds of lasagna (crab and sausage), a green salad with slices of strawberry, and Yvonne's just out of the oven-still warm bread. It was a congenial group of people who loved Crane Island — current and former residents. I could report on the water system and the Board's policy review project. We all told boat problem stories — though Yvonne and I had the best — or worst ones — perhaps because our coming and going to Orcas is so constant, sometimes three round trips in one day. After Lou talked about how his garden fence had fallen down and he could no longer keep the deer out, Margaret asked him whether he'd be willing to have a Crane work party spend a morning restoring his garden, deck, and whatever else needed attention. He said he would think about it. He talked about how affectionate Rollie was — more than his previous two miniature dachshunds — a companion to him like Coda was to Iris. About 8:00 everyone was ready to go home — except Iris and Coda who would stay the night with Margaret. I thought about inviting Iris to come and see the new kitchen but then thought better of it — an opinion Yvonne confirmed. Iris had talked about how she missed the beauty of Crane and in Bellingham had only the house across the street to look at. Yvonne, thinking about the future pointed out that tenure on Crane is aways limited but a gift in any case.

Yvonne was the youngest person at the table, Margaret younger than me but everyone else older. Over the last weekend I had been painfully aware how old we're becoming compared to the younger people that visited us, how much more vitality they have than we do. After this dinner Yvonne and I both felt rejuvenated after being part of a group that for the most part moved slower than we did, had less energy, but of course were doing very well for being 85 or whatever.

Two-hundred-twenty-nine: Not again?

"Life is a shipwreck, but we must not forget to sing in the lifeboats."
- Voltaire

Spring had dragged on, cool and wet, but now summer was here, signs of it everywhere. Northwest winds or very little wind had become more common than southeast winds that last from October until May, sometimes very strong, and with the high winter tides pilling up waves and flotsam (not to mention jetsam) in our cove. The lilacs were gone, some rhododendrons were left, and peonies coming. The early June sun on moist soil had caused the grasses to grow inches per day — it seemed — the grass in the meadow north of the house more than three feet tall — the seed heads darkening suddenly without warning — and I thought drying but looking closer I saw that they were in fact flowering, bluestem and Canada rye, each with tiny lavender flowers that made them look dark and not green at a distance. I had never before paid attention to the life cycle of these grasses and I was surprised at what I saw. They changed quickly, day to day, and had a kind of noble beauty.

We were at the Deer Harbor Community Club by 8:30, much of the crew had already arrived, as well as a few early birds who were looking over what would be offered on the tarps on the lawn in front of the historic building. Pam and Steve had already removed the covering tarps from the outdoor goods. Nothing had been disturbed overnight. We then spread the goods out so as to be more visible laying down one of the cover tarps to hold building supplies. Now shoppers arrived in earnest, filling the lot and parking along Deer Harbor Road, crowding around the outdoor sales area, some walking into it and having to be shooed out. Just before nine, Bev rang the old school bell in the belfry above the entrance, prompted by Judy, and shoppers streamed into the building and through the outdoor area, some like Howard and Michael rushing to the objects they had picked out as true treasures and bringing them to the checkout area under the canopy Pam and Steve had raised. Michael picked out the table saw rollers Gene had donated and Howard the Force 10 boat grill I had stored in my shop and we'd never used. Blake saw the oars Gene had brought in (and that I had considered buying) and bought the pair for $20. And Nancy picked up one of Mike's rain barrels for $10, a steal at twice the price. Cal's two professional style, and very heav, crab pots went.

229: Getting ready for the multitudes soon to appear

Kat had come with Michael and I hadn't seen her for at least six months. She looked better and clearly had enough energy to make herself look nice enough to go out — something she hadn't been able to do then. She was still rail thin and still weak and she reported that social events greatly tired her even though she had been a year with her new liver, the transplant having come after doctors in the midwest had been unable to diagnose what was wrong with her and she had nearly died. But she was better now because she could talk continuously, almost without taking a breath, about what she had done and what she knew.

Mike, having opened a marine service business recently after being laid off when his Carousel Buffalo Ranch employer died, picked out all the oil and filters Joan and Roger had donated, the shop lights Steve and I had each brought over, filling the bed of his pickup and running up a $140 tab. About 10:00, after the choice items were gone, Joyce and Larry appeared, and once he found nothing to interest him, he and I sat on a log and talked about the computer needs of the Food Bank. I had volunteered, through Yvonne, to make them operational in their new building but I needed to know exactly what he wanted to accomplish, what he had in mind, which was pretty basic: Windows, desktop, internet access (he had made arrangements with Century Link), MS Office, maybe QuickBooks, email, a multifunction printer/copy machine and I added to that virus protection, and automatic external drive backup. Windows 7 was apparently an improvement though I hadn't used it but would need to when Yvonne and I bought a netbook to replace the injured Averatec notebook. I told Larry I'd do some research and provide him some proposals. He said that BestBuy had a small business service that might be worth investigating.

Once I put Erik, who had donated a chipper, with Jennifer, who thought she might want to buy it, together, I decided I could go home for lunch, coming back in time to take what was left over to the Exchange (or the transfer station for what they wouldn't take). Yvonne had spent most of the morning inside the old school house with the household goods, providing direction to the crew and at times the check out line was long but patient, one woman with a big pile commenting on the sale's low prices when her total came to $11.25. Though at times Yvonne was worried that she had priced too low, we both agreed that people weren't likely to spend more with higher prices, they'd just buy less and there would be more left over to dispose of. Who knows?

Since the bed of the truck needed to be empty for the run to the Exchange after the sale, I took the string mower, full gas can, and filament roll home with me and put them away in the tool shed. After lunch I got back in the *Huginn*, had some trouble starting the engine, and then pulled out into Pole Pass, the tide running out, east, with a west wind breeze. And the engine quit. I tried to start it again but got only a sputtering response — just as I had the Monday before, followed by Ian's coil replacement on Tuesday. The *Huginn* was drifting southeast quickly. I had no cell phone but could call Vessel Assist on my VHF radio — and had insurance so that it wouldn't cost anything. But that would take a hour and I was due back at the Community Club to help clean up. I was drifting stern first now, the heavy end leading. I had to stop or slow the drifting and so climbed along the side of the cabin to the bow, pulled the pin out of the anchor holder and tossed it into the water and the boat slowed but didn't stop its drifting. By now I was 200 yards east of Margaret's and I yelled in the direction of her house. I regretted not having an airhorn aboard. She didn't respond but I saw a teenage boy with his dog on the Becker's beach and yelled for him to go to Margaret's and tell her about my need. He headed that direction and at that point Margaret came through the trees in front of her house and saw me. She signaled that she would come rescue me with her boat — and she did. In the meantime I sat in the sun under an intensely blue sky watching the occasional boat pass by, studying the Crane water line — green above, gray below, noticing the distribution of madrona among the firs along the island's bank, and generally enjoying myself. Margaret pulled up along side, created a harness, cleat to cleat with slack to clear her outboard and then looped the line I offered her through the harness and back to me, where I secured it to the anchor rode cleat along with its other end. Soon we were back at the Crane dock and I was on my way to Orcas in Margaret's boat. Resolution of the starting problem would have to wait until Monday. We'd already received a bill for Ian's services: $230.

Back at the Community Club I was surprised to see that almost everything outside had sold, including both chippers, and almost everything that I'd brought from my shop. The bake sale table was almost empty, Sue, Anne, and Lois having served coffee and treats to many of the shoppers. Inside probably twenty percent of the donations remained. At 1:00 I began to load our pickup with what was left in the yard and Bob, Erik, and Howard filled their truck beds and one trailer with what Yvonne's crew was boxing up. By 2:00 the yard and old school house were restored to their usual condition and the four of us men had been to or were at the Exchange. That worthy organization accepted virtually everything we brought to them, except the baseboard heaters I had (from my shop and Howard's), and David's old laser printer. San Juan Sanitation was already closed for the day so I couldn't drop off the heaters. I brought the laser printer back to the community club and Yvonne would call David to come and get it. At the Exchange, Arthur had been very helpful as usual, chuckling when I handed him a Kegel exercise device someone had donated to the yard sale and I wondered where he would put it among the enormous variety of objects waiting for a second use.

Pam S, the club treasurer had done a quick count of the receipts before the small group remaining left the club and reported sales just under $2900. Later in the day she called Yvonne to say the sale had made just under $3000, the club's best fundraiser ever. Yvonne had done a great job organizing and directing the effort, having become an expert over the years, beginning with the enormous Boulder Unitarian Church sales she directed 30 years before. It seemed to me that the women working on the sale enjoyed it as a kind of reverse shopping exercise that made use of their considerable knowledge of what things were worth.

Checking the Amazon KDP site, I saw that *Metamorphosis* was no longer locked. I changed "Kruze" to "Kruse," clicked on the "Publish" button and wrote everyone that the correction was in process. Yvonne said she felt like she was now on vacation. I felt a sense of relief and accomplishment. We were both tired. Yvonne took a nap and I sat near her in the living room alternately writing and falling asleep sitting up, something I can do without effort.

At dinner we talked about the sale, the people, living on Crane, and her appreciation for Joyce Carol Oates' *A Widow's Story*.

Two-hundred-thirty: "I Want to Do Everything"

"Live in each season as it passes; breathe the air, drink the drink, taste the fruit, and resign yourself to the influence of the earth." - Henry David Thoreau

A beautiful morning, the rising sun reflecting off the calm waters east of the house, and Yvonne on the deck doing something. What? Hanging a four-sided humming bird feeder she'd bought at the Community Club yard sale the day before and that had soaked overnight in a big bowl — to clean it presumably. She stuck a bird feeder to the kitchen window two weeks before but it hadn't seen much activity. Then at Margaret's for dinner Friday evening, her two hummingbird feeders on stakes just east of her waterside deck, we saw them alive with the tiny colorful birds, Margaret commenting that she'd seen as many as nine visiting simultaneously. Yvonne wanted that too — and thus this morning's project. Dean and Iris had installed a curved, movable aluminum armature to the the eaves over the living room deck to hang a bird feeder the squirrels couldn't reach but in the four and a half years we'd been in the house we had done nothing with it. Now Yvonne put it to use, hanging the feeder and then rotating the armature out over the space beyond the deck. Coming in after completing her project, Yvonne declared, "I want to do everything! Everything! Put that in your log!"

Later, while we ate lunch on the deck, 20 feet from the feeder we watched the peculiar choreography of hummingbirds recognizing and then coming to use this new food source. One aggressive bird made continuous inspection passes, not landing, but from time to time sitting on a nearby madrona branch, observing and chasing off any other birds coming close to the feeder. In one scene, a third hummingbird dined on the far side of the feeder while the first bird chased away a second. I'd been reading about raven feeding habits and status orders and was looking for clues here with hummingbirds.

230A: "I want to do everything!"

Early emails from Jens and then Chris reported that the Amazon catalog now listed "Kruse" rather than "Kruze" as author (eNotator) of *The eNotated Metamorphosis.* The marketing process — distribution of courtesy and review copies, changes to the Website and Amazon author pages, broadcast emails, and so on could finally begin. We were finally in business with our first literary classic and Jens reported that he wasn't far from a first draft of *In the Penal Colony*.

As I'd been for much of the last week, I wanted to be outdoors now as much as possible, feeling strongly as I had when young that being outdoors, especially in a beautiful place, is exhilarating and when combined with work on projects deeply satisfying as well. Inside air is always stuffy, though that's not always noticeable if one is only indoors or if the outside air isn't clean, at least it's a little bit cool. The Crane air, the San Juan Islands air, the Pacific Northwest air, for the most part, is a pleasure to breathe and feel, like certain spring waters.

With the *Huginn* out of commission and its return to service uncertain and the untenability of continuing to borrow Margaret's boat for our almost daily commutes, we needed an alternative way of getting back and forth to Orcas and two possibilities presented themselves: our 8' Livingston tender and our kayaks. We had three forms of power for the Livingston: oars, a tiny electric motor, and an old 4 horse Johnson two-stroke that we hadn't used in several years — since it fell off the Livingston into the water when I was being pushed backward by the wind and the motor ran into a rock in the Crane marina. Neither rowing nor the electric motor could take us through Pole Pass against the tide and the Johnson probably wouldn't work, so to use the Livingston we'd have to keep it on east side of Pole Pass, the same side as the Crane dock on Orcas, and that meant keeping it in our cove — and that meant cleaning the cove and creating a place to store the Livingston above high tide. So I went to work cleaning out Raven Cove, as we call it.

Our house sits on a shallow peninsula, with Raven Cove on the south and Och's cove on the north. Margaret's house is south just across Raven's cove. We own both sides of the cove and so, extending work Dean had done years ago, last spring I cut a new path and installed stairs down to an intermediate level, widened that level, and then put a railing on the heavy plank Dean had left as a ramp from what acted as a landing to the beach below. The high tides, east winds and waves of November had dislodged the ramp so that it had hung by a thread (chain and heavy rope) from a willow stump above until put back by Matt this spring with some help from Ron and me. I needed to find a way to fasten the bottom end of the ramp to the beach — though I had no expectations that anything would hold should incoming floating logs bash it over the winter. The right solution was to have steps I could pull up — but I wouldn't do that today.

I rolled a large log left by a ten foot winter tide higher on the beach and stuffed rocks under it to keep it from rolling back down and then began to carry fir branches up to the rain shelter burn pile area and moved drift wood to the back of the beach. Then raking the beach above the high tide mark, I carried that debris up the ramp, path, and stairs and deposited it next to the upper path at the head of the cove that leads from the house to the stairs. I wasn't happy with the landing above the ramp; it sloped too much toward the cove, so I added another layer of wood boundary and carried up gravel from the beach to regrade the landing and path just above it. A big improvement.

230B: Putting together a drip irrigation system

I found two heavy aluminum right angle mounting brackets I'd pulled out of my shop the week before and piled with other metal I didn't think I would ever need and used a sledge hammer to pound them into the beach gravel at the lower end of the ramp and then put stainless screws through them into the bottom of the ramp. That would hold it against most wave at-

Two-hundred-thirty: "I Want to Do Everything"

tacks. Next I found two painted steel right angle hanging brackets from which the garage door tracks had been hung, pounded them into the beach gravel four feet below the log I rolled up the beach and hung a four-inch driftwood tree trunk with wire from what were now posts. This would hold the aft end of the Livingston above high tide, the bow resting on the log. While I worked on the cove beach Yvonne was putting together a drip irrigation system that would use water from the newly installed 450 gallon catchment tank at the northwest corner of the house just outside the deer fence to water her front garden. She has created an irrigation system out of bits and pieces of existing hosing and from time to time asked for my help forcing a connector into a raw hose end, impossible for her to do with her arthritic hands. In the afternoon she demonstrated the system to me and then put it to work, intending to let it run for several hours or until the tank was empty or the water pressure from the tank too low. By evening the north end of the garden was well watered and she was very satisfied — and we hadn't used any water from the Crane community system.

Taking a break after lunch, with Margaret we moved the Livingston from its off-season location next to the path approaching the house from the meadow, the north, down to the Och's beach and then because the tide was very low across the beach to the water. I rowed and Yvonne encouraged me with "stroke, stroke" as we moved south toward Raven Cove a 100 yards away. Carrying the Livingston twenty feet above the current water line, we left it there until the afternoon when I brought the battery and electric motor down to the beach and installed the system on the Livingston. Yvonne suggested we cruise to the Orcas dock and back to see whether the motor would move the boat adequately and to get some idea of how long it would take. It was a pleasure to be out on the water with the nearly silent and effortless system and Yvonne suggested during the summer we use the *Huginn* less and the Livingston and kayaks more. When we had little to carry and the weather was right that would provide exercise and near contact with the water — a pleasure.

Margaret wanted to get her long, narrow, sea kayak in the water, and had a two wheel carry for it — but one tubeless tire was totally flat and her compressor couldn't output air fast enough to close the gap between tire and rim fast enough to allow the tire to be filled — but it turned out the output from my compressed air carry tank could and she was soon in business.

Two-hundred-thirty: "I Want to Do Everything"

While Yvonne made exceptional chicken, bean, rice, and green chili enchiladas for dinner, I called Noah and we caught up. He was pleased that Kelly and Tim had named their baby boy Noah, not after Noah but because they liked the name and thought it immune to being turned into a nickname. The Olympia school district hadn't approved the next year's budget so he wasn't certain he'd have a job, though odds were in his favor. Natasha had turned down an employment offer because it was too clerical given her background and skills. Morgan was doing well with guitar, enjoying his continuing reading of mythology-based books, and succeeding in fourth grade. Opal loved her swimming classes, had done some at a recent birthday party at a classmate's grandparent's lake house, and was much appreciated by her kindergarten teacher.

Two-hundred-thirty-one: Gemütlichkeit

"Nature is not a place to visit. It is home." - Gary Snyder

Stopping on the rise just south of the community center on Circle Road, I could barely see the tank level indicator and markings through the greenery. At 13' 9" the 35,000 gallon Crane community water system tank was close to overflowing but also had plenty of capacity to respond to sudden increases in transient population. On a typical winter's day the three full time households use only 200 gallons total. On Memorial Day weekend, the island's daily usage was close to 4000 gallons. At 14', the overflow point, the tank has about 16,000 gallons of water available (2500 gallons per foot) before it reaches the fire reserve point at 7 1/2 feet where normal outflow takes place. By opening a valve from the bottom of the tank the remaining 7 1/2 feet, (19,000 gallons) can be drained to fight a fire. Keeping the tank at close to capacity without overflowing was desirable but difficult with our completely manual environment. Gary, our water system manager and I had been talking about how to accomplish it for some time but had yet to actually do anything.

A week or two earlier I'd been puzzled by what looked like bark shavings in two places along Rocky Road, one near its junction with Circle Road. In each case the strips, all about 1/2' wide and 3" long were concentrated in a small area on the road. It was possible but unlikely that they had spilled out of an islanders truck bed, Gator, or trailer. They must have fallen from the tree above — but I as I searched the branches above I couldn't see any sign. And what had done this bark stripping and why? This morning I came upon three new bark strip sites on Circle Road, this time on the other end of the island, near Lou's and then farther east by Skip's. But this time, for the last two sites at least, I could see where the bark had been stripped, in one case about 30 feet above the ground in a Bigleaf maple, about 4 feet had been stripped from a three inch diameter branch, all the way around, at least as far as I could see. At the third site, near the intersection with Dock Road, a foot long section had been stripped from a smaller branch at about the same height. The branches that had been stripped would die. How often was this happening? What was stripping the bark in such a methodical way and how was it stripping not just the top and sides of the branches but the bottom side as well. And why? Or was the bark just falling off? Or was someone climbing the trees with a draw knife? Of course not, but the bark strips could have been created by one.

231: Our homestead - looking west from a bluff above the Salish Sea

While Yvonne did "office work" in her studio, I caught up on my emails and generated many new ones relating to the publication of *The eNotated Metamorphosis*, — after talking to Betsey at West Sound Marina, describing how the *Huginn*'s engine had failed in Pole Pass — just as it had less than a week before and then been fixed by Ian. About an hour later Ian called and said he could come to the Crane dock and would call before he left West Sound Marina. At noon Yvonne came into the house from the attached studio, saying she'd finished her inside work, couldn't stand another minute of it, and wanted to spend the rest of the day outside. Then Ian called and by 2:00 I was on the Crane dock watching him go through a series of experiments to determine why the engine wouldn't start. He quickly found that no gas was getting to the carburetor. Was there gas in the tank? The gauge showed just under a 1/4 tank, or more than 10 gallons — although it could be overstating the actual level. Was the electric fuel pump operating? Yes, at least it sounded like it was pumping. Ian checked the mesh filter right in front of the carburetor and the line feeding it. No problem. Then he checked the fuel pump by having it pump from a jar of gas back into the jar. No problem — though he couldn't be certain that the pressure was adequate without a gauge — which he hadn't brought along. What about the anti-siphon device between the tank pickup and the line to the fuel pump. He pulled it out of the tank, inspected it and blew through it. It seemed OK. By sloshing the pickup pipe back and forth in the tank, he said the fuel level seemed lower than the fuel gauge reading. Maybe the problem was simple — too little gas — which triggered the anti-siphon — which made it impossible for the pump to pull any gas from the tank. But he wasn't sure and suggested that I drive the *Huginn* — which he was confident would start now (I added 1 1/2 gallons of gas I'd bought for the string mower on Friday to the tank) and once in West Sound he could test the pump's pressure and then fill the tank and test it.

 Yvonne and I needed to be in Orcas Highlands at 5:00 and it was now 3:30. Margaret, now on the dock to take Iris back to Orcas so she could go back to Bellingham, said she'd be happy to take Yvonne to Orcas at 4:00 and if necessary pick us up when we returned after 9:00. Ian said he could lend me a boat — so the plan was that I'd drive the *Huginn* to West Sound Marina, Yvonne would pick me up there and then on the way home drop me off. I'd take Ian's boat to the Crane dock on Orcas and pick Yvonne up and we'd go on to Crane. And it worked just like that. I left the West Sound Marina about 9:00, after sunset but plenty light, in Ian's ancient Bayliner Trophy and was at the Orcas dock then minutes ahead of Yvonne.

 Jens and Susan had invited us for dinner and we sat on their west-facing deck from 5:00 until 8:45 enjoying the conversation, a meal of salmon, wild rice, and homemade carrot cake, hot sunshine, a 50 mile view from the side of Mount Constitution, and gemütlichkeit — a mood of fellowship, good-feeling, and calm in an extremely beautiful setting. Since they were "trying out" Orcas as a possible retirement venue we talked a good deal about the climate differences between Boston (and New England) and the San Juans, about how some of his colleagues dismissed the west out of hand, never having visited, about the friendliness of Orcas compared to New York City — Susan saying people treated one another as obstacles — the cultural, if amateur richness of the community, and about boating in the Salish Sea (its costs and charms), the responsiveness of the medical care system on Orcas, and on and on, topics Yvonne and I knew well and were happy to comment on. The only thing I couldn't understand — not from an intellectual point of view but a feeling point of view — was why Jens and Susan were tentative about Orcas — compared to Wellesley. I explained how the move had been a rebirth for me, in a very real sense the start of a new life, and though it was a great deal of trouble sometimes — witness the ongoing boat saga — having another, new, open ended, challenging, satisfying life, was worth every cent of cost and every minute of work. And Yvonne felt the same way. But not everyone had the same reaction or saw the same reality. Instead of an opportunity for a phase-shift, as Jens said, some saw the ferry as an inconvenience, and island life too insular and inconvenient.

Two-hundred-thirty-two: Trophy Case

"Happiness is not a state to arrive at, but a manner of traveling." - Margaret Lee Runbeck

Looking out the living room windows about 6:15 a.m., I noticed a hummingbird checking each of the four stations on the feeder Yvonne had recently installed and finding them empty. Over the last two days the zippy little birds had consumed all the nectar Yvonne had provided, nectar being colored sugar water. The water and wind were calm and the morning sun and its reflection on the water so archetypal of summer on Crane, I took my Nikon 7000 off the counter by the telephone in the kitchen and carried it outside to take pictures. I walked to the edge of the point, about 25 feet from the house and took a few pictures looking back into Raven Cove, the sun lighting it directly; later in the day it's shaded by the trees on Margaret's side of the cove. I wanted to admire the work I'd done in the cove, thinking ahead to how we'd be using it over the next three months. Then I looked south along Crane's shore, seeing Jim's Sea-Sport at his dock and Tom's Bullfrog at his dock and a yellow Santana sailboat moored to his buoy. Then I turned around and took some pictures of the luxurious heather blooming behind the deer fence Yvonne had raised this spring around the rockery where daffodils had bloomed for almost two months and lilies would later make an appearance, protected this year from the Island's voracious deer. The two aluminum deck chairs nearby were standing now, often overturned by east winds. Through the clear water gently lapping the rocks below the point I could see brown and green seaweed beyond the low tide mark. Looking north I took a picture of the twisted madrona trunk, one of four small trees that make the house hard to see from the water though easy to see through looking out.

At 12:30 Yvonne and I left the house and walked across the meadow to the community dock, seeing the ancient Bayliner Trophy Ian had lent us and that we'd come home on at dusk the night before. As I understood it, Betsy used it for fishing and crabbing and related equipment was scattered around inside and out. A pot puller extended over the port side of the cockpit. The engine compartment hinges were broken. In the cabin spare parts and tools were everywhere, along with charts, newspapers with fishing articles, a pair of blue rubber coated work gloves, a manual bilge pump, and a variety of other objects that had found their way to the boat and not left or were once part of the boat but hadn't been reinstalled. I liked this old boat a lot. It was clumsy to maneuver, at least given my limited experience with it, but it ran very well over the water, much less skittish than our smaller SeaSport. A deluxe fishing boat forty years ago, now looking very dated, the Trophy had good visibility and a sense of spaciousness. And it had, somehow, survived decades of hard use. But, I noticed as we motored to Orcas, the fuel gauge showed empty. Was it?

We stopped at the Deer Harbor Post Office so Yvonne could mail back the black, patent leather dress sandals she'd received the day before but which had turned out to be a half-size too big and I took our mail out of our mailbox and then Crane Association mail from its box. We'd received a small red envelope, a thank-you note, with an ink drawing of a hill with something on it — I couldn't tell what — a child's drawing with no name. Probably Jackson, Yvonne said.

Now in Eastsound, Yvonne parked the van in front of Home Grown Market and walked across the street to the Chamber office to fill out an application for the Food Bank to join the Eastsound Fourth of July Parade, where it would have a chance to thank the community for funding the new facility and that she later reported after the Board meeting, would have its grand opening and open house July 10th. I walked to the bank with a check to deposit for Yvonne, did, walked out, and then back in to put an envelope in the OPALCO payment box next to the door for a woman in a motorized wheel chair. The cashier called my name; the check was to the IRS and for a different amount than was on the deposit slip. I walked back to the van and laid the check and deposit slip against the dashboard above the steering wheel. I stopped at the Library to print out an email from Jens that had arrived too late to print out before I left home but which might be important for our imminent conversation, waved at Phil, Library Director, in his office wearing earphones for some reason and had help from Holly figuring out how to print from Word on Windows 7.

232: Bell Island in the background

Arriving at Ezno's just before 2:00 I ordered tea and looked for a place to sit — only to be called over by Jens who was sitting close to the service counter. He had completed much of his work on Kafka's *In the Penal Colony*, and it was time for an editorial/planning meeting. *Penal Colony* could use some of what he'd done for *Metamorphosis*, with modification. I passed him the two no-knead bread recipes he'd asked for and Yvonne had printed out — the eighteen hour (James) and one-hour (Natasha). He'd prepared a list of images he wanted to use that would supplement the images he wanted to carry forward from *Metamorphosis*. And we reviewed the situation with complementary copies. Leaving business we spent some time talking about Kafka's writing style, its resistance to being reduced to allegory and how the images he unpacked had surfaced after stressful periods in his life — for instance when

Two-hundred-thirty-two: Trophy Case

Felice broke their engagement after subjecting him to something like a hearing or tribunal. The Food Bank having adjourned their Board meeting, Yvonne appeared and we headed for Deer Harbor.

The possibly empty tank on the Trophy was troubling so I called Ian on Yvonne's cell phone from the lumber yard, on Crow Valley Road and he said that the fuel gauge wasn't reliable and that neither he nor Betsy could say with certainty that the tank wasn't nearly empty so I walked inside, bought a five gallon plastic gas can and filled it using the pump outside. Dropping Yvonne off at the Crane dock I motored to the Deer Harbor Marina, holding the five gallon tank in reserve and pumped seven gallons into the Trophy. Ian had confirmed that the *Huginn*'s problem was a marginally performing fuel pump that couldn't cope with a low tank fill level. The new pump might be in by Friday. I'd call him. In the meanwhile we had transportation from and to Crane Island in the interim. Yvonne wanted me to ask him whether the first fix, the coil, had really been necessary and whether it was the fuel pump all along. I told her I'd discuss that with Ian when the time seemed appropriate. The issue now was to have the *Huginn* repaired and to have reliable boat transportation.

Two-hundred-thirty-three: Trapped

"The illiterate of the 21st century will not be those who cannot read and write, but those who cannot learn, unlearn, and relearn." - Alvin Toffler

Because I was a little ahead of schedule, that is not yet late, I took a few minutes to inspect the rubber doughnut hinge that connected the breakwater floats with the east float on the Orcas dock. It was now torn half way across and when a wake passed under the two hinged sections they didn't move together, the breakwater rising higher where the rubber hinge was torn, little by little tearing it further. I used a pen to mark and date the current position of the tear. After notifying Blair a few emails had passed by me that suggested some action was afoot but I had seen nothing for a month now. My guess was that the more the hinge tore the faster the rest of it would tear and once the hinge broke the second hinge could be compromised quickly.

Howard and I were it for this week's Greybeards. Chris was in Spokane at a utility meeting, I hadn't heard from David in a week (traveling?) and Brian was a no-show. Howard said Becky had heard from Sheldon that Brian had been medevaced from Orcas but didn't know for sure — and would try to reach Brian later on. I handed Howard a strip of maple bark I'd retrieved from Circle Road on Crane, representative of five different locations where I'd found strips scattered together and which I observed had come from stripped branches above. After hearing my account he had two suggestions: first that perhaps some animal, maybe a squirrel, liked to lick maple sap, and second that perhaps Lou, the state wildlife group, or a Google search would generate an explanation.

Barbara had been doing eNotations on Willa Cather's *My Antonia* and was now ready to talk, so we'd arranged a 9:30 meeting at her house in Spring Point, the southwest corner of Orcas Island near Bev and Dave. She opened her door as I walked down the stairs to her house below the road and she and her friendly Norwegian Elkhound greeted me. She'd been through the entire book now creating two kinds of eNotations, glossary entries and theme citings. The glossary entries provided definitions and historical and cultural background for words and phrases with meanings not obvious to the contemporary reader. The second set of entries identified words or phrases where Cather was developing an underlying theme that ran through the entire novel, for instance about the influence of the landscape on the lives and psychology of the characters. She'd written or outlined essays on the themes she was elucidating — independent of the citings she'd done — and in fact had entered no text to the theme eNotations. She hadn't seen how Jens had approached the same task — making theme citings complete discussions of a specific appearance of a theme and then bringing those notes together in a complete discussion of a theme or topic writing additional, connective tissue to make the collecting of notes on a theme into a coherent essay. The reader could read the notes along the way, one at a time and commingled with glossary entries and then read them together in one extended essay to appreciate them in concert.

Once I showed her *The eNotated Metamorphosis* she understood. She'd cut and then copy elements of her long essays into appropriate theme citings, leaving pointers in the now depleted essays then would insert that text back into the essay at the appropriate point to make the essay whole. She reported she was having a great time and looked forward to the next book. She apologized for taking so long — I assured her she wasn't — but being a member of the Fire District Board, working on a long range plan it would make use of when its tax assessment came up for renewal in 2014, had agreed to do a comprehensive policy review, a major undertaking this spring. Barbara had a Nook, which required EPUB format (which I had yet to create for *Metamophosis*) and since being able to read Jens' book would be very helpful to her, we installed the Kindle reader software on her Mac and then copied the MOBI file from my Mac. She was in business.

When I got home for a late lunch, Yvonne reported she'd been doing office work all morning, had more to do and was tired of it. I turned my attention to the Crane Island Association creating an end-of-year Cash Report projection and based on that as well as special needs I knew about for the coming year created a draft budget that the Board would discuss at the Board meeting Saturday. The process lasted all afternoon. Yvonne had managed to get outside early in the afternoon.

Two-hundred-thirty-three: Trapped

233: Where the wild wide world pauses its spinning

I was trapped with paper files and my Mac. The process made me lethargic. Yvonne liked the idea so right after dinner we took a brisk walk around the island and I had a chance to show her some of the places I'd found maple bark deposits on Circle and we fruitlessly hypothesized about the cause. She showed me the white globular deposits of harmless spittle bugs on grass stems as we crossed the meadow north of the house and I pointed to the deer line on the salal, trees, and bushes. She told me it was usually called a browse line. Ah, that made sense.

Two-hundred-thirty-four: Boys in Transit

"Children are the hands by which we take hold of heaven." - Henry Ward Beecher

Out of bed before 4:00, I worked some more on the Crane Island Association year-end projections and next fiscal year budget before sending it on to Martha for distribution to the Board in anticipation of Saturday's meeting. Because James and Keith would pass through Prague on their way to Grindlewald and points south and because we'd be publishing more Kafka, I hoped they could take some relevant photos in Prague and perhaps pick up Kafka-related documents so I composed an email and attached examples of what we were looking for. Yvonne was already up when I went to wake her at 6:50 to get ready to leave for Seattle. Lois and partner were also having coffee (or tea?) in the Orcas Hotel while waiting for the ferry. Lois, with scarf on her head, was recovering from chemo and the couple were on their way to Bellingham for an MRI. She suggested we get together in a few months to see how we might be able to help the Library with technology, both of us having served together on its Board. On the *Elwah* heading up to the second passenger level we saw Jim and Nancy with three grandchildren, all on their way to pick up a used Boston Whaler they found on Craigslist to replace their current model with holes in its hull. I confirmed that they were going ahead with their house addition — they were — and that the Architectural Committee had provided the pre-build review service due him and he reported that Tim had come to the house and they'd discussed the project. Jim said he might reroute his water lines outside so I reminded him that Gary should inspect them before they were buried. He seemed to think that was too much trouble and expense for the Association and I assured him that inspections were part of Gary's job description and were important and he seemed to agree he'd give Gary a chance to look before covering his work. Jim and Nancy were committing to Crane and would live on the island, at least part-time, as long as possible, but finally with a more spacious and comfortable house. But the addition would be expensive given the modest increase in square feet. A contractor was already at work and cost $1000 per day. Jim, wanting to hold down expenses, had made himself part of the construction crew, putting in an eight-hour day of heavy work and was finding it challenging. I told him how I had paid two sheet rockers to hang sheetrock when I was converting the garage into the studio and how they could hold up a 4′ x 8′ sheet with one hand and quickly cut it with the other. They had done in a day what would have taken me perhaps two weeks to accomplish.

The ferry was a bit late arriving in Anacortes but even after stopping at Costco to buy gas on the way south we arrived at SeaTac just as James and Keith arrived from LAX. We parked in the Radisson lot across International Blvd waiting for them to tell us which door they were waiting by, checking email via the iPad. They each had a rolling suitcase and a backpack and were clearly excited at the prospect of being in Stockholm the next day. At Costco south of downtown Seattle, I spotted Henry the Fiddler's truck with homemade camper atop the bed, and Henry driving. I'd seen neither for nearly 30 years, since he left Boulder. I knew he was in Seattle so I wasn't entirely surprised but he was was gone before I could flag him down. Yvonne made a return and we all checked computer alternatives that might fit the Food Bank's needs. An HP tower, an external drive for backup, a printer/copier/scanner, and Microsoft Windows 7, with tax, would cost about $1000, what I had expected. I'd do more research but had a benchmark. Yvonne wanted a two-flush toilet for the guest bathroom that I would install when I redid the floor and she thought the Eco store had what she wanted. Located near Costco, the store catered to homeowners, architects, and builders who wanted to build "green" but as I'd seen in previous visits the business wasn't well run and they didn't have what Yvonne wanted in stock, even though their inventory system said they did, and the sales associated did have access to a price list that would allow her to quote an alternative. The episode reminded all of us of one from *Portlandia* in which a shopper at the Women and Women First feminist bookstore isn't allowed to buy a book he wants sitting in plain sight on a shelf.

After Kelly returned from a brief trip outdoors, Tim confirmed that we could come and visit them and baby Noah — and Michelle, Kelly's mom, who would be in Seattle for a month helping out her daughter cope with her new life. Just 10 days old, Noah was every inch a newborn, with skinny legs and tiny fingers and toes. James and Keith were amazed.

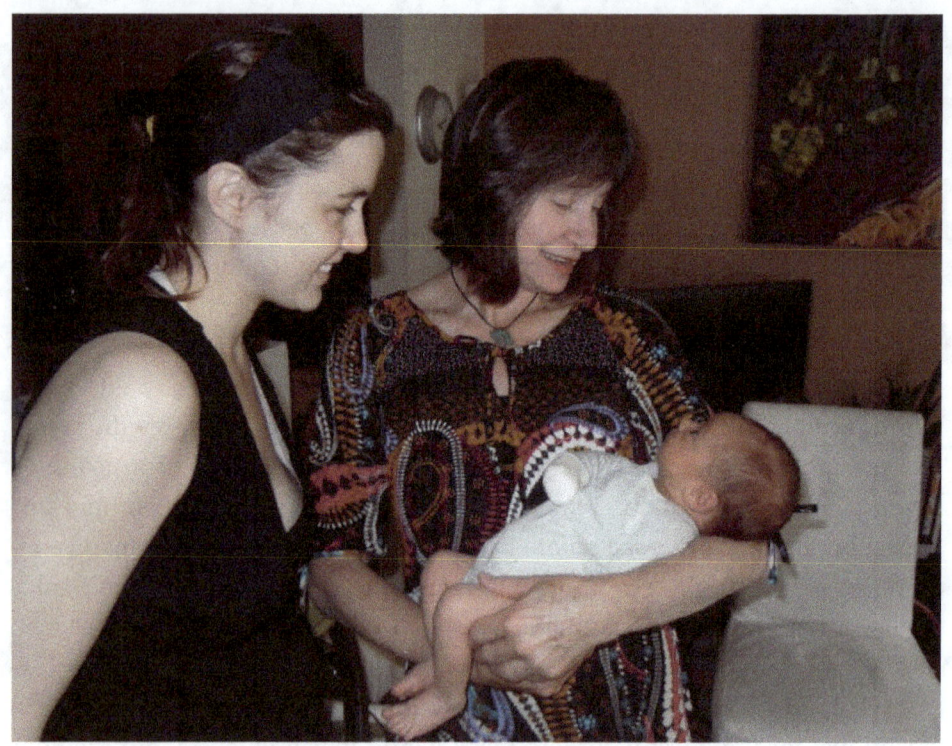

234: Kelly, Yvonne, and newborn Noah

Kelly looked tired, Tim shell-shocked Yvonne thought, and Michelle happy, cool, and confident. Tim confirmed that he felt that the birth process and emergence of his new son had been miraculous, while Kelly reported that labor had hurt a lot, more than she had expected. Yvonne gave Kelly a lovely edition of *Mother Goose* she'd bought at Elliott Bay Books where James had bought me a copy of Marilynne Robinson's *Absence of Mind* after I expressed interest in it and briefly considered buying a copy. On Capitol Hill we picked up a take-out pizza and salad and then met Jen, cats Lola, and Gypsy (who

Two-hundred-thirty-four: Boys in Transit

Corrina had left with Jen when she began her drive East a few days before to begin art graduate school in Philadelphia). The boys had been pre-adjusting to the time zone change they'd experience, nine hours, and had gotten up at 3:30 and wanted to be in bed this evening as early as possible — which turned out to be about 8:30. Yvonne and I had inflated the mattress we'd brought with, made the bed, and then left the Belltown Gardens where Jenny's friend, Emma, had helped us rent their guest studio and went around the corner to the Coffee Bedlam shop where we shared a hot chocolate and checked email. By this time I was very tired and while Yvonne read by flashlight (we'd forgotten to bring our head lamps) I quickly fell asleep.

Two-hundred-thirty-five: Turnaround

"The true community is the one in which the members arrive at a feeling of togetherness through the free acknowledgment of their differences." - M. Scott Peck

James and Keith were already up by the time I rolled out of bed at 5:30, Keith using James' MacBook Pro and James reading his iPhone. I hadn't heard a peep even though Keith had awoken at 2:30 and James an hour later. They were continuing their process to get ahead of jet lag. Yvonne had ordered a wake up call for 7:30 so the three of us were soon on First Ave — not bound for nearby Starbucks but Street Bean Espresso on Third Avenue, a not-for-profit coffee shop that employs young people leaving homelessness — according to Faithventure Forum, and were their first customer of the day. Out of necessity changing my order from English breakfast tea to French (I couldn't tell the difference) and a raisin scone (the boys had decorated foam lattes and scones, my treat), we then spent the next hour looking at Jens' *Metamorphosis*, loading copies on James' MacBook Pro and their iPhones and then talked about the Wagenbach *Kafka Prague* travel guide I had gotten after Jens showed me his German language version. I'd printed out Jens' note about how to get copies of the Kafka "Haus zum Schiff" apartment layout. They looked forward to taking as many Kafka relevant photos as they could in Prague, understanding that the more we could use those that were our own the better.

By 8:00 we'd said goodbye — the boys could stay in the condo until 11:00 and didn't need to be at SeaTac until after 1:00 — Yvonne and I headed out of the city, the detour on Broad taking us by the fancy new Gates' Foundation building across the street from the Seattle Center and Paul Allen's Frank Gehry designed Experience Music Project building and then to The Five northbound. Yvonne climbed in the back seat and slept almost until we reached Mt. Vernon. The cars waiting in the Orcas ferry line had spilled over to lane 5 but there was plenty of room for us and many cars behind us.

Tourists were everywhere, especially outside their cars, talking to one another and clearly excited at the prospect of leaving the mainland for the San Juans. The tourist season was underway.

235: The Livingston on our pocket beach

The ferry was late arriving at Orcas Ferry landing and unloading took forever. We were home before 1:00 and once we'd dumped our baggage in the house, we walked up to Circle Road and then to the other end of the island to attend Bob's 80th birthday party, arranged by Sue and at Stacy and Doug's, a pretty house facing west with a separate bunk house that would sleep at least a dozen, water supplied to the compound that would eventually have separate dwellings for three families (a second house partially completed) by a sophisticated catchment system as well as the Crane water system.

We knew at least by sight the better part of those in attendance, many coming from Deer Harbor and the balance, probably, from the Community Church in Eastsound, transported to the compound's dock by a large powerboat. The first summer we lived on Crane we hosted the UU summer picnic and service, bringing at least 40 to the community dock on our Finnish Nauticat sailboat and Roger and Joan's Ocean Alexander powerboat. I was happy to have a chance to talk to Roger briefly now, having seen less of him as he'd become frail. During Pastor Dick's rambling grace, the Unitarians in the group looked around, catching one another's eyes and we were soon sitting together around the fireplace heating the patio enjoying Sue's offerings. After congratulating Bob and thanking Sue, Yvonne, Lynn, and Sheila took Circle Road to the south and Howard, Chris, and I to the north, agreeing to meet at our house. I'd then take our friends to the Crane dock on Orcas and they would borrow our van to get home in Deer Harbor. Howard and Chris hadn't seen this part of Crane and were interested so we detoured to the little farm Rachel and Marilyn had built then sold to move to Orcas Island a decade ago, still vacant and now on the market. I showed them several stripped bark sites and neither could come up with a plausible theory. We stopped to see how Josh was coming on the remodel of Ilze's house. By the time we reached the dock area the women were already there, but not especially impatient at our meandering.

When Margaret was ten minutes late appearing at the community dock, Yvonne went to fetch her and I opened the canvas on her boat to make it faster to get underway once they both returned. We easily convinced Margaret to use her boat to take the three of us to Orcas and then her car to the Deer Harbor Community Club for the June potluck — where we could pick up our van borrowed by our UU friends. This was the first year Deer Harbor Community Club would have potlucks in the summer and though not all the places were filled, it was crowded enough to feel satisfying — but the fare, in my opinion, left much to be desired and the only thing I could find palatable was Yvonne's potato salad, a rice salad, and some bread. After talking with Sheila about her complex quilting projects and sitting down to eat, I sat directly across from Sheldon and our conversation eventually turned to Brian, his father-in-law, and the struggle he and his wife Dawn were having convincing Brian that his back problems, Parkinson's symptoms, and overweight condition required changing his living arrangements, at least to bring in part time care but even after totaling his Volvo, falling and not being able to get up, hardly being able to walk, and struggling to cook for himself, not unexpectedly but impossibly he wanted things to be as they had been. I told Sheldon that the Greybeards had talked much of this through with Brian and that we were eager to help him adjust to his new reality, my theory being that if he could see clearly how a different life style would work and be satisfying he might consider it. This potluck was Howard's last as Club president and I made a toast to him at the end of the meal, appreciation flowing to him from all directions. More than anyone over the ten or eleven years coming to the potlucks he'd done the most to create a warm and party-like atmosphere, a celebration of community and friendship, especially through his hosting of these dinners, and this night including a flash-mob singing of "June is Busting Out All Over" from Carousel, which, as Yvonne pointed out, we all knew but our children probably didn't.

Two-hundred-thirty-six: Budget

"Aging is not lost youth but a new stage of opportunity and strength." - Betty Friedan

Thick clouds blocked the sun and wouldn't break until the afternoon as I took Yvonne through Pole Pass on the borrowed ancient Bayliner Trophy. She'd join Sylvia and Julia at the Master Gardener table at the Eastsound Saturday Farmers' Market, dispensing information to worried gardeners. Today's experiment was to take the iPad and use it to access relevant data on the internet. As Yvonne reported later, their customers didn't have the time or patience to wait even ten seconds for an answer; they wanted it right now. One woman commented that if it meant looking something up in a book or on the internet she could do that herself at home. Another woman described symptoms she was seeing on her new cherry tree and Yvonne and her colleagues, not hearing something that was necessarily a problem, referred her to the source of the tree, Bulloch's Permaculture Homestead, which also had a booth at the Market. She came back to report they told her the tree was fine and acting as it should. At dinner Yvonne told me that three recent Master Gardener graduates of the Washington State University extension program were top notch and she looked forward to recruiting them into leadership positions in the Orcas group to relieve her and Sylvia who had shepherded the group for the last five years.

Back on Crane, I walked the quarter mile from our house to the Crane Island community center (and fire station), finding Martha, Kate, and Dan already setting up tables for the Board meeting. I retrieved the carton containing the conference call speaker phone from the cabinet next to the fire engine and with Dan's help ran a long extension cord from the fire engine area to the meeting area and set the phone up on the picnic table the five of us on the island would share for the meeting. Kate hadn't been attending Board meetings regularly and I was pleased to have her with us today. When Yvonne and I

Two-hundred-thirty-six: Budget

saw them at the Crane dock on Friday she and Steve greeted us and Steve carrying cedar 2 x 4s explained that he was putting the finishing touches on a replacement deck that their son had worked on the week before. Kate had also brought homemade blueberry coffee cake and three of us accepted her offer of a slice. We could hear Jason's Gator come up Circle Road and then he walked through the big doorway after pushing the sliding door open. The Crane Community enter served as venue for the members annual meeting in August and housed a ping pong table, several picnic tables, a piano, and memorabilia from 51 years of serving Crane residents.

Martha, Board Secretary, called into the conference call service and the voices of Blair, Pat, and Dave soon made themselves heard through the conference phone. Only Tim was missing, his life in transition his brother Tom later reported, with a divorce and job change in process. Jason, approaching the end of his productive tenure as President of the Board called the meeting to order. From my point of view the crucial item on the agenda was next fiscal year's budget that we had to mail to members 30 days before the annual meeting August 21st, the date of my high school class' 50th reunion and which I had't yet decided to attend — or not. After approving the minutes of the previous meeting, in April, which I had missed because Yvonne and I were traveling in Colorado and New Mexico, the group turned its attention to our current financial situation. Though revenues were under budget expenses were as well and according to my projections would remain so through the end of the fiscal year, July 31st. Dan asked where the $1500 annual expense for airstrip and verge mowing appeared in the Cash Report. I'd heard that Jim was paid to do the mowing but had seen no sign of it in the current year's financial statements — but it would need to be there and would also have to appear in the budget for the next year. After everyone felt comfortable with the year-end projections we reviewed together policy drafts for roads and parking, Board operation, and a miscellaneous catch-all and with a few changes the new policies were accepted unanimously and Martha was directed to mail copies to the membership with a cover letter with content from Jason, Dave (on the policy process and product), and me (on the water system Cross Connect Policy we'd adopted earlier in the year in response to a Washington State Department of Health regulation). Later in the afternoon I'd have Tom B fill out and sign the last Cross Connect Survey I was looking for and I scanned and emailed it to Gary to add to his stack of returned surveys.

Two-hundred-thirty-six: Budget

My budget for 2011-2012 assumed reduced revenues, in part because responding to our campaign for water conservation usage was reduced and therefore revenues and also because the return on our healthy reserves was so anemic in the current economic climate. On the other hand our expenses really couldn't be much lower or we would compromise the viability of our fire and safety, water, docks, roads and other systems. My draft budget allowed for our normal $30,000 contribution to reserves but as the other Board members pointed out, it was inadequate in a number of areas. By the time we'd included what they felt was truly important we were about $5000 out of balance — that is, wouldn't be able to make our customary contribution to reserves. I said that since doing a rigorous study to determine long term needs and then to figure out the best approach to funding them was a big job we couldn't finish by the time of the annual meeting so it would be prudent to scale back budgeted expenses but that set well with no one. Jason suggested we look at raising either the annual dues from $800 per year to perhaps $900 or $1000 per lot per year or raise the water connection fee from $100 to $200. Dan objected saying we should consider raising use fees, for instance the price per gallon of water, per foot moorage fees, and so on, reasoning that those who actively use island infrastructure should pay the lion's share. I pointed out that the members would balk at adjustments to use fees much more than a flat increase in dues, that raising variable fees would just result in members finding a way to reduce their use or underreport (both of which would further erode revenue) and that absentee owners benefit from the quality of inland infrastructure since it increases the value of their property even if they never set foot on Crane. Raising use fees on full time residents would, in my case certainly, make me less likely to put in all the volunteer time I do for the benefit of the entire membership. In the end the Board agreed unanimously to include a $100 increase in the annual dues as part of the new year's budget, unembarrassed to raise a modest fee that hadn't been adjusted in ten years. After all, we had two interlocking responsibilities: one to keep expenses as low as possible and the other to provide adequate safety, water, and other infrastructure.

We broke up about noon, Jason having received a series of distress calls from Theresa who said she was at the Orcas dock and couldn't start the motor on their Whaler. I volunteered to take him to Theresa and their two kids and he pulled the jump-start battery from the Crane dock cart shed and we head-

Two-hundred-thirty-six: Budget

ed to the Orcas dock. They weren't there, it turned out but at the Orcas Ferry Landing. I waited until Jason got the Mercury outboard started (it had been flooded I think) and returned to Crane to enjoy a lunch and wait for Yvonne's call to pick her up at the Orcas dock on her return from Eastsound.

236: Looking south at the east side of Crane Island

When I did pick her up later and was waiting at the Orcas dock I used the time to pour some of the spare five gallons of gas I had aboard into the fuel tank. With the fuel gauge registering empty and undependable and not having experience with how much fuel the eight-cylinder Volvo engine used, it seemed prudent to add another few gallons to the seven I'd put in five days before. Back on Crane with Yvonne already walking back to the house I talked

Two-hundred-thirty-six: Budget

with Tom B briefly at the dock parking lot where he and his nephew were repairing the split rail fence that borders the meadow and then fetched a blank cross-connect survey for him to fill out for his family. I now had surveys for every lot that had a water meter and scanned this one and sent it as an email attachment to Gary along with another email that told him the tank switch project was funded and that the Board was looking for a somewhat detailed estimate.

Two-hundred-thirty-seven: Flower Sunday

"The Earth is what we all have in common." - Wendell Berry

Yvonne, Lynn, and Sheila rotated responsibility for coffee for Unitarian Sunday services on Orcas. Today was Yvonne's turn. I carried the two big thermoses; one for coffee and one hot water for tea. Yvonne carried a vase with three kinds of flowers and maidenhair fern as greenery. In the Trophy cruising to Orcas I was struck at how beautiful the blue lupin was; a seven inch head, the flowers a rich, light blue topped with gray. After picking up the *Sunday Seattle Times* at the marina, we drove the three miles to West Sound and parked next to Kathy and Ray in the yacht club lot, built on top of a Native American midden, perhaps by Lummi, that had developed over hundreds of years of summer residence, and we all walked down to the door of the West Sound Community Center and I unlocked the door to let us in. Others soon joined us and we set up tables, chairs, all putting the flowers they brought in vases on the table next to the lectern that held Ruthie's ceramic candle stand (our "flaming chalice") and ceramic bowl filled with sand where joys and concerns candles would burn.

A number of times in the past I'd been moderator for our Flower Communion service, a May tradition in many Unitarian Universalist congregations, and one with particular poignancy. Norbert Capek, founder of Unitarianism in Czechoslovakia, created the service in 1923 for his congregation in Prague that would symbolize their connection as a group, the bouquet beautiful because of the variety of the flowers it contained. Capek was later arrested and killed by the Nazis but his wife, who survived, brought the tradition to the US where it persists. At our Orcas service in past years we would collect the flowers at the table in front and then come up one by one to remember and acknowledge someone important to us now gone from our life.

Nineteen were in attendance today, five new to the group, but none of our friends who, like us, had found less and less to draw us to these services, imitations of what had come before but without understanding or even much interest in what lay behind our local and general Unitarian meetings and group. This day Yvonne was particularly disappointed at the low quality of the service and as we drove back to Deer Harbor said she didn't want to waste her time being part of something so lame. Since my standards, at least in some areas, are much lower than Yvonne's I didn't have as strong a reaction and continued to feel some responsibility for the group I had led for about six years but was no longer willing to, believing that someone else needed to take his or her turn.

Jason, Theresa and kids were recreating at the community dock when we returned from Orcas so I dragged Jason home and had him provide the second signature on checks that had come in from Linda. Mike had forwarded a letter he had gotten from the accountants saying that Elise had left to pursue other opportunities, i.e. been let go and that Linda who was a returning employee would be taking her place. In the short time I'd worked with Linda I already had more confidence in her than I had had in Elise. Jason passed on a tidbit. He'd seen Tom at the Orcas dock and Tom, cool to Jason, had told him that he'd had five meetings with Jim in the last two days and would be sending Jason an email. Hmmm. Had our conversation with Tom had a positive effect?

Back home on Crane I couldn't bear being inside on this beautiful day so after making myself a two-egg sandwich, I walked out to the area outside my shop to deal with the the pile of what I no longer wanted or needed and which I couldn't take to the Deer Harbor Community Club yard sale. I'd checked the County website and found that the transfer station would take dried latex paint as garbage but other paints and various toxic substances could only be presented once a year, schedule to be announced. So first I turned my attention to paints and chemicals. Only one can of the collection I wanted to get rid of was latex and it was already dried out. It could be garbage. I found about a dozen oil-based paint cans, opened each one and put them in two boxes to dry out. Dean had left me six cans of wood preservative, not something that I expected would dry out so I stacked them along the front side of my shop and would figure out what to do with them later. Then I looked through a carton of other containers I wanted to get rid of, mostly left by Dean, that included rat poison and other presumably highly toxic substances. I put this carton in the carport tent, its door now rolled up and open,

Two-hundred-thirty-seven: Flower Sunday

Yvonne testing her hypothesis that mink and otters wouldn't use it as a privy if it wasn't private — and so far, after more than a week, it held up. The big mink that came up from the cove, finding the ramp, path, and stairs I'd set up convenient to its purposes, hadn't even looked in the direction of the carport as it crossed the yard and took the path toward the community dock and the west side of Pole Pass.

237: Getting help at Pole Pass

After moving what was left, garbage, closer to the outhouse-cum-trash shed, I began to dismantle furniture displaced by what had been our kitchen cabinets and which better suited my purposes. A dresser, a tall cabinet, a medium sized cabinet, and a set of shelves were made mostly of particle board. I'd have to dispose of their remains on Orcas. A tall, oddly shaped cabinet was made of plywood and perhaps it could be burned, not legally, but without doing damage (or much) to our environment. Along the way Margaret came by and wanted to borrow the Livingston dingy to snag logs on the beach next to hers and float and secure them on hers, in preparation for being pulled out and to her yard for cutting with a come-along hand winch. Something she'd done in the past. By 4:00 I'd created a stack of flat trash elements that would fit in a dock cart to be transported to the transfer station. A second pile contained wood that Yvonne would burn in the next week or two before the county closes burn pile permissions for the summer.

Two-hundred-thirty-eight: What Goes Around

"He who works with his hands is a laborer. He who works with his hands and his head is a craftsman. He who works with his hands and his head and his heart is an artist." - Francis of Assisi

I looked again, squinting to see better. Yes, the tank was at 13' 9". That was good because it provided a cushion against heavy use when summer people, like Howard B's friends, a young couple he didn't introduce us to when we saw them arriving in the Orcas lot Sunday afternoon, spend idyllic time on Crane without realizing that they should flush the toilet rarely and take showers quickly. On the other hand, with overflow at 14" there was a chance we'd waste water. Presumably having a tank float switch would allow us to have a full tank without running over. I hadn't yet heard from Gary about Board approval for this worthwhile project.

On the west side of the island I found three more bark strip cases, two maples, with about twenty and ten strips lying on the gravel road and then half a dozen strips under a fir. Farther on at Skip's the number of strips under the big maple had increased significantly and I could see several branches that had suffered this peculiar, unexplained fate.

In an email to Jason and to me, Tom said that he was resigning from the water committee, not surprising because he had told us that he was withdrawing from involvement in Crane activities, in part, I assume, because he felt persecuted and unappreciated. Since he knew more about the water system than anyone else, it was a loss, and I forwarded Tom's message to Gary, who sometimes depended on him, saying than sometime I would provide background. I replied to Tom thanking him for his services to Crane over many years and asked whether he was willing to help in an emergency. A later email from Jason to Tom said the same thing.

Two-hundred-thirty-eight: What Goes Around

I'd been feeling overwhelmed over the last few weeks, having to-do lists that seemed to grow longer each day even though I was up working at something by 5:00 every morning. A big item was cleaning and staining the house, faced in clear cedar siding that had darkened over the years and was looking worn out. Yvonne thought I shouldn't even think about it until after Borgfest, our family gathering in August. She was more sanguine than I about the external appearance of the house; what counted most was her garden and the interior and the most important interior project was a new floor and toilet in the guest bathroom, the current toilet, like the one in the master bath suffering from accumulated mineral build up visible in the outflow drain, and sitting on home made wood pedestals that added four inches to their height presumably to make them easier to get up off of. When we moved in four and a half years ago Yvonne worked hard to clean the scale from the bottom of the toilet bowls but had no success and had been embarrassed with company ever since because it looked like she didn't keep a clean house. And the high toilets weren't comfortable to use. She didn't like the light colored vinyl on the bathroom floor and worse because we had replaced the sink unit bare plywood was visible, if you looked for it, under the sink unit.

Jens had supplied me with everything I needed to assemble another ebook, this one an eNotated version of Kafka's *In the Penal Colony*, and I was determined to provide him a Kindle version draft by the end of the day. His brother would be coming from Germany soon and with other visitors he'd have little time for writing and editing the rest of the summer.

But Yvonne would be meeting with Joyce in the early afternoon to work on a mailing to Food Bank donors to invite them to the coming open house to celebrate putting the new building in operation that they had donated to and she would be seeing Larry as well who needed to approve the purchase of a computer system to be operational before the grand opening and which I had volunteered to take care of (with Yvonne's encouragement). Larry had talked to Best Buy but after 10 minutes on hold I gave up on them. After trying some alternatives, Amazon, with the use of supplementary sites for more information. turned out to be the best place to shop and after two hours of research I provided Yvonne a list, with prices, of what I thought would best serve the organization, given what Larry had told me they needed. Coming home later in the afternoon Yvonne told me Larry had approved the purchase so I'd need to order, assemble the system, and then install it.

Two-hundred-thirty-eight: What Goes Around

238: Making the new Food Bank building ready for the Grand Opening

Yvonne said that she and Joyce had talked about island yard sales and that before she knew Joyce, she sold her a classic orange tablecloth she'd gotten at a yard sale for use in our Deer Harbor home, then sold it to Joyce when we'd redecorated because the color was wrong, then when we moved to Crane buying it back at Joyce's sale since the color was now right. Joyce regretted selling it since she now realized she liked it.

By late afternoon I'd sent a draft *Penal Colony* ebook off to Jens, and cleaned up my desk, gathering up the bark strips I'd brought home for no good reason and putting Crane, Classics Unbound, and personal materials in separate piles, each crying out for attention. That felt better anyway.

We almost finished the potato-chard gratin and braised spinach (with a little bacon), leaving enough for Yvonne's lunch the next day. The chard and spinach had come from Ken and Kate, but not without a struggle. Because Yvonne couldn't pick some up when they were at home Kate told her to come and cut some from their garden whenever she wanted. Pulling into their driveway, with the rental cabin on the left and rental yurt on the right, Yvonne was distracted and didn't see the electric fence wire stretched across the driveway until she almost drove through it. She parked and crawled under the line, Cassie, their grey muzzled, red Lab mix, bounding toward her, and their four big horses somewhere inside the fence grazing. Would the half-ton horses stampede, knock her down and trample her? She thought that could happen but then saw they were confined by another temporary electric fence to another part of the property a hundred yards away — but they had all come to the fence to watch her walk to the house and garden, cut the spinach and chard and then return safely to the car. All in all it had been a terrifying and exhilarating experience but worth it; the chard gratin and spinach were delicious and very satisfying.

Two-hundred-thirty-nine: Grind

"The best way to find out if you can trust somebody is to trust them." - Ernest Hemingway

Not such a nice day but not cold, just overcast and a little windy. No trips to Orcas planned. With a draft version of *Penal Colony* to Jens along with an export text file of the contents of the annotations and supplementary pages, he was now on the critical path and I could turn my attention to tasks that had been languishing for a week or more.

First I wanted to continue the thread on Marilynne Robinson I had begun two days earlier, citing two reviews (Karen Armstrong and Rowan Williams) that shed some light on this dense challenge to reductionism and positivism. Then I wrote sisters Marcy and Julie in Colorado about Barney Rosset and Grove Press and his love for cousin Nancy Ashenhurst and both responded with interest, Marcy replying with a report on Cory, to whom they'd given their old van and who would be returning to California shortly — his symptoms not related to alcohol and so his seizures a mystery though they disappeared when he discontinued his prozac prescription. Paul and Marcy would see him in a week when Paul was in the LA area to visit sales prospects. I thought the rest of the family should know about this development so I excerpted that part of Marcy's email and forwarded it to our Borg. Then an email to Jim Johansen to find out whether he'd billed or been paid for mowing, I made arrangements with Jens to meet at Enzo's the next day and then sent him a copy of the *Penal Colony* database I'd changed as well as an export file of all the text he'd written that he could make changes to and return to me for import into the database (rather than make the changes directly, which would actually be more time consuming).

A key goal was to provide our Canadian translator with a copy of *Metamorphosis* in an ebook format his KOBO device could read — and according to online specs that included both MOBI and EPUB. Weeks before I'd found that writing my own EPUB generator for our books was more complicated than it should be given that I was following directions in a how-to book. Rather than carry on that time-consuming and so far fruitless exercise, I downloaded the newest version of Calibre and used it to convert our MOBI file to EPUB. Then I downloaded the KOBO software onto my iPad and Mac but could find no way to transfer this new EPUB file into the KOBO software's library on either device. Apparently that can only be done if you have their hardware device and I didn't. Then I tried the new EPUB file in iBooks on my iPad and it worked very well and looked great. I tried it also with Stanza on my iPad and it worked pretty well. I could find no way to move the book into the Barns and Noble software on my iPad. Until I actually tried it on KOBO I couldn't be certain the Calibre conversion would work but rather delay longer I sent the MOBI and EPUB files to Ian Johnston and asked him to let me know whether either one worked for him. If the Calibre converter worked, it would be reasonably simple to put our books into the Barnes and Noble catalog, KOBO, and others that required EPUB.

I forwarded two ebook marketing services emails to Natasha and then replied to Barbara's paper letter of the previous day. After I'd met with her the Wednesday before she'd been discouraged and in effect resigned from the *My Antonia* project. I'd been thinking about what to say and finally decided I'd be positive, tell her she had done a great job so far, that I'd help rearrange what she'd written to make it fit our format better, and that I'd do whatever it took to get it to publication.

Then I ordered the computer, printer, external backup drive, MS Office and virus protection software for the Food Bank and forwarded the Amazon receipt to Yvonne. It would be shipped to the Orcas parking lot and put in the locked storage shed by the UPS contractor on Orcas. Friend and former business partner, Loren, had written about his New Zealand and Australia travels and the fact that he was changing houses in Boulder, moving south and east, and that son Casey and wife Jodi would occupy the bottom floor of this very big house. Marcy had reported that son Kevin and girlfriend Lauren had just become engaged, at Tivoli in Copenhagen, Kevin having delivered a paper there and they were taking advantage of that occasion to visit our relatives in Munka-Ljungby and Bredaryd in nearby Sweden, shortly before James and Keith would appear. He might be interested in the Barney Rosset-Nancy Ashenhurst connection so I sent him a note. With the need to complete the

Two-hundred-thirty-nine: Grind

2011-2012 Crane budget and because some of what I needed to do wasn't obvious I wrote Treasurer Mike a note asking six questions about the budget and financial reporting. That morning I'd read four provocative columns and articles in the New York Times: on evil as lack of empathy, a report on a young man's success in proselytizing for religious tolerance on college campuses, a column on the failure of either political party to address the real needs of the country, and a study on how being able to make bad arguments is adaptive and not, in a sense, a human flaw, and I forwarded them to the Greybeards as possible discussion topics when we'd meet at Howard's the next morning.

239: Going in a Circle

Then I received an email back from Jens, responding to the *Penal Colony* draft I'd sent him, with a list of changes and corrections attached. By this time, 4:00 in the afternoon, I'd been sitting with my MacBook Pro on my lap for almost twelve hours and had almost cleared my inbox. I couldn't stand another minute of sitting and headed out the door for a walk around beautiful Crane Island. The water tank level was still at 13′ 9″, just below the overflow point, and that was good. The sun had come out and the day warmed up. I saw a few more places where a few pieces of bark had been stripped from branches of trees overhanging Circle Road. The grass bordering the path from the dock to our property through the meadow was now four feet tall in places, the seed heads so heavy the stalks were bent over, brushing against me as I passed by. I held out my arm, sliding the seed heads through my right hand as I walked, something I'd done from the time I could walk and there were seed heads to feel.

Two-hundred-forty: Welcome Home

"The best way to cheer yourself up is to try to cheer somebody else up." - Mark Twain

The all-aluminum boat once owned by Bill, the owner/builder of our house in Deer Harbor that he lost to a divorce, now belonged to a Cranian, I wasn't sure who, and usually sat on the inside of the inside finger of the Orcas dock, never moving, as far as I could see, year in, year out. But now it was parked at the Crane Community dock so I hoped to find out who owned it, another piece of the Crane puzzle. For now I was bound for Orcas and the Wednesday morning Greybeards' assembly. In my hand I had four printouts of New York times articles and columns I thought interesting enough to act as starting points for discussion and had sent links to the others the day before. The morning was sunny with a very light wind out of the southeast. Beautiful. I started the Trophy loaner and backed away from the west side of the Crane dock (the Trophy was set up for a port side tie), turned and passed through Pole Pass on an ebb tide, that is, the water leaving Deer Harbor, counter-intuitively heading east through Pole Pass, then south and west through Wasp Passage between the south shore of Crane and north shore of Shaw Island, into San Juan Channel, and south to Cattle Pass and then into the Straight of Juan de Fuca and out into the Pacific perhaps 50 miles away.

A tad late, Howard, Brian, David, and Chris were already in the honeymoon cottage sipping tea, David talking about his 50th DePaw college reunion he'd attended in Greencastle, Indiana the evening before. He'd enjoyed the experience and had been impressed with the new president. Howard asked Brian how he was doing, having been flown off Orcas the week before by Mercy Flights, a volunteer program, for a spine MRI in Bellingham. Brian had looked at the images on his computer but wouldn't really know what they meant until he had visited a new-to-him orthopedic surgeon in Bellingham. He'd had three surgeries over the years but none had relieved the significant pain he felt when in any position other than supine. He was hopeful that new techniques in arthroscopic surgery would give him relief without the trauma of more intrusive procedures. As it was now he couldn't stand up properly and could only walk slowly, needing to sit down and rest frequently. With his Parkinson's Disease and the side effects of more than a dozen different medications he was struggling and now in his early seventies was frustrated and anxious. Howard pursued the topic we were all concerned about since having a long discussion with Brian a few weeks before: how was he going to cope with the diminishment of his mobility — especially relating to driving after having totaled his Volvo by crashing into a rock and then careening to the other side of the road into the ditch. His daughter didn't want him to drive but he needed to get to Eastsound twice a week for shopping and physical therapy — and to events like our mens' group. Last time we had discussed the topic he had told us he had been disappointed that successive tenants in the cabin he owned next to his house, having it rent free on the understanding that they'd help him with house work and transportation, had been unreliable. We'd made two suggestions: one that he look into ride and expense sharing with Jim, who lived in Deer Harbor and was immobilized with MS and who went to town regularly and was running out of money; and two that rather than having informal arrangements for his cabin he charge competitive rent and use those funds to pay for transportation — to the renter, to a third party, or for a cab ($20 each way) and to understand that he couldn't count on either his daughter and her husband or friends to provide anything but rare volunteer transportation for him. As far as we could see he hadn't followed up on either suggestion. Rather he wanted confirmation that it was just fine for him to continue to drive.

He had recruited Chris to be an observing passenger on a trip to town the previous Friday so now he turned to Chris for what he hoped would be a report confirming his opinion that his driving was sufficiently skillful — but Chris demurred, observing that Brian's small motor control of his feet and thus action on the pedals was less than ideal and while Brian wasn't the worst driver he'd evaluated, Chris didn't think Brian belonged on the roads, especially if he was tired, a condition he often, but unpredictably found himself in. Then we turned our attention to alternative forms of transportation, talking about the possibility that someone could offer some kind of subscription bus service from Deer Harbor to Eastsound — but that didn't exist and the thought of starting one was daunting — so we came back to how Brian could use existing alternatives and afford it. A round trip, with physical therapy and shopping would take three hours or six hours if twice a week. If he were to hire someone at $17/hour, the going rate for home care, that would come to about $100 per week. He could rent his cabin for $500 per month and had been willing to forego all the rent for help. Why not just use the $500 to have scheduled transportation and I recommended Nancy. As it turned out she was already providing home help and he, as Yvonne and I did, thought highly of her. But, he said, he wanted to drive himself whenever he felt up to it. I pointed out that would never work; to have reliable transportation he'd have to make a schedule with a provider well in advance and stick with it.

Then I had to leave to pick up Yvonne. Howard followed me out and told me sotto voce that he had little confidence that Brian would respond to our suggestions, that he wanted to believe he could drive safely (and I thought — that surgery would fix everything). He was in denial and was making life very difficult for his daughter especially, and his son-in-law and friends. It seemed to me that the persistence that had made his life successful in the past had become a stubbornness that was holding him — and others hostage. When Yvonne and I discussed the situation later she repeated what we all knew — that Brian's story was typical and one faced by our aging cohort — as their strength diminished. But she also suggested we be sympathetic with Brian and acknowledge the pain associated with the loss of independence and help him understand that he couldn't really change things he didn't like, he could only change himself and the way he saw his life, to be realistic and to embrace a new, different life, with its own advantages, as Bob had finally done and become much happier.

Docking on Orcas, I realized the aluminum boat that had followed us from Crane was the Fischers and I said hello before following Yvonne up the ramp. I'd put the four baseboard heaters that had been in the bed of the pickup following the Community Club yard sale into the van, intending to drop them at San Juan Sanitation on the way to town, something I hadn't been able to do that Saturday because their gate was locked. Today it was open but no one was in the office. The sun bleached sign on the door said we could drop off scrap metal free but that refrigerators cost $45. We dumped the heaters in a huge dumpster and then I saw another sign that said appliances cost $15 to leave. Were the baseboard heaters appliances? I'd have to call them later and then see about paying. The heaters were perfectly good, two brand new, but they hadn't sold at the yard sale and the Exchange wouldn't take them. An open item.

I ate half my lunch as we approached Eastsound. The tide was out and very low, the little island right off the Eastsound shore now an extension of the beach and tourists were on the island and plentiful on the beach. Yvonne driving, she dropped me off before continuing to the east side of the island for the Garden Club picnic. Jens came in shortly and we sat and talked, sipping tea for the next two hours talking about the finishing touches *The Penal Colony* required, eNotator prospects at Wellesley, the Modern Language Association and its January Seattle convention as a marketing opportunity, mailings to lists he provided, the possibility of him having some ownership in the business, whether and how he'd use the two Kafka eBooks with his fall class, and finally his advice for helping Barbara with *My Antonia*.

On our ride back to Deer Harbor Yvonne told me that she had enjoyed the Garden Club picnic — especially because she had been recognized for her special contribution to the club over the years with a Lifetime Membership, the highest award the club makes with only a few other recipients ever so honored. She was especially pleased and I think perhaps feeling a bit vindicated five years after completing her term as President and succeeded by a retired professor who ignored her contribution, whose great ideas crippled the club, and who had the social sense of a rock. It had taken her years to undo his destructive influence. Good!

Picking up a voice mail when we arrived at home, Yvonne learned that the *Huginn* was ready to go so I went back out the door, down to the dock, and took the loaner Trophy east and then north in West Sound, parking it at the guest dock at the West Sound Marina. The repair dock was surprisingly warm, at least six men at work on boats on the repair dock, high above the water or nearby on one of the floating docks. High season for repairs and maintenance. Ian came upstairs from the shop and then discussed what he had found and done. He couldn't explain the coincidence of the coil going out and then the fuel pump, showing what appeared to be similar symptoms. For this latest repair episode he would charge us for the pump and labor but not his travel time. Fair enough. It was a pleasure to take the *Huginn* home. Smaller and much more agile than the Bayliner Trophy, with very responsive steering, and easy to fit into small places, I had a renewed appreciation for this 19' cudy-cabin power boat. Yvonne was pleased as well, having not been interested in even trying to pilot the old trophy. Now she could get herself back and forth from Orcas without needing my help.

240: Garden Club recognizes Yvonne's service

Before dinner I'd received five emails from Jens with additions and corrections to the second draft of *Penal Colony* or responses to open items created during our mid-day meeting. My highest priority now was preparing for a Friday meeting with David and Chris but I accomplished little by dinner time, by decision the end of my work day.

Two-hundred-forty-one: Good Deed

"The purpose of life, after all, is to live it, to taste experience to the utmost, to reach out eagerly and without fear for newer and richer experience." - Eleanor Roosevelt

Yvonne and I sat on the porch of the Orcas Hotel in the warm June sunshine, she sipping her latte and me Earl Grey tea (they were out of Awake this morning). Across Harney Channel, a mile away, we could see the Shaw Island ferry dock, empty for now, as was the one below, on Orcas. Yvonne had picked out a cherry danish and cut me a slice for tasting. Tasty! I'd had oatmeal, toast, and grapefruit juice at home. That was enough for now. Thirty feet away, just east of the Hotel deck, the gray-haired gardener worked the border between grass and plantings, close to the spot where Kelly and Tim had said their vows not quite a year ago, now their lives joined by baby Noah, who we'd seen when we visited them a week before in Seattle. The hotel coffee shop was packed this morning by a group wearing orange tee-shirts who were leaving the island on two charter buses having attended some kind of conference, adults and kids.

Then the *Elwah* came into view, making a wide sweeping turn and in a few minutes the ramp was down and islanders and tourists walked and drove off and then through Orcas Village, many on their way to Eastsound, eight miles north. Leaving the hotel by the east deck we walked carefully across the exposed rock that made the path to the fence and gate and then to a walkway that led down to the ferry and up to the vehicle waiting area. We passed under blue wisteria, then between irises and lavender, more June blue, and then up the stairs to our brick-red F150. Sarah Jane called to Yvonne and they talked awhile while I read more of the *Seattle Times* in our pickup. The air was very clear and the big green and white ferry moored to the loading ramp was sharp and distinct. At 9:00 the ferry backed out of its slip, turned around and made a pickup on Shaw and then at the Lopez Island Landing two miles to

Two-hundred-forty-one: Good Deed

the east, then threaded its way through Thatcher Pass, docking in Anacortes a few minutes late.

241: Orcas Hotel at Orcas Landing

Because the tide was very low and the ferry packed, the attendants unloaded the upper car level first, then the tunnel, and then the lower car levels and it was nearly 10:45 before we were off the ferry and driving through Anacortes, taking the back way to save time. Yvonne had called the Burlington Costco Eye department, advising them that she would be late and she was, by about 15 minutes. After filling the truck with gas, I went into the store, looking for their low-flush toilet special. Only one left, the display model, and because it was banded to a pallet I needed help getting into our cart. Then a Kirkland

Two-hundred-forty-one: Good Deed

Chardonnay and a Pinot Grigio (with screw top so Yvonne could enjoy the wine later at the ferry landing on the return trip) and then for dinner a chicken Caesar salad for Yvonne and a wedge of combo pizza for me. Her eyes checked, Yvonne ordered new glasses (the clerk sold her on anti-glare coating) and I dropped her at Ross Dress for Less and put the truck in line at Jiffy Lube for an oil change. With a year of trees dripping on it, the truck had a rough, golden sheen but with not enough time, I retraced my route, picking Yvonne up and then dropping her at the dentist's, rushing north to Bellingham to pick up a freezer for the Food Bank, Larry having picked up the twin the day before. By the time I returned to Burlington Yvonne had already left the dentist. We would rendezvous at the back row of the Target parking lot under the little shade in the area where in the past we would leave 'Mantha Moo Moo in the van while we shopped. It was only 3:00 and we had agreed to meet at 3:30 so I walked over to Office Depot to see if they had any ebook readers. Just Pandigital. Then into Target where they carried Apple and Amazon devices. No help there. Getting into the van I saw Yvonne coming across the parking lot from J.C Penny. She told me she had seen a Borders inside the Mall but that she wanted to go into Target. So I went to Borders and had a chance to experiment with a Kobo reader but didn't have enough time to figure out how to successfully copy an EPUB file from my Mac. We didn't want to miss the 6:30 ferry — by ending up in overflow — now that we were in the high season. At the ferry landing we were directed to park in the overflow lanes — but that's because the last ferry had been full. We would get on this ferry. Yvonne ate her salad — with wine — and I finished my Costco pizza slice. Back on Orcas we put the Costco low-flush toilet in the dock cart with the few other items we'd purchased. We were home before 9:00, both tired and once we'd soaked in the hot tub got into bed and read until lights out.

Two-hundred-forty-two: Purple Grains

"The Earth has music for those who listen." - William Shakespeare

Another sunny morning, that at our house would start at 48 and rise to 62 over the course of the day. Away from the water it would be warmer in the afternoon, perhaps close to 70. A perfect day to be outdoors working and Yvonne soon was. She stood for some time evaluating the flower bed against the black nylon net deer fence south of the studio deck next to her bamboo sunrise gate. The lupin, with foot long blossom heads, a rich, milky blue and matching gray were dominant now but would be succeeded by lilies, though, Yvonne reported to me later, were not growing as much as they had the year before, for whatever reason. Shortly she called me outside to help her move her one tomato plant, in a large paper pot, wrapped in red cellophane, from the studio deck to the south house deck, up four stairs, and put it against the house, sheltered by the extending bay of the kitchen window from the winds off the water where we could admire it evenings from the comfort of the hot tub at the edge of the deck. Later in the day I watched a hummingbird study the red-wrapped plant hoping it was a huge bird feeder filled with nectar.

On the studio deck in late morning I studied the Douglas firs that were shading Yvonne's raised beds. I had assumed that they were far enough from the deck not to matter — but they did. Fifty or sixty feet tall they captured the sunlight that was needed for the onions, potatoes, broccoli, lettuce, and other treasures of the raised bed. I hadn't been sure but now was: we'd need to take down another ten trees and should do so soon since the summer burn ban would soon be in effect.

All morning Yvonne worked on her pond, just outside the south fence, having become unhappy with its ineffectiveness. She'd siphoned out most of the water, using a five gallon bucket to remove the rest, pulled out the black plastic sheet liner and stretched it out on the grass of what had been the driveway to dry out. Then she'd removed the rocks she'd placed around the edge of the pond, about ten feet across, and had begun to fill it in with top soil I brought from Orcas in our pickup the previous late summer when we had it on Crane. It was heavy work and I wasn't helping — but would.

242: Crane June evening

At 1:00, Chris and I would meet David at his house on the palisades 200 feet above and west of Deer Harbor, our monthly "Executive meeting", at which we reviewed and planned. To make the meetings effective and organized, I'd been creating reports each time in the same format, emailing them out for review before we got together but was late this time, finishing it mid-morning. At least they'd have some time to look at it before we talked.

I called Natasha for an update of the review seeking process for the recently published *The eNotated Metamorphosis* — no one yet interested. She'd sent out twelve gift emails to Jens' list and six had picked up their book from Amazon. We'd had nine sales month to date — so we'd actually sold three copies — not bad given that almost no one knew the book was in the Amazon Kindle catalog but a random shopper would be unlikely to see it mixed in with scores of other editions, many less expensive or free. She reported that she continued to enjoy working on the publishing project — when she had time — but that continued to be rare with the demands of family, house, work, and garden.

Chris had already arrived, as usual, and while David and I took our places at the dining room table, he lay face down on the floor; his back was going out again and he could stand or lie but not sit and so the meeting went. Our first important topic was whether and in what way to offer Jens ownership. We all agreed we'd offer him the same number of shares David and Chris had but at twice the price we'd all, as founders paid, so his 500 shares would cost $200 rather than $100. We were uniform in our praise of his contribution and complementary role he could play in the group. And we decided we'd make the January Seattle MLA convention the major focus of our activity for the next six months, agreeing that it provided a unique opportunity to market, recruit eNotators, study the competition, and get feedback on our product. Another important focus would be to provide our books in EPUB format.

Home again I convened our own executive meeting and Yvonne and I scheduled major tasks for the next several weeks, anticipating the arrival of our first guest group mid July. Saturday, we'd take the freezer in the bed of our pickup to Larry and Joyce's and he and I would deliver it to the new Food Bank building and then work on the pond. Sunday we'd move the pieces of the cabinets and shelves taken out of my shop and broken down to Orcas and the transfer station. During the next week I'd put down a new floor in the guest bathroom and replace the toilet with the one we'd brought home from Costco. As soon as possible we'd cut down more trees south of the house. Over the next few weeks I'd clean the windows, the decks and railings, painting the former, and staining the latter. I'd need Yvonne's help to inspect the septic system, a good idea before the guests began arriving (we'd had a crisis the July before when we hosted ten people for Kelly and Tim's wedding) and the County had sent me a postcard reminding me a report was due them.

I invited Yvonne along but she demurred so I made my island circuit alone as I usually do. The tank was down a bit, to 13 feet. I'd send Gary an email report. I restudied the first location where I seen bark strips in the road, at the intersection of Circle Road and Rocky Road (more lane than road) and saw the tree was a fir not a Maple. A hundred yards along Circle, on the south side of the Island, I found another fir with new strippings. Coming home, crossing the meadow from the dock area, many of the seed heads on the grass stems, now five feet high, looked purple in the late afternoon light, each of the three different kinds I saw glowing with the same shade. Was I seeing things? No — they really were purple and I picked samples of each and brought them home. Out of the sun they no longer glowed but they were purple and cutting off the ends with a scissors Yvonne kept for the purpose, I found a small vase in the cabinet on the deck outside where Yvonne told me to look, put in the leaves of grass, and filled it with cool water. Green to purple; and then in a while they'd be golden. A lovely pallet really, all appropriate and matching one another. Why?

Two-hundred-forty-three: Timberrrr! Uh-oh....

"No man is an island, entire of itself; every man is a piece of the continent, a part of the main." - John Donne

The ferry landing, two miles away, wasn't visible through the morning rain and mist. Shredded cotton floated here and there just above or among tall firs on Shaw and Orcas. An almost calm wind created a slight shimmering, not waves, in Raven Cove, the water green like the trees above and the rocky bank uncovered by the falling tide revealing yellow green seaweed. A plop-plop of dripping water from downspouts was steadily filling our 75 gallon and 450 gallon catchment tanks, depleted by Yvonne's garden watering during a three week dry spell. The hummingbird feeder suspended outside the living room windows was almost empty. Then the rain fell harder and the ferry landing became visible. A wonderful morning.

Twice before Yvonne had been to one of Joyce's garage sales, once with me, and I had remembered the occasion, admiring the order of their compound and Joyce's graciousness. Though we didn't know Joyce and Larry then, Yvonne immediately liked her and was certain she would get to know Joyce through the Garden Club. Instead it was the Food Bank, where Yvonne became Board Secretary to Joyce's Vice-Presidency and Larry's Presidency during a transition that moved the operation from a rat-infested, and poorly managed (though well-intentioned) borrowed OPALCO building to the Community Church basement and shortly to a new building on the Church grounds. Another garage sale day, Yvonne would visit with Joyce and Larry and I would take the freezer in the bed of our pickup to the new Food Bank building and install it next to the one Larry had brought in Wednesday.

The rain had all but stopped by the time we turned off Orcas Road, near Indralaya, a Theosophist camp and spiritual home to a handful of locals and thousands I suppose across America. Larry had backed their RV out of its stall so the sale could continue out of the rain and I immediately noticed a small fold-up plastic golf cart like the broken one we had at home Yvonne would use to carry groceries from van to boat and boat to home, so I pointed it out. Just the ticket. I found Larry at the house and he and I drove the two miles to the Community Church and unloaded the freezer and brought it into the building I had yet to enter. It was packed with cartons of food, one freezer, one refrigerator, two stainless steel tables, and would get a three sink unit and perhaps two more refrigerators, office equipment, and more food. Larry observed that they would have preferred more space but a bigger building wouldn't fit on the small site at the rear of the Church parking lot.

Back at the garage sale, Yvonne had Joyce ring her up (Joyce said they'd acquired the cash register at a sale but couldn't remember where or when, and then we were off to Island Market (and me to the bank to get some cash). Then farther on to a sale at the American Legion hall and while Yvonne shopped I went next door to Crescent Service to talk about the squeaky brakes on the F150. The rear pads were almost metal to metal was the report and the front pads not much better. Since the station had access to the NAPA dealer's inventory, the good news was that the pads and calipers were in stock. I'd talk with Yvonne about our schedule and call to make an appointment. Since the work could require half a day, they'd be happy to drive me to and from the Library.

The day threatened to clear and the sun shone brightly by late afternoon, about the time we were finishing our afternoon project. Yvonne wanted more sun on her raised beds on the east and west sides of the studio deck and she had her eye on one particular fir she wanted down in the worst way. My analysis was that perhaps as many as ten trees were to blame. Little by little we'd been cutting trees south of the house and had done ten since last fall — of the 20 we'd cleared here over four years. As we looked at the trees I could see two problems: first, because they were so close to one another they would have to be taken down in a sequence that reduced or eliminated the possibility that they'd become entangled with one another; second, some of the trees were bigger than I felt comfortable cutting, having so far cut trees perhaps up to ten inches in diameter, these were up to fifteen inches and probably at least 60 feet high. The first tree, an eight-inch, fell the wrong direction, just the opposite direction Yvonne was pulling a rope I tied to the trunk from. It wasn't possible to overcome the tree's natural lean. The second tree, nine inch diameter, came down just about right. The third tree, nine inches, leaning on a big-

Two-hundred-forty-three: Timberrrr! Uh-oh….

ger tree, and in a very tight environment got caught in a third tree, remaining on the stump and with intertwined branches looking pretty stuck. I knocked the trunk off the stump while Yvonne pulled the upper trunk away from the capturing tree but that did nothing — except make the partially fallen tree a bit safer to be around. Yvonne said we would need to call an arborist. Instead I went to see Margaret to talk to her about her "come-along" hand winch. Yes, I could borrow it.

243: Clear waters of the Salish Sea

And, taking a break from a paper she was writing, came along to show me how it worked. In twenty minutes I'd been able to pull the bottom of the tree far away enough from the stump that the crown pulled away from the embrace of the nearby tree and it crashed into the driveway. Margaret went back to her work telling me she'd much enjoyed the diversion. Yvonne continued to feed the burn pile with greenery from the three trees she'd cut off with her long-handled shears or that I had cut off with my chain saw. Once I'd cut the logs into sections light enough to carry and stacked them in the driveway for cutting down to 16" sections, I inspected the cabinet section pile I'd created a few days before and used the chain saw to cut anything longer than about three feet into smaller sections easy to carry in a dock cart. We'd have to take it all to the transfer station the next day.

James and Keith had posted more pictures from their time in Sweden and we could see, almost hour by hour who they had seen and what they did — Janne's new building project, skeet shooting with Lars-Erik. We missed our family in Sweden.

Two-hundred-forty-four: Seven Hundred Pounds

"Community is a place where the connections felt in our hearts make it truly a home." - Robert Hillman

The madrona outside the living room window and elsewhere in the San Juan Islands, growing from the thin soil above the archipelago's basalt foundation, were filling out with new leaves, the old ones turning dark, to fall off in July, and the fragrant flowers of May and early June were growing into berries the crows would eat during the coldest days of December and January.

As soon as Yvonne emerged from the bedroom at 8:30, as usual, for her breakfast, I took a shower, then took the dock cart to the back of the yard near our Ranger sailboat, not yet launched for the season, and systematically loaded the cart with pieces of cabinets and shelving I'd removed from my shop to replace with the old kitchen cabinets, broken down and then cut up when necessary to manageable size, placing the pieces upright like pages of a book, spine down and closed. Though some of the material was plywood most was particle board, sawdust and glue, heavy and not something legal to burn — for good reason. I set the pieces upright between the port side gunnel and engine cover and after the third load, Yvonne was at work at the old privy we'd moved and now used to store trash and recycle in four big rubber cans, beginning to consolidate cardboard into a heavy duty big plastic bag and I made one more trip with particle board, leaving two dozen cabinet doors — many from kitchen cabinets I'd put in my shop and didn't want to cover with doors and others from cabinets I'd pulled out of my shop and broken down for disposal.

With the cockpit full and the cabin packed, the stern low in the water, and the *Huginn* listing to port, Yvonne cast us off and we made the ten minute passage to the dock on Orcas, Yvonne seated on trash in the cockpit, outside, and happy in part because she was outdoors and in part because this ballast would leave our boat and island life. In November we had spent two days bringing cartons of IKEA cabinets to Crane in preparation for remodeling the kitchen. Now, more than six months later we were dealing with one of the consequences of that effort.

244: Packing for the transfer station

The tide was on its way out and getting the heavily loaded dock carts down the ramp on Crane required us to pay attention, shuffling our feet on the roughened surface of the aluminum ramp so as not to slip and lose control of the cart. The issue on Orcas was to get the material up the steepening aluminum ramp and then the long wood ramp and then steep concrete ramp to the parking lot where we could load everything into the bed and back seat of

Two-hundred-forty-four: Seven Hundred Pounds

our pickup. Each of us taking one trash can and dragging/sliding it up the ramps to the lot we brought back two dock carts and began an arduous process of wheeling, dragging, and carrying the material we'd moved from our property to the *Huginn*, about thirty feet vertically and two hundred and fifty feet horizontally and then lifting it into the bed of the F150. And then it was loaded. Yvonne wanted to stop at the Post Office for Saturday's mail and now that it was 11:40 and I was starving I decided I'd better eat something so while Yvonne visited the PO I picked up a breakfast burrito and the *Seattle Sunday Times* from the dock store, eating the burrito while Yvonne drove the six miles to the transfer station.

The transfer station was unaccountably empty. Now, as a county cost cutting measure, open only Friday, Saturday, and Sunday, 10:00 to 4:00, it was usually crowded with cars and trucks. After checking in with the attendant I drove onto the scale, she recorded the truck's weight and then I drove to a huge shed, its floor usually covered with trash waiting to be pushed into a trailer at the back of and below the level of the floor, now completely clear. We pulled all the particle board out of the bed of the truck to the shed floor and then emptied the two garbage cans, leaving the two remaining cans for deposit into the recycling trailers when we came back to the attendant's shed and recycle area. Two other vehicles joined ours in the shed, piling trash on the floor and giving the ravens waiting in the trees outside something to pick through whenever the shed was unoccupied — but the trash had not yet been pushed into the transport trailer. Then we drove onto the scale, now from the other direction, and waited for the green light that would tell us the attendant had recorded the total from the second weighing. We'd pay for the difference.

Our truck back at the attendants window, Yvonne made out a check for $122 — all but the $5 recycling fee to pay for leaving our trash. How much did it weigh? I explained we'd carted it all from Crane Island. Seven hundred pounds. Good exercise we told each other. Not as much as when we cleared the sheetrock scraps left over from finishing the studio, but enough that Yvonne said she was taking the rest of the day off. I backed the truck up to the nearest recycle trailer and we dumped the two remaining cans and drove off satisfied — only to realize — when Yvonne happened to look in the back seat that we'd forgotten a big bundle of cardboard. A return trip and then soon we were home.

Yvonne lay on the couch reading drafts of my writing and I sat, her feet against my right hip, with my Mac in my lap, creating photo albums for our family website with pictures I'd taken over the prior five weeks; I was way behind. Then Yvonne shut her eyes for a little nap and after a while, unable to keep my eyes open, I put my Mac on the coffee table and moved to the love seat, lay down, and was soon asleep. A half hour later, rested, I made myself an orange Italian soda, took a fresh home-baked chocolate chip cookie from the cookie jar and sat down in my regular wicker chair, picking up my photo albums project while Yvonne slowly woke up.

It was Father's day and I was hearing from the kids during the day, all calling but James, who was in Berlin. And then there were eCards and Barnes and Noble gift certificates via email I would use to partly finance buying a Nook eReader. And I thought about my father and that I missed him, gone now sixteen years, who would have been delighted at the ubiquity and ease of eCommerce and the emerging revolution in publishing I was contributing to (or trying at least), writing and small scale publishing having been part of the family culture for at least five generations.

At 6:00 Margaret arrived for dinner carrying a blackberry crumb pie and we sat down to an Indian dinner, a chicken and vegetable curry Yvonne had prepared while I tried to finish the photo albums. Margaret noticed the leaves of grass, three different kinds, I'd put in a small vase, now on the kitchen counter, reporting that in a prior year, out walking with Moonie, the cat, on the meadow path she too noticed the beauty of the grass, and having had a grass-expert boyfriend years ago so that she knew something of the subject, began identifying species in the meadow, eventually finding seventeen. Conversation moved from Margaret's sister-in-law, a widow for less than a year, Yvonne recommending Joyce Carol Oates' recent book, "A Widow's Story," to the coming Crane Island 3rd of July parade and picnic Margaret was managing, to the yard cleanup and chipping project Margaret had begun with our jointly owned chipper that would jointly benefit our effort to keep the shared path, the one around the house, not to it, mud and water free. Margaret and Yvonne talk at length about a seaweed class Margaret had attended the Thursday before — when we'd been to America — agreeing that they'd take the next class together, Margaret repeating. The talk was of varieties of kelp especially and the different ways they could be prepared for eating — all delicious apparently — though nori didn't grow in our waters. I'd reserve judgement. When I went back to my album project, Yvonne made her way to the hot tub, then got in bed and was asleep shortly after I joined her, staying awake long enough to get through some more pages of Marilynne Robinson's *Absence of Mind*, trying to distill what she was saying and connecting it to what else I had recently read and questions I had been preoccupied with for sixty years. And then I couldn't keep my eyes open.

Two-hundred-forty-five: Helpmeet

"One of the marvelous things about community is that it enables us to welcome and help people in a way we couldn't as individuals." - Jean Vanier

Having agreed at our Friday meeting that we'd exhibit at the January MLA meeting in Seattle, I called New York to make sure booth space was available and then completed an exhibit application and put it out on the bench in the front hall ready for mailing and then ordered a Nook using my Father's Day gift certificates and then a Kobo, needing the first to test our books in EPUB format on the Barnes & Noble platform and the second to make sure our *Metamorphosis* translator would have an ebook version that would work correctly on his Kobo. By mid afternoon I'd gotten confirmation that each had been shipped and would arrive in a few days.

With a to-do list so long I couldn't find the time to write it down, I started early in the day trying to complete items faster than they added themselves. I wrote Father's Day thank you notes to the four kids and then responded to Gary's reply to my request for a tank float switch budget, copying Jason and Martha, with Martha then replying to me that her notes on the Board meeting differed from my memory and what I was telling Gary, though practically speaking the difference was nil. My sisters hadn't been able to read James and Keith's Europe Picasa album so I wrote James in Prague and before he could reply Julie reported she had gotten into the album. And then the Belltown Condos claimed to Emma that we hadn't returned the key to the guest apartment we'd used with James and Keith so I wrote James and before he could reply Yvonne heard from Belltown that they were mistaken, though now Emma had been put out. Jens had forwarded an email from the Wellesley library about having his ebook available there. Blair had written to be reimbursed for dock ramp non-skip paint so I scanned that invoice and forwarded it to Linda and then remembered that I hadn't been reimbursed for a quart of that paint either and scanned and sent that on. Blair and Molly had donated to the No Wake Zone effort so I created a thank you letter to mail, a deposit slip, and then an email to the committee apprising them of this latest donation and the committee's bank balance (good). I'd sent Howard B two pictures of the footing for a new porch on Ilze's cabin that Howard and Chris and I had looked at walking back from Bob's party to the community dock and now he asked whether I had one of the roof line showing the new raised center section so I sent that off. I sent a note to Phil, at the Orcas Library asking whether the Library subscribed to any services that would let them lend ebooks to patrons for use on their own devices, something the Wellesley librarian was hoping we could do and wanting to understand the implications and approaches better. Chris had sent an email recommending the *Time Magazine*'s coverage of the Tea Party to the Greybeards and I replied with a link to a discussion of Nozick's repudiation of his *Anarchy* book, having had him as one of my undergraduate thesis advisors and having had a class with him on Freedom. I confirmed that the five albums I'd added to the family website were complete and emailed the family to look for them. I had promised Barbara I would get back to her about how to continue with *My Antonia!* (she'd approached the structure in a different way than Jens) and studying what she'd done saw that her approach, though different, was fine and wrote her to continue as she was, suggesting she add two more essays, one on women on the prairie and one on the conflicts between immigrants and the established community, asking whether she'd like to see her work in prototype format, her later answer being yes. Then I looked for cover art for *In the Penal Colony*, found images of the Legrande paintings, and wrote for permission.

Two-hundred-forty-five: Helpmeet

245: Orcas Landing from the ferry

In the meanwhile Yvonne was working her own to-do plan that included preparing guestbooks for the upcoming Garden Club Garden Tours and I don't know what all — but by 2:00 she was frustrated because I wasn't helping her fix her pond — that she'd drained and taken apart because she was unhappy with the way the black plastic lining was visible. She didn't know what to do and didn't have the strength to dig in the rocky soil in any case. She needed help and so we spent two hours in the afternoon sun applying a level to see how the bank would need to be adjusted and then I dug a new shelf to hold rocks that would in turn hold and cover the sheet liner. During this process Margaret came over to ask where she should put a cart load of chips (I'd helped her get set up for chipping some of the dead branches that covered the ground around her house) and I apologized for not distributing the chips, having said I would the day before. My head was spinning. I had

Yvonne inspect the pond shelf I'd created, suggesting we stop for the day and move deliberately with the pond re-do, thinking through each stage.

After dinner Yvonne reported that Margaret had seen an eagle harassing a Merganser mother and her six chicks in the shallow water off the farm's beach, the babies diving and mother flapping until the eagle decided the effort wasn't worth the payoff and flew away. While Yvonne caught up on Facebook, I opened the box with the Food Bank's new computer I'd ordered a few days before (with printer and external backup drive) and began the setup process. This HP unit was a thick bodied monitor with the computer guts inside so a separate tower wasn't required. After watching *Mao's Last Dancer*, I read a few more pages of *Absence of Mind* and Yvonne turned out her light. Too much today. Too much.

Two-hundred-forty-six: Summer Solstice

"The summer night is like a perfection of thought." - Wallace Stevens

Having parked the *Huginn* at the Orcas dock, I started up the ramp and then saw that Ken and Kate were only 30 feet away, Ken carrying a bouquet of peonies and fragrant mint greenery. They were early. Home again, we moved outside to the deck and started to work on the vegetable rolls Yvonne had made. What was their good news, we wanted to know. After a long drought as realtors — they had helped us buy and then sell our Deer Harbor house — their client had made a cash offer on a high-end house near Friday Harbor — the inspection due in the next few days. And another potential sale was in the offing. Congratulations were in order and we toasted our friends, our first on Orcas.

Yvonne grilled Thai chicken on skewers while the rest of us talked and soon we were enjoying the chicken and a Thai salad. Kate and Ken were more relaxed than we'd seen them in a while and Yvonne and I were happy their prospects had picked up significantly. We wondered together whether the housing market in the Islands was about to turn around; they reporting that a friend had seen very positive signs in the Northern Plains states during a recent trip. Crane had so much property for sale, especially since Jim Jannard had put his parcels on the market that it would be years before the current inventory was exhausted.

Back in Boulder our friends would be having dinner together to observe the summer solstice. Generally that would happen at breakfast but now as "softies" as Barb explained in an email, dawn was much too early. Missing them, we did the next best thing, and would celebrate Midsummer on Crane, much as we had done years ago in Sweden with cousins Peter and Ann and their friends, watching the sun take forever to set into the North Sea, sharing

Two-hundred-forty-six: Summer Solstice

new potatoes, strawberries, and pickled herring, and talking about our lives in our two different countries.

At about 8:20, Yvonne put fresh-baked chocolate chip cookies and a vacuum carafe with hot ginger tea into a cloth sack and Ken and I collected four folding beach chairs I'd brought from the *Huginn* into our "new" small dock cart and we set off for the northwest corner of the Island, about a mile away. I pulled two bark strips from my jacket pocket and began to tell Ken about our island mystery and he quickly interrupted me to describe a bark stripping case he'd come upon near their Deer Harbor house recently, in this case the bark being stripped from a three foot section of the truck of a small tree, girdling and therefore killing it. He suspected Pileated woodpeckers because they're big and they can form holes in trunks very quickly but he admitted that he'd never seen them strip bark or even why they might be interested in doing so. Maybe our warming climate resulted in some under-bark insect infestation that birds were going after. Maybe.

I pointed out some strips under a fir near the intersection of Circle and Dock Roads (two wide paths really) but we couldn't imagine the motivation for the stripping. At the north end of the airstrip I had Yvonne, Kate, and Ken pose by the "stay off" warning sign, my habit with new visitors and then we descended the steep hill at the head of the strip, and passing Jason's house, I spotted fresh bark strips under a big leaf maple. About twenty lay near the trunk in the spring grass, having come from a branch about eight feet off the ground. Some of the strips were damp and therefore very recently shaved from the branch. We saw no sign of claw marks on the stripped areas of the branch and could see no teeth marks on the bark strips. And the cambium layer had not been eaten. Farther on I pointed out a live tree trunk from which I'd heard tapping about three years before, never being able to explain it to myself and never having heard it again. And there we saw more shavings, hundreds of strips that had been created perhaps a month earlier.

At Sunnyside we left Circle Road and walked past Lou's and then to the "Girls'" house. The sun was very low in the sky now, rays finding their way among a thicket of firs to set branches, even whole trees ablaze while their neighbors became harder to see in a hint of semi-darkness to come. The sod roof, luxuriant in past-its-prime grass was greener than the grass on the bank facing northwest toward the setting sun. The Salish Sea, calm water stretching west to Reef Island was dark blue like the cloudless sky.

Two-hundred-forty-six: Summer Solstice

246: Ken, Kate, and Yvonne as the solstice sun sets

Madrona trunks glowed red and orange in the setting sun and drying grasses yellow, gold, and pink. Not a breath of wind on the water, the highest and snowy peaks of the Olympics visible to the southwest over Shaw Island though 50 miles distant and across the Straight of Juan de Fuca, Vancouver Island to the west and north, Speiden, Stuart and behind them the high slopes of Salt Spring Island, stepping stones to the west. Ken walked out on a small rocky point so he could look back the house, the sun tinting its gray cedar board and batten siding. The scene gave us insight into why the Girls had chosen the site and what it was like to live here, with their center-pole barn, cow, chickens, goats, and elaborate vegetable and flower garden fenced from the deer. With the sun approaching the top of Stuart Island and sliding at a shallow angle toward the northwest, we walked back out to Circle Road, then south and east to Gull Lane and then into Stacy and Doug's property (having had an invitation from Stacy to enjoy the view) and found our way down the ramp to their year-old dock and then out onto the 40 foot float. We set up our chairs and Yvonne served the tea and chocolate chip cookies and we toasted the fiery sun as it slipped and then disappeared behind darkening firs about five miles away. Taking Circle Road on the south side of the Island on the way home, we stopped long enough for me to show Ken the location of the osprey nest and we swapped bird stories all the way back to 120 Eagle Lane.

After dropping them at the Orcas dock I returned to Crane Island. At 10:30 the sky and water were still light but not enough to read by though once I left the dock and was under the trees it was clear night had fallen. Going out to the hot tub I saw a dark shape scurry off the deck. A raccoon had been tempted by the grill Yvonne had left open to cool after cooking chicken. The longest day of the year has the shortest night, though here never really getting completely dark. Tomorrow the day would be three seconds shorter. Now it was summer but to make up for it Nature reminded us that fall and winter were coming.

Two-hundred-forty-seven: Pirate Booty

"Humanity is acquiring all the right technology for all the wrong reasons." - R. Buckminster Fuller

The shortest night of the year lasted until about 3:45 for me, the sky now brightening, brighter than it had been at 11:00 the night before. Might as well get up. To the east, nine miles away, Blakely Island was invisible behind a cloud bank that covered its 1500 foot summit to the Salish Sea below. The Orcas Ferry landing, two miles away, was barely visible, and nearby Shaw and Orcas were blanketed in a cloud layer that descended to about 100 feet. The clouds and fog had come in from the Straight of Juan de Fuca, ten miles south and the passage to the Pacific. Years ago I'd flown over the Straight, returning from the East Coast, seeing it covered with a fog blanket, only the superstructures of a few ships showing through. Fall is fog time in the San Juans and today was the first day of summer. By mid morning the low clouds had disappeared, revealing another, though scattered layer above.

I was up earlier than I'd intended but made use of the time by installing MS Office and an external backup drive on the Food Bank computer now being staged on the dining room table and then unpacked the Kobo Reader and was impressed with the design and screen clarity and the touch screen was acceptably responsive. The important question, for me though, was whether the Kobo would work with our books — since the report back from translator Ian on Vancouver Island was that he couldn't exercise the links. Loading a EPUB version of *The eNotated Metamorphosis* I'd created with Calibre doing a conversion from a MOBI version, the book looked good and the Table of Contents the Kobo created allowed access to the various sections of the book. I displayed Part 1 and tapped the first link, to an eNotation discussing the title. Nothing happened. The Kobo, unlike every other eReader device or software, did not support hypertext links, the core of our books. Then I checked online and found my experience confirmed. Though the Kobo would support links for pages displayed in its browser it wouldn't for links in books. What foolishness! I'd return it.

I was last to join the Greybeard's in Howard's honeymoon cottage for our weekly tea time, late in part because crossing to Orcas I'd stopped the *Huginn* to observe two, seals probably, a hundred yards apart, creating a rumpus in the water, perhaps as part of a fishing technique. The night before Yvonne, Kate, Ken, and I had seen something similar several hundred yards west of Crane as we enjoyed the solstice sunset. Howard added that Tom, one of our local whale watching boat captains, reported that orca whales had come through Pole Pass again on Thursday, almost exactly a year since Yvonne and I had stood on the rocks at Pole Pass as we watched the orcas parade come through.

After lunch my lack of sleep caught up with me and I napped for a few minutes until Yvonne found me and said she needed help moving rocks for her remodeled pond. She was using the hillside behind her shop as a quarry, moss covered rocks, mostly brittle basalt, everywhere. I carried about 20 down to the open area in front of the shop and she used the two-wheeled hand cart to move a few to the pond area and I moved the rest. We'd dug a shelf around the edge of the pond at what would be just below water line and then laid the plastic liner back in the excavation, folding under the edges so the liner would be slightly higher than the water line and then put rocks on the shelf. The previous version of the pond didn't hide the liner adequately. With this version, the black liner would be invisible.

Yvonne's pond building book showed a few ponds with small wooden docks extending out over the water and she wanted one on the other side of the pond from the Japanese lantern she'd set on a little rock peninsula we'd constructed. Rooting through the scrap wood pile behind my shop I found six 2 x 4 and three 2 x 6 pieces that would do and showed Yvonne what I had in mind. OK. I took my chop saw out of my shed and set it up on the ground next to the yard power post and cut the scraps to the size of the smallest piece and then laid them out and screwed them together, the three 2 x 6s crosswise carrying the six 2 x 4s lengthwise. The boards had all been painted, intended initially for use with the house deck stairs project of two years before. We found a 200 lb smooth granite rock next to what had been the driveway, hidden in the salal and I forced it out of the ground with a long heavy pry bar from the tool shed. Using the hand cart we lowered it into the pond depres-

Two-hundred-forty-seven: Pirate Booty

sion and arranged it to support the outer edge of the "dock." I drilled five holes in the 2 x 6 on the land side of the dock that extended two inches past the ends of the 2 x 4s and pounded large spikes, three vertically and two at an angle through the holes and into the soil to keep the land end of the dock from moving. Yvonne then completed laying rocks around the edge of the pond, finishing the area on either side of the dock. We knew the grandchildren would want to touch the water but we didn't want them walking on the rock edge. The little dock was the solution.

247: Getting the pond right

Two-hundred-forty-seven: Pirate Booty

In late afternoon I downloaded the solstice pictures I'd taken to my MacBook Pro and added a photo album to our family website. Though the images didn't capture the extraordinary visual quality of the setting sun on all that it touched the evening before, they did hint at it.

During dinner Margaret called, describing a coin treasure she'd found on the community beach. A horde of small coins, all in a group, showed itself through the sand, and she'd dug it up, mostly pennies, the newest circa 1975. She opined that they had been in a sack, the sack left by accident on the beach, buried by the tides, the sack disintegrating over the years, the coins remaining together but now revealed — for who knows what reason — beach erosion? The buried treasure, now found, had become another kind of treasure, and Crane lore.

Two-hundred-forty-eight: Remodel

"Architecture is a visual art, and the buildings speak for themselves." - Julia Morgan

Yvonne finished the remodel of her little pond outside the deer fence south of the studio deck — including adding a pump to the side and below the Japanese stone snow lantern perched on a large rock at the east, water facing side, and the pump created a burble on the surface of the pond and would, she said, keep mosquitos from successfully breeding there (we have few in any case). She painted the little dock with dark brown deck paint, the same as the house trim and decks. Rocks, many moss covered, lined the bank of the pond and behind them plantings, grasses, on one side and salal on the other framed this water feature in a pleasing way. And just inside the fence the yellow day lilies were beginning to open up, in the same bed as the lupins, their tall creamy blue and gray flower heads having brightened the area for the last month.

Later, walking Circle Road the leafed out forest understory made it difficult to see the tank level gauge on the hill 200 feet away. Just over twelve feet; down a bit. I'd send Gary an email. Perhaps he'd need to add an hour or two to the well #6 timer. A few minutes from completing my circle I heard a vehicle behind me and stepped off the road; it was Lou on his weekly trip to Orcas and Eastsound to visit, shop, and do laundry. We talked about the weather (very nice) and walking on Crane (very nice) and I considered asking him whether he'd thought about a work party coming to his house to repair his deck and cleanup the yard — but I didn't. Perhaps Margaret, who knows him much better will ask. He values his solitary lifestyle, his privacy, and only seeks company when there's an emergency of some sort (telephone doesn't work, heat doesn't work). Neither of us having much to say this morning and both enjoying being alone right then, Lou, in his golf cart, continued to the dock and shortly I noticed an unopened bottle of cranberry juice lying in the grass off the north side of the road. Whose? Did it fly out of a Gator hurtling down the road? Matt had been on the island for the first time since fall, to repair his water system he'd failed to drain, though at his request after a cold spell in November, I'd drained the system, too late as it turned out. I stood the plastic bottle upright so it would be more visible for someone to recover and when I was near the dock and could see Lou getting ready to castoff, I turned left instead of right and walked to the beach to see if I could spot signs of where Margaret had found the buried treasure the day before. To the left of the tracks in the beach created by a tractor perhaps, someone had dug a hole a foot across and two feet long, perhaps six inches deep — the site of the treasure trove apparently.

By 1:15 Yvonne had finished packing books for niece Gina and her daughter Cresi and the cookware she'd found at the Deer Harbor Community Club yard sale for Natasha and put them in the dock cart in a rush to get to the Post Office before it closed at 2:00. My Nook ebook reader had likely arrived and I was eager to try it out on our eNotated classics. Neighbor Rupert, from Vancouver, B.C. was aboard his C-Dory working on the outboard engine. It had caused him trouble crossing from the mainland and now wouldn't start at all. We talked about possible reasons and then I had to go. Tom, Margaret, and Lou were all on Orcas and I parked the *Huginn* at the far western section of the transient dock. Debris or garage sale items perhaps were now in the shared dock cart parked against the side of the shed with no one in sight. Why? What if someone else needed to use the cart — Lou, for instance, when he came back from town. Fortunately I had brought our dock cart with me on the *Huginn* (the first time ever) and so had used it to bring the cartons to be mailed up to the parking lot. I put the cart behind Dan's van where it would be out of sight until I returned.

The Nook had arrived. A new toy. While she weighed the cartons for mailing I asked Pat how it was that the Postal Service and UPS were working together. Somehow the Nook had gotten to Deer Harbor through the joint efforts of these competitors. She didn't know about UPS but said that FedEx was bringing her packages daily now and thought that the two groups were sharing resources. What an interesting development!

248: Success!

Back at the Crane dock Rupert was still struggling with his outboard and I stopped again to offer encouragement and to commiserate. He'd removed the gas filter and found no water. He removed one of the three spark plugs from the two-cycle engine and asked me to turn on the ignition while he watched for a spark. Though I couldn't see behind me I could hear him get a shock. Could the engine be flooded? He removed all the plugs and did see that the cylinders were wet. I told Rupert to ask for help if he needed transportation to and from Orcas (Rachel was due to arrive the next day) and to come to the house to call Mike if his cell phone coverage was inadequate.

I continued my guest bathroom little remodel. The sink and cabinet were now in the wall. I removed the screws holding the toilet to the 3 1/2 inch high wooden base it sat on — Iris and Dean had liked their toilets high — and used

Two-hundred-forty-eight: Remodel

a pry bar to separate the toilet from the base it had been glued to — and then put the toilet on the front porch. I cracked the base apart and removed it and was left with a closet flange 3 1/2 inches off the floor. I'd have to cut it down. But how would I attach a new flange? On the internet I found that Ace Hardware carried a twist-on adaptor. I called Harold to find out whether Orcas Hardware had one — but Harold was busy and didn't call back.

Then Margaret called from the Orcas dock. Could I give her Dick and Nancy's phone number. She thought the shared dock cart I'd seen was filled with their stuff and wanted to offer to bring it to Orcas. Yvonne had decided that it made sense to bring the F150 to Crane for two months — to launch and later pull out our Ranger daysailer, to collect fire wood, and to have a chance to thoroughly clean it — so I sent Gary an email asking that he let me know when he would next be bringing his *Mud Puppy* landing craft barge to Crane and got an email back saying he would the next day. That meant we'd need to think through and organize whatever we wanted to bring from Orcas to Crane the next day.

Two-hundred-forty-nine: Wheels

"You can't go back and change the beginning, but you can start where you are and change the ending." - C.S. Lewis

The old toilet was on the front porch and though Yvonne hadn't yet suggested it be moved somewhere out of sight I wanted to get rid of it as well as a smattering of other trash that hadn't made it across to Orcas and the transfer station the previous Sunday so I pulled the partly filled garbage can out of the repurposed privy and added metal and plastic trash I'd laid on the grass outside my shop when I'd cleaned it out — including old cabinets and shelving in order to replace them with what we'd taken out of the kitchen when we did the remodel last fall and to find items for the Community Club yard sale and, of course, generally reduce our ballast. Whew!

Yvonne and I crossed to Orcas about 9:30, she bearing fresh baked chocolate cookies for the weekend's Garden Club's Orcas in Bloom garden tour (she'd make more in the evening to eat while we watched "Babies"). We'd meet at the Cayou Quay Marina at noon. I brought the F150 down from the Orcas side Crane Island marina upper lot, loaded the trash, toilet, and vinyl flooring I'd torn out of the guest bathroom, the paddle ends from two oars I'd replaced in the Pronto, Crane's backup rowboat moored underneath the aluminum ramp on the Orcas side, a seriously messed up florescent shop light, and the 3 1/2" split wooden stand the toilet had perched on, covering it all with a bungie cord web to keep it from falling over.

First stop: the transfer station — except as I approached I could see that at least twenty cars were queued along Orcas Road waiting to get in. Last Sunday had been quiet at the dump. Apparently everyone has the same idea — get to the dump at 10:00 Friday morning, the first of three days it's open each week. It was now twenty past ten. I didn't have time to spare so I drove past the line and continued to Eastsound to the hardware store. I was looking for a 3" PVC Oatey Twist-N-Set closet flange to replace the flange now sticking up 3

1/2 inches from the guest bathroom floor. I'd need to cut the waste pipe at the floor and then needed a way to add a new flange to hold the toilet to the floor and after spending hours on the internet looking for a solution this seemed to be the best. Ace online listed the Oatey. Harold hadn't called back the previous day to tell me whether they carried it but I was hopeful they did. But they didn't. And they didn't have a pond liner patch kit Yvonne asked me to look for — worried that the reason the water level had fallen in her newly remodeled pond was because of a hole.

Next stop: the lumber yard. No Oakey and no liner repair kit but I loaded three 100 lb bags of sand Yvonne intended to use to mix concrete to lay a footing for the memorial grotto she intended to raise over 'Mantha Moo Moo's grave next to the compost bins. Yvonne wanted a scoop of topsoil from Island Sanitation. I'd intended to go there last, once I'd been to the dump but since it was now 11:15 I stopped there before going back to the dump reasoning that I could take the trash out of the bed of the truck, have the top soil loaded, put the trash on top of the load and then deposit it at the transfer station. A friendly attendant greeted me, asked what I needed (top soil) and then asked about the trash in the truck. I'd take it out and then put it back. He thought about the absurdity of that for a few seconds and then offered to take the trash, for what it would cost to leave it at the transfer station. He too had seen the long line. Great! Did I have any scrap metal. Yes. Did I know I could leave it in the blue dumpster for free. Yes. That answered the question I was going to ask and didn't. Yvonne and I had left four baseboard heaters in the dumpster the week before and then read the sign that said we had to pay for appliances. Were the heaters appliances? No. We had done the right thing. Case closed.

He and I moved the trash to a dumpster and I positioned my pickup near the soil and mulch bins while he started up his front loader. While it warmed up we positioned a tarp I carry in the truck in the bed and over the sand bags to make cleanup easier once the soil is unloaded. He dumped a scoopful of soil into the truck bed and then he and I shoveled what had spilled behind the truck onto the pile in the bed. I hooked the ends of the tarp together over the load to keep them from flapping and to reduce blowoff and drove to the Cayou Quay marina parking lot where I'd leave the truck for its trip to Crane later in the day. I took my MacBook Pro out of my backpack and confirmed that the unrestricted WiFi was still available at the marina and checked my email — and Yvonne pulled into the next parking spot in the van. We stopped at the

Two-hundred-forty-nine: Wheels

Deer Harbor Post Office (Yvonne got some shoes in the mail) and then back in the Crane parking lot I opened the UPS locker and found that the Canon Pixma 880 printer/scanner/copier had been delivered so I put it into the our dock cart which I'd hidden by the side of the shed and we headed back to Crane.

After lunch Yvonne went to work on her pond and I began what turned out to be a 2 1/2 hour internet and telephone search for an Oatey Twist-n-Set. No one in Burlington or Seattle had one in stock so I ordered one from the only source on the internet I could find that claimed to have it in stock and paid extra for three day delivery. I had less than three weeks to make the guest bathroom operational before our first batch of guests arrived.

Yvonne came into the house and asked me to come look at what she'd done with her pond. She'd discovered the source of the leak: the liner was too low on the east side, the low side of the pond. She'd removed all the rocks she'd stacked around the edge of the pond to make certain that was the only problem and had raised the lining on the low side, then replaced the rocks in a more pleasing arrangement. The right way to do the pond she now realized was to place a few rocks, then add water, then rearrange the lining top, and then finish the rock wall around the edges. The pond looked great — much better than her beta release.

Yvonne cooked an early dinner of stir-fried tofu and vegetables served with rice while we watched for Gary's barge to come around Caldwell Point from West Sound with Jim and Doug's loads from Orcas. I walked down to the community dock not knowing whether the barge would come in there or at the concrete ramp below the airstrip. It was close to 6:00, with no sign of Gary so I called Yvonne at home with the walkie-talkie she suggested I take with. She buzzed me back after talking to Gary on his cell phone. They were on their way and would be coming into the concrete ramp so I walked the half mile along Dock Road, Circle Road, and then Reef Road to get to the ramp and walked out on the rebuilt private dock to look for Gary. A pickup pulled into the lot: it was Doug. Soon Pat pulled into the lot driving his not-so-small bulldozer. Doug and Pat had been building an 80 foot bocci ball court next to their shared bunk house. Doug's house was complete, Pat's house framed, and Larry's an idea. The barge appeared, docked, and Gary let down the landing craft ramp, Wilma taking the helm to hold the barge against the beach while Gary helped with the unloading and loading. Doug S and Jim J were aboard, Jim's green John Deere tractor facing out with Doug's pickup face out right behind it. A log splitter lay on the deck below the tractor scoop and a small boat trailer was turned on its side leaning against the transom next to Doug's pickup. Doug W backed his Gator up to the ramp to receive the wheeled log splitter and towed it away and Doug and I talked about the satisfaction of splitting wood by hand instead of using a machine.

249: Packing the Mud Puppy on the second day of our move to Crane (January 9, 2007)

I also told him, in his capacity as Road and Parking chair, that he might get a call from Dick who was worried about two dead trees near Rocky Road behind Dick's cabin where the 3rd of July picnic would be held. Dick had called me the week before asking me, as Treasurer to provide him proof that the Association had liability coverage and I called the insurance agent to find out. Neither one of us could quite understand why Dick needed paper proof. Before dinner I had walked the half mile to the intersection of Circle and Rocky Roads to look for dangerous trees but hadn't seen anything more dangerous than anything else. I called Dick to understand better what he was concerned about and he pointedly said that the Board would have liability now that it had been informed about the two dead trees. He then went on to talk about the fire hazard that all the brush and dead trees represented on the island. I agreed with him but didn't say that Crane was dangerous to children and adults. There was the water all around the island a person could fall into and rocks a person could fall over and crack their heads on and trees and brush and houses that might burn (he mentioned lightening but I'd never seen any in the San Juans) and the cute raccoons might bite or bucks impale with their antlers. But that's the way it was. I could see clearing imminent dangers (trees about to fall over the road and combustibles away from houses) but otherwise there wasn't anything to do about it nor did the other residents. One of the prices of rural living is exposure to certain kinds of dangers one doesn't see in the city. But on the other hand, the city has its own dangers not present on Crane. I suggested to Dick that he call Jason, Board President about his general concerns, Pat about road related dangers and Dan about fire dangers, excusing myself because I, as Treasurer and Water chair, didn't want to intrude into their territory. Sigh.

Jim drove his tractor off and then Doug R pulled his truck forward and he and Gary lowered the trailer and hitched it to the truck and Doug drove off. Pat backed his bulldozer onto the barge, to the back, and Gary, now at the helm, backed the landing craft off the beach, turned it around and headed for the Cayou Quay Marina ramp where my pickup waited.

Wilma and I talked about her youngest daughter, Ruby, who had just graduated from high school, and was in a quandary about what to do next because her older sister, Edie, back from eighteen months in Vietnam teaching English, wasn't certain now she wanted to leave Orcas for California where the sisters had intended to live together and go to college. But Ruby wanted to be out on her own, away from home in the worst way, and was thoroughly frustrated now living at home. With Pat's dozer off the barge and my pickup on, Wilma and I continued our conversation, now on their progress building their house. Their well had come in the day before, a relief, their building project now practical and they planned to lay the foundation and floor before winter and then do the construction themselves as they had time, Gary competent in all aspects of residential construction (years before he'd hung the drywall for Dean and Iris in what became our house). Back at the concrete ramp on Crane I drove off and Doug R drove on, his enormous outdoor grill now waiting at his house for installation and wanting to get his pickup back to Orcas. As I drove Circle Road and then Eagle Lane to our house I was struck at how narrow and overgrown these "roads" were. Never wide enough for cars to pass, the salal, not trimmed sufficiently by the resident black-tailed deer, bushes, and trees were expanding into the roadway, and would if left alone make it impassable in a few years. I hadn't noticed when walking. Now that I had wheels again on Crane I did.

Two-hundred-fifty: Blooming

> *"To live content with small means; to seek elegance rather than luxury, and refinement rather than fashion; to be worthy, not respectable, and wealthy, not rich; to study hard, think quietly, talk gently, act frankly; to listen to stars and birds, to babes and sages, with open heart; to bear all cheerfully, do all bravely, await occasions, hurry never; in a word, to let the spiritual, unbidden and unconscious, grow up through the common."* - William Henry Channing

Yvonne left for Orcas by 9:30 under cloudy skies to meet with Lynn and together visit the six gardens on this year's Garden Club "Orcas in Bloom" garden tour while I stayed home to work outside. The pickup, now parked back by the rain shelter, held a yard of topsoil, and three 100 lb bags of sand. The topsoil belonged on a tarp shared with mulch I'd brought from Orcas at the end of last summer, but before I could unload it I needed to make room on the tarp. The sand would be stored on the floor in Yvonne's shop near bags of cement. Consolidating the mulch to the north side of the storage tarp, I emptied half the bed to the other side and then swept out the bed liner and covered the mulch and top soil. Yvonne would now have a planting supply for her garden projects. Time for lunch.

The week before we'd cut down three more trees on our property and I'd stacked trunk sections in what was once the driveway to the Eagle Lane cul de sac and they needed to be cut up and moved to the firewood area outside the deer fence at the north side of the house protecting Yvonne's garden. The sun had come out and the day had turned beautiful. The cutting work was dirty and required lots of bending over. I was happy to finish and to have contributed to the to-be-split wood pile. Then I did some minor repair work on our dock cart (an Agri-Fab 7 cubic foot model) replacing side bolts that were working their way into the surface of the 1/4" plywood sides with larger head versions and tightening all loose bolts. A few months before when I'd replaced the spa water filter I'd noticed that rats had gotten into the 4' x 3' x 4' structure under the deck and I sealed the openings around the PVC pipes with hardware cloth and left an open box of moth balls inside before sealing it up again. A month later Yvonne noticed that insulation had been torn out — by something or other — in the structure next to the spa and through which the pipes run. A rat had probably been trying to get into the "pump house" and had been thwarted by the hardware cloth and then tore out fiber glass insulation around the pipes trying to find another way in. Now finally addressing the mess I thought I would completely close this side of the structure with hardware cloth but when I took a good look I realized that I'd really need to use wood to close the bottom and part of the exposed side and that was more than I wanted to do right now so I got a "contractor's" trash bag from the converted privy and filled it with the insulation I pulled out. I'd finish the job before the weather got cold again.

While I was moving cut wood from the driveway to firewood area Margaret came by on her way back home and I asked whether she needed the cart to move the chips she'd been making. Not today. She was struggling to finish a paper she'd been writing. I also told her that with our truck on the island I'd be happy to pull her boat out if she wanted to clean the hull — and she said she would, probably in August. She'd return to Ohio State in Columbus to complete her last teaching year before retiring full time to Crane but not before finishing the spring semester and then attending a number of meetings in Europe, with a side trip to Afghanistan, her area of expertise, if possible. She was trying to bring into focus when she would put her Ohio house on the market, what furniture she would bring to her smaller and already pretty well filled house on Crane and what she should do about her thousands of books. A daunting prospect with all her time already spoken for.

It was about 5:00 before Yvonne came home and as we ate warmed up stir-fry, we recounted our days. She'd enjoyed the garden tour with Lynn, for the first time in many years without any responsibilities on tour day. Yvonne had initiated the tours when president of the club as a substitute for a fair at the park in Eastsound, a very big project. The garden tours were a reliable fundraiser and appreciated by islanders and visitors since they offered the opportunity to see a variety of gardens in a variety of settings — and to see how the people who had them lived. Three in Deer Harbor were nearly adjacent and the two women walked between them on Deer Harbor Road. Lynn had suggested that we join her and Chris, Sheila and Howard for a trip to the Olympic Peninsula during the winter. Yvonne and I had already talked about a trip that would include a stay at Lake Quinault, in the rain forest, a place we hadn't been to in almost 30 years. Yes, that would be something to look forward to when the weather turned cold, wet, and dreary in late October.

250: Dinner in the Gumption (July 2004)

Two-hundred-fifty-one: Let's Get Together

"Technology is a useful servant but a dangerous master." - Christian Lous Lange

Neither of us slept well, for whatever reason, me only until about 2:00 and when I couldn't fall back asleep I decided I might as well get up and found that the DSL internet service wasn't working and later that though we had a dial tone no call could be completed through the CenturyLink system. And our Verizon cell phone had no bars — no signal was coming from the transmitter two miles away at the ferry landing. By 10:00 everything was back in service. A mystery islands outage.

I'd made some efforts to understand why Calibre's MOBI to EPUB conversion wasn't 100% successful with our *Metamorphosis* book. Two items in the table of contents pointed to the wrong section of the book. Two hours of experimentation and narrowing down led me to understand that in two places the book used second level heading tags for emphasis and the program took them to indicate structure. I took them out and now had a clean EPUB version. We could now began the process to publish on Barnes & Noble and generally be compatible with Apples iBook and just about every other reader device and reader software.

Yvonne was up by 7:00, much earlier than usual, she too having given up on trying to sleep. Not a propitious way to start the day.

Suzanne and John were hosting the UU group's annual meeting and picnic. We'd skip the first and attend the second. Once the phones were working Yvonne called Margaret to ask her whether she wanted to come along. She was way behind where she thought she should be with her paper. Then she called back; she would come along. Yvonne made a bowl of her signature potato salad and filled one of the UU thermoses with coffee and the other with hot water for tea.

Two-hundred-fifty-one: Let's Get Together

I'd put three boxes of books into the *Huginn* to join Yvonne's three that she would take to the Everett Half Price Books store on Tuesday on her way to Seattle, another small step to lighten our Crane home ballast and be paid a pittance for it. I held back one box of books I had determined were worth enough to sell on line — fantasizing I would post them on Amazon when I had time in the fall.

We arrived at the picnic site just as the annual meeting attended by about a dozen broke up, Yvonne hearing Suzanne confirm with one of the attendees that they'd agreed to continue for another year. Two new couples had volunteered to help Suzanne carry it off. I was happy to see others step into the breach others of us had created when, after some years of service, we'd retired. I was no longer willing to put time into the Sunday mornings that proved less and less satisfying.

The core group, Suzanne, who was feeling better after an MS episode she thought was brought on by stress, Margot, Babs and Peter (founders in 2000), Kathy and Ray, Ruthie and Andrea (a widow for one year), Susan and her husband, Michael and his wife now made up the core group, with late arrivals like Chris and Lynn, Kate (who said Ken was busy writing up an offer document for a client and it looked like they'd be involved now in a second sale, this one in Deer Harbor after an extended drought) and us adding to the group. Sitting in the sun the day turned hot and I was scolded later by Yvonne for not putting on sunblock something I so far hadn't worked into my daily habits. I talked to John, an arborist, about dropping some trees for us on Crane and we made arrangements for me to pick him up at the Orcas dock Wednesday at 9:00.

Most interesting and enjoyable were Sharon and Mike, Orcas music fixtures, who had sung at every UU picnic for at least the last eight years, four times at our house on Cayou Valley Road and twice on Crane when the UU summer picnic was held here. Sharon has an opera quality voice. Both compose, Sharon's songs serious and yearning, Mike's serious and whimsical, she accomplished with violin and guitar, Mike with bass and guitar. Earnest and idealistic New Yorkers, still — forever — using music in the ancient prophetic tradition of folk music — the call to peace and love, the eschewing of war and hate. Suzanne passed out lyrics sheets and we sang together song we knew and didn't know, Chet Powers "Get Together" evoking for me strong feelings from the 60's and 70's when it looked like basic change was possible. How far we'd all come in the last 40 years in our return to a new gilded age like 1890's.

251: Sharon and Mike at the Unitarian picnic

After my call to Noah, naps on the couches and dinner, we made a round of the island, Yvonne suggesting we make the route counterclockwise, something I would never have thought of on my own. Jason had told me the day before that another tree had come down at well house #4, narrowly missing the little building and obstructing entry. Yvonne and I stopped to look. I'd cut it up and bring it home for firewood. A few steps farther on we met Ormond with son Will, who we'd seen at last summer's Crane 50th Anniversary party.

Two-hundred-fifty-one: Let's Get Together

Just across Circle Road I pointed out a dangerous broken tree situation, a fir, broken about 25 feet up, the top leaning against a nearby tree at about a 60 degree angle. If the base of the top section came loose it could fall almost anywhere. I would show it to John Wednesday and see whether he had any ideas. Coming home along Eagle Lane, we met Rachel and daughters on their way home from the community dock. The daughters excused themselves because of the appearance of mosquitos, rare near the salt water, and we talked briefly with Rachel about the software system she was developing to help film and TV casts, crews, directors, and producers track what was going on in a production — on iPads they would carry with them — a great idea and something she understood the need and solution for since she and Rupert both worked in that industry. Their C-Dory outboard was now working perfectly after Mike's ministration. They'd be heading back to Vancouver the next day but hoped to be back later in the summer. Yvonne and I had enjoyed having Rupert for dinner many months back, with his stories of encounters with film industry celebrities, some for whom he had great respect and admiration.

Two-hundred-fifty-two: Refulgent Summer

"The song is ended, but the melody lingers on." - Irving Berlin

On Sunday, with Yvonne driving and chatting with Margaret in the back seat as we drove up Crow Valley Road at the base of Turtleback Mountain on our way to Suzanne and John's, I had a chance to really look at the road side, valley, and mountains to the east (Mt. Constitution on the east side of the East Sound fjord and Mt. Woolard on the west), I could see, even feel, how happy and full the vegetation felt (if it could feel) with plenty of moisture in the soil, long, mostly sunny days, and air temperatures optimum for growth.

The fir and cedars were extending their branches, the new growth, at least six inches now, obvious in a lighter green. The Nookta wild roses that grow all over the San Juans as head high bushes, several at the Crane dock, were flowering now, a pink daisy shape with a yellow middle. Here and there the ubiquitous blackberries (though strangely absent on Crane) were beginning to flower and Yvonne noted to Margaret that we'd run out of blackberry jam so she'd make a batch in the late summer and we all commiserated that last summer's blackberry crop had been very poor.

Orange California poppies had appeared in abundance in their regular spots, one bordering Deer Harbor Road just east of Crow Valley Road, the site of an historic Native American summer camp and midden. A hardy geranium joined the poppies against the south wall of the Community Club building just west. Queen Anne's Lace, elegant and tall, rose above the grasses along Orcas Road, and flowering Foxglove had returned to the slope descending from the north end of the Crane airstrip to Circle Road. And the delicate ocean spray flowers would bloom in a few days.

The water in the cove that held the Crane dock at Pole Pass was in bloom as well, noctiluca plankton having turned the normally clear water a murky brown, almost orange, spreading through Pole Pass to the east and evident at the Orcas dock though not as pronounced, the first time I'd noticed this condition in the San Juans, perhaps associated with the warming of the Salish Sea, into which warm water dolphins had appeared now unexpectedly.

This morning I watched a robin stand in the half-inch deep water covering the rock next to the snow lantern in Yvonne's pond take a bath, ever alert to danger but apparently enjoying flipping the water up over itself with its wings. Sunday evening we'd seen our local raccoon, a young adult, cross the yard and enter the forest near Yvonne's shop and Yvonne told me, now, Monday, that lying in bed in the morning looking out the north windows at the bay that extends from the house, she saw the raccoon descending the large, green Douglas fir, with its top 40 feet missing, apparently broken off during a storm years before we came to Crane. Now we knew where it lived.

Mike, replying to my query about whether he had any comments on my proposed Crane Island Association budget replied that he hadn't had time to reply because he'd been with his son in the hospital being treated for a nasty staph infection (his first report had been two weeks before) and I forwarded his note to Jason and Martha who wrote back saying she would send a card from the island to Mike and family.

While I was cleaning up after dinner, a delicious gorgonzola white sauce over pasta, a balsamic vinegar dressing and chopped walnuts on spinach and sweet potatoes with kale braised in olive oil, I heard an "Oh no!" from Yvonne who had been doing her nightly Facebook session in my office. She'd received an email that had gone out to all the Garden Club members: Roger had died a few hours before. Roger and Joan had been UU stalwarts for many years but moved to the Community Church when I retired as moderator. Both had been very active volunteering on Orcas and had boated up into the Straight of Georgia and skied at Kamloops every year until the last two or three, Roger saying at one UU meeting that he refused to get old — but by this spring he'd become very frail. What would Joan do?, Yvonne said. He was her world. She loved him so much. She would be lost. Joan had been an irregular regular at Yvonne's Friday afternoon knitting sessions at the Deer Harbor Community Club during the cool rainy months and they'd had many conversations about their lives.

252: Gumption in Desolation Sound (July 2004)

Yvonne and I would reach out to her soon — after understanding more. At a yacht club get together on Thetis Island, in July 2004, Roger had given me good advice about how to cross the notorious Straight of Georgia on our way farther north in the *Gumption* to Desolation Sound, suggesting a route through Gabriola Pass, past Flattop Island and then across the Straight, very likely with the wind astern, more comfortable than abeam. Even so that crossing had been nerve wracking for me with three foot following waves trying to push the boat broadside, I felt like I was driving downhill on ice and was so focused I couldn't even talk to Yvonne for fear of being distracted. Coming back, a week later, we took the same route back but now heading into the wind and perhaps because I now had more experience and because we were following another yacht club couple we'd come upon in Prevost Harbor, the crossing was almost, but not quite fun. Roger, who'd served as corporate counsel for a major corporation had integrity and perspicuity and had been consistently friendly to Yvonne and me from the first time we had met him and Joan at a yacht club dinner on the Saanich Peninsula at Deep Cove Chalet. We'd miss him.

Two-hundred-fifty-three: Off on a Tangent

"The best way to predict the future is to invent it." - Alan Kay

A crow perched near the top of the wooden handrail for the steps leading down to the lawn below the Orcas Hotel and it slid slowly down the rail, putting its beak down to the rail to steady itself, stopping, and then sliding again, very smoothly and very slowly, interested more than worried, it seemed to me and when it took off after sliding about three feet I turned my attention back to what Jens was saying instead of staring over his shoulder at the crow. Later, farther into our discussion I could see a half dozen crows cleaning the plates of two tourists who had departed on the noon ferry without bringing in their plates and the coffee shop staff having been too preoccupied to go out on the deck facing the water and the ferry dock and bus the brick red heavy filigreed metal tables. At 11:30 the coffee shop had been filled with noisy diners. By 11:45 they'd all cleared out and were sitting in their cars in the ferry line or down at the landing waiting to walk aboard.

Yvonne had left for Seattle on the 8:30 ferry taking the van. The pickup was now on Crane for the summer. I wanted to meet with Jens after his session with Chris in Eastsound about doing more book promotional videos and talk especially about whether college and university libraries might be a promising marketing and sales entry point for our eNotated Classics as well as a literature learning platform I was considering creating to be called Blab School, recalling the 19th century American response to being able to afford only one volume of a book to be studied, sharing it, and students and the teacher taking turns reading it aloud to the class. What I had in mind was something a little different but I liked the name, the idea to provide a net-based service that would allow teachers and students to share and annotate literary classics together out of an extensive library that contained both annotated and non-annotated classics. Academic libraries and their information technology department partners were providing an increasingly rich menu of technical services to faculty and students, replacing paper "on-reserve" material with "e-reserve" students could access through their computers and perhaps smart phones and tablets. They wanted to be able to do the same thing with books — in effect being able to supply ebooks to students for class without each student having to buy one and optimally for interaction with the books — by faculty and students (such as annotation) also to be possible. Existing paper publishers weren't enthusiastic at the prospect of losing volume sales of paper books to lower margin library multiple user ebook purchases. Maybe there was an opportunity for us in this evolving shift from the paper to the digital world.

About 2:00 Jens headed home by way of Killebrew Lake and Dolphin Bay Roads in an attempt to avoid the Orcas Road resurfacing project that was applying a layer of tar and fine gravel — called chip seal, a simpler way to build up something like a asphalt road in thin layers every few years. I walked down to the county dock where I'd left the *Huginn* and noticed a 26' Macgregor hybrid sailboat like the one we bought and used for two years before buying a Camano Troll 31' pocket trawler that we used to cruise up and down the Salish Sea — as far north as Desolation Sound and south to Olympia. The Macgregor was a passable sailboat but because it had a semi-planing hull, used water ballast, and a centerboard that could be raised, could also act as a passable power boat, moving along smartly powered by a 50 hp two stroke outboard, quite a sight for other boaters unaccustomed to see small sailboats moving along at fifteen knots. But it was too small, in our opinion, to cruise in more than for a day or two and close to home although we'd meet Macgregor owners who were out for weeks over long distances.

The sun was warm inside the *Huginn*, the water barely rippled, as I flew back toward Caldwell Point where I'd have to slow down for the mile long no wake zone that extended west through Pole Pass into the south side of the Deer Harbor area. I was thinking about next steps in developing our business and the need to spend more time on the MOBI to EPUB conversion because I'd noticed for the first time with the Nook that it wasn't clearing images from the screen when pages were turned. Back home and experimenting with the Nook I found that the images wouldn't clear because I hadn't used paragraph tags in the ebook source files but was using break tags to create a blank line between what in fact were paragraphs and stored that way in the book database.

Two-hundred-fifty-three: Off on a Tangent

253: The Gumption - our pocket trawler

I'd taken the paragraph tags out to solve a problem with the Kindle, namely that it would arbitrarily carry text formats from one paragraph into another, ruining the formatting I intended. So I found myself in a pickle. I wanted to use only one source file for all books but the Kindle and the Nook were mutually inconsistent; I couldn't satisfy both devices with the same source — apparently. But likely there was a third way to create the source that would work for both but that would mean more research, coding, and testing. By 10:00 p.m. I understood the dilemma but not the solution and couldn't get to sleep thinking about it. I had broken one of my rules: no work after dinner and without Yvonne around to moderate my sometimes obsessive pursuit of a project had gone off on a tangent.

Two-hundred-fifty-four: How It's Done

"Trees are the earth's endless effort to speak to the listening heaven."
- Rabindranath Tagore

The rain was light, almost misty, and then picked up. John was scheduled to come to Crane to cut down six of our trees, too big for me to handle safely. Would he bail because of the rain? Not likely. I wouldn't. The rain would probably abate or in any case wouldn't really matter to any islander with things to accomplish outdoors. I pulled up to the Orcas dock before 9:00 and John, wearing a black raincoat was already there with his STIHL chainsaw, red can containing gas mixed with oil, a quart of chain oil, two yellow plastic wedges, and a spare chain. I had driven my pickup to the Crane dock so I could show him a broken tree across Circle Road from the community center. He agreed that it was dangerous and suggested throwing a weighted line over the top half leaning on a neighboring tree, use it to pull up a stronger rope and then tie a bowline on one end of the rope, and using that as a loop pull it up to and against the broken trunk — and then pull — away from the road, using a come-along or set up a pulley system to pull the rope from the road with a vehicle. He thought the problem could be solved without hiring him or another arborist to do something we could do for ourselves, being especially careful not to stand under the broken tree, obvious perhaps, but not, he knew from experience, to everyone.

I left the truck at the top of the driveway we share with Margaret. With trees likely to be falling all over our property there was no place for it close by. John and I eyeballed the six trees Yvonne had marked with yellow Xs, talking about what order they should be felled in, their bias to fall in one direction versus another (because they were leaning, bowed, or had more vegetation on one side (south) rather than another and came up with a plausible plan. I had told Margaret that John would be coming over to Crane to knock down some trees and Yvonne had consulted with her before deciding which should go —

Yvonne interested in getting sunlight to her garden and Margaret pretty much reluctant to cut any trees. Since Margaret would look at and pass through our property on her way to the dock and because her more than forty-year association with the two lots (her parents had been friends with Iris and Dean) it was right for her to have a say in how we were going to change it — not by cutting down some small trees — but some big ones. When John began his first face cut, Margaret came out of her house to observe, as interested as I was, to see how an expert arborist felled crowded, good-sized Douglas firs (the largest with a nineteen inch diameter trunk and nearly 90 feet tall (measurements I took once the tree was lying down). Cutting into the tree about three feet off the ground on the side it was to fall, perpendicular to the intended direction of fall and horizontal to the ground (so it wouldn't start to fall slightly to the right or left from the intended fall line), John cut about a third of the way through and then started a new cut about eight inches above the first, coming down at an angle to intersect with the deepest point of the first cut, popping out the wedge he'd created. I knew how to make the face cuts though I had thought I should cut half-way through and I wasn't vey good at making the first face cut perfectly horizontal though I usually made it pretty much perpendicular to the direction I wanted it to fall.

John started the back cuts from just above the two ends of the face cut rolling the saw blade toward to back of the tree so he could see exactly where to make the back cut across the tree parallel to the face cut. He made a cut a bit deeper than the width of the saw bar, took the saw out and tapped a wedge (he had borrowed a hammer) into the back cut. Then he worked the saw into the cut from the side and cut deeper — toward the face cut, stopping to add a second wedge and tapping the wedges farther into the cut. With about an inch of uncut tree between the face and back cut John pulled out his saw, put it down and began to whack the wedges. They forced the back side of the tree up just enough to tip the tree in the direction of the open face cut and the tree began to fall, accelerating until it hit the ground with a thump, breaking some of the branches at the crown.

In a crowded environment Douglas firs grow up not out and self-prune as they go, leaving a bare trunk up 80% of their height. This first tree fell right in the middle of the driveway, its crown passing between two other trees on either side but far enough apart that the crown passed among them without a fuss. The next four trees, one to the east across Samantha's grave where the daffodils had already flowered and the leaves were beginning to dry out, and the other three along and across the "public" path that winds through the salal west of our house, all fell perfectly, all within inches of where John intended them to fall. Margaret and I were amazed at John's skill. The sixth tree, it tuned out wouldn't be so simple.

The last tree, the biggest, stood next to the 12 x 12 rain shelter I'd built three years before, two smaller, though still large firs next to it. They were the constraint on the right side of John's intended fall line. A half-dozen trees were lined up loosely on the left side of the fall line. The crown of the falling tree would have to pass through the crowns of several other trees, breaking limbs or pushing them out of the way to make it to the ground. If it fell a few inches too far to the right or left, the crown of the falling tree might tangle itself in the crown of a neighboring tree and then we'd have a problem. John made his cuts, the big tree fell but only six feet. It's trunk now lay against the next tree on the right. The danger quotient had risen.

Margaret retrieved her two come-alongs and I supplied a rope. John got the line tied to the partly fallen trunk about 30 feet up using the technique he had described to me when we looked at the broken tree at the community center and began to try to pull the trunk off the stump with the come-along, just as I had done with a smaller tree when I'd gotten into the same kind of pickle. It wouldn't budge. He then began shaving the contact point where the trunk sat on the tree, making it smaller and smaller, almost a point, shaving the stump as well so that the point was only inches from a falling off place. He then used my steel wedge, whacking it with a sledge hammer in the direction of the falling off place and then it did — rolling off the stump and then the crown rolling out of its embrace with the neighboring tree. Fascinating.

Margaret went home to continue her work on an article and I took John back to Orcas, very appreciative of his help getting the trees down and the up-close look at how he did it — including coping with a big tree that wouldn't fall.

Returning on the noon ferry from Anacortes, Yvonne had packed the car with food and other essentials, three dock carts worth and it was nearly 3:00 before we were home and everything put away. I gave her a tour of the field of felled trees and told her the story of each, with plenty of detail about the last, biggest, and most challenging tree. She said she was very happy not to have been anywhere nearby with the trees falling all over the yard. She would have had to go to the other end of the island. Like riding in a speeding boat, the prospect and then the actuality of trees crashing to earth caused a feeling of terror she could barely stand — even though she knew she wasn't in danger.

254: Solution to a hung up fir

Two-hundred-fifty-five: Long Days Burning into Night

"Nature never did betray the heart that loved her." - William Wordsworth

Before 9:00 a.m. Yvonne and I were both outside looking at the six trees splayed across the lot, looking like a pile of huge pick-up sticks, deciding what to do first. Yvonne would start the burn pile. I'd cut and carry branches and greenery to a pile near the fire and Yvonne would strip the green from the branches, burn the former and stack the latter for an eventual chipper session. Because the San Juan Islands have such scant rainfall in the summer, fire danger increases from the almost non-existent in winter to the extreme by August, beginning the change in June. June 30th would be the last day burn piles were permitted until the summer drought broke in October. We had to finish our greens cleanup today or pile it for three or four months.

The burn pile and sometime campfire site was in an open area, no overhanging trees above, near the rain shelter and Yvonne's shop, a three foot circle trimmed with rocks. Since one felled 85 foot tree occupied Margaret's driveway, making it difficult for her to walk along it, I started there. Most of the branches had been knocked off the trunk when it passed between other trees or when it hit the ground falling. I used a hand saw to cut the remaining branches, not wanting to disturb Margaret with a chainsaw. As I dragged the bigger branches to the pile near the fire, a doe visited the compost bins not 20 feet away, unperturbed by my presence. When what remained was only greenery, I opened a tarp, raked it into piles, moved the piles to the tarp and carried or dragged them to the pile near the fire. Before I finished the tree in her driveway, Margaret walked by on her way to the dock. She'd be gone most of the day to Orcas so I topped up the gas and chain oil tanks on my chain saw and put it to use. Though 80% of the length of these Douglas fir trunks were bare, the crowns were thick with branches, some more than 10' long, and they all had to be cut away and then moved.

Yvonne took the branches and used a small hand clipper or long handled, more powerful model, cut off the greenery, stacking it in the pile to burn, added the stripped branches to the chipping pile and the bigger branches, especially those over three inches in diameter, to another pile that I'd either chip or carry to the firewood storage area. I'd add to the input pile and Yvonne would process and feed the fire and though at the beginning I got ahead of her, by the time I began working on the last three trees, less accessible than the first three, having fallen into a big patch of salal and small trees and bushes, impenetrable even to the deer, who seemed to be able to go anywhere in spite of their size, my efficiency fell off and Yvonne began to process faster than I could supply. Because the fallen trees made walking across the lot to the burn pile area difficult, I cut some sections from the butt ends of two to allow passage between stump and trunk.

One of the trunks had fallen into a part of the yard I'd never been into, impassable because of the salal and the unevenness of the ground, frequently falling away into holes, invisible from above through the salal and disconcerting to step into. And there'd been no reason to fight through the salal. We had just let it be. Now I was in the middle of it, only 30 feet from the public trail through our property — from the meadow on the north and its path to the dock and access to Margaret's as well as the driveway that rose through the trees to Eagle Lane — and the world looked completely different. This previously unexplored space now felt like it was ours — and I liked that. Our world had gotten larger in an unexpected way, right off the path we frequently walked on and pushed our dock cart through carrying trash cans to the *Huginn* to take to the transfer station on Orcas. I hadn't paid attention to the wood chips Margaret had added to the path a few days before and now I did. She knew the parts of the path that turned soggy in the winter if not covered in chips and she had laid a four inch layer in three different sections. Perfect. She had gathered more downed branches to chip but I would likely borrow back our jointly-owned chipper soon so that Yvonne and I could take turns adding to the chip pile.

Two-hundred-fifty-five: Long Days Burning into Night

259: Bad roads and good signs

By 4:00 I'd moved all the branches and greenery to the processing pile, the last hour Yvonne asking me frequently, is that all? Not quite. A little more to come. And the little more turned into another little more. She was tired of it. I went in to take a shower and then do some email. Then I spelled her while she made dinner. The pile of ash, coals, and burning wood and greenery was now about six feet across and three feet high at the center and most of the time created a dense white plume of smoke that most of the time rose to the south, in the direction of Yvonne's shop and the very big Douglas fir and western red cedar pair that flanked both ends of it, features of the site we took into account when planning where to put the shed. Because the hill began to rise here I'd had to excavate the hillside a bit to accommodate the rear of the shop.

The burning went slower than I expected, new greenery significantly slowing down the fire until its intense heat could boil the moisture out of the needles. Not long after 6:00 Yvonne came out carrying a tray with our dinner on it and we sat at the lavender colored picnic table inside the rain shelter, the translucent polycarbonate roof above, needles partly filling the valleys in its corrugation, one or the other of us getting up to feed the fire from time to time. And it seemed to both of us we should make the shelter a some-time dinner venue when guests are on hand and the weather is warm enough. I told her about the review of a new book on Susan Sonntag I'd read in the *New York Review of Books,* the current state of eNotated Classics, and my ideas for making the Crane Island Association bookkeeping process more efficient and less expensive. She told me how she would be taking a meal to Joan next week, Joan a widow now, after Roger, 92, suffered a massive stroke while they visited Glacier National Park and then lived another nine days in a nursing home nearby, long enough for his family to say goodbye. And she told me about how she would appear twice in the Independence Day parade on Saturday on Orcas, with the Food Bank and the Garden Club. And we talked some more about brother Ron and his experiences in Seattle where he was building an acupuncture practice and playing a leadership role in a mens' group where one of the problems some of the men were having was convincing their partners (a woman, a man?) to be polyamorous or as Yvonne said what used to called wife-swapping. Ron, single and nearly 60, couldn't quite figure it out. This was an aspect of Seattle we didn't know — were too un-hip to know but it sounded to me like the men just wanted to have sex with as many women as they could. For time out of mind.

About 8:00, with the coals raked out and no visible flames, though still very hot, we left the fire and went inside, smelling, not bad though, of wood smoke. Later Yvonne made a check. The fire was safe. I had begun reading William James' *The Varieties of Religious Experience* and was finding it surprisingly relevant to the current debate on the topic, more insightful, in fact, than most of what was being written. His science was out of date but not his argument. The fire was still safe when I checked it at 3:00 a.m.

Two-hundred-fifty-six: Six Big Firs

"Age is an issue of mind over matter. If you don't mind, it doesn't matter." - Mark Twain

Because the Crane Board meeting was only eight days away and because we'd have to adopt a budget we could send to the members at least a month ahead of the annual meeting in August, I wanted the two-member Finance Committee to review the budget and make recommendations in the next five days so I put my latest budget draft in the form we've presented them in the past and sent e-mails with explanations and Excel spreadsheet attached early in the morning, after reviewing the numbers several times. By raising lot dues from $700 to $800 per year we'd have enough revenue for necessary road and dock maintenance projects, even with declining use fees (members were conserving water as we'd asked them to and therefore water billing was falling, and they were storing their boats elsewhere or using their own dock, which we'd encouraged).

The six big firs, intersecting lines that made it difficult to walk across the yard, the result of Wednesday's tree massacre, had been stripped of branches and greenery and that either burned or stacked waiting for the chipper, had to be cut and moved to the firewood area in the front yard. Using a conversion table I found on the internet I calculated that the six trees represented about 2 1/2 cords of firewood and weighed 6 1/2 tons.

First I created entry to all parts of the yard by cutting sections out of downed trunks large enough, at least, to get our dock/yard cart through. One trunk, lying on top of another got in the way of the outer, public path through the salal that neighbors used as a shortcut to their properties, so I cut eight 14" slices from the overhang. The 85' plus tree extending along most of the length of Margaret's driveway was my first target. Margaret, John, and I had rolled her boat trailer out of the way before John downed the tree, none of us sure exactly where the top would land and that had been a good decision. Since this tree lay across another extending up our common driveway, at a right angle to Margaret's, it made sense to take advantage of the target tree being raised more than a foot off the ground, about 1/4th its length up the trunk. I put blocks under the butt end where I'd make a cut and pushed wedges John had made when creating face cuts under the trunk to prevent it from rolling once I'd made a cut, at about the 1/8 height line. Once cut, a portion of the tree now overhung the log underneath, making it very simple to cut 14" to 16" sections. That done, I turned my attention to the longer section of the log extending from the supporting tree to the tip, up Margaret's driveway. I picked some 2 x 4 and 1 x 4 pieces from the scrap wood pile behind my shop and used them to support the areas where I'd make cuts, top to bottom. Because the ground wasn't perfectly level and because the trunk lay on the stubs of branches that had broken off when hitting the ground, I could find places here and there under the trunk where I could tap wood scraps under; in some cases two 2 x 4s and a 1 x 4 under the trunk. It's important to hold the trunk up when cutting through or the cut may cause the two sides to bind the saw and twice I hadn't supported the to-be cut area adequately so that before I could finish it the two sides had sunk lower, closing the gap above and binding the saw. I retrieved a wrecking bar from my shop and pried the shorter portion away from the rest of the trunk, freeing the saw bar.

With all but the bottom 10' of the trunk now sliced up — in 14" lengths for the thicker sections and 28" to 30" lengths for the upper part of the tree, I could begin to cart them to the firewood area in the front yard, fortunately mostly downhill. Since much of the area I used in the past for wood to be split was already occupied by three trees Tim had cut, three I'd cut, and three that I had brought from the community beach where they'd landed after escaping from a log boom, I established a new area where the six big trees, 2 1/2 potential cords, could dry out over the next 18 months. By 3:00 I'd had enough cutting and hauling.

256: Moving tree sections by dock cart to to front yard splitting and storage location

Yvonne had worked on her garden all day, on the water side, within the deer fence, cutting back drying daffodils and transplanting from pots she'd brought to Crane recently. With the sky blue now, the afternoon sun drenched her garden surrounding the studio deck, the payoff from downing the six tall firs I would spend more days slicing, transporting and then eventually splitting to burn in our wood stove. Before our first house guests arrived July 14th she wanted to clean the green growth from our brown decks she'd stained two years before when I'd rebuilt and modified the house deck next to the lower studio deck to make easy passage between them. I provided two approaches, a commercial wood cleaner and an oxy bleach powder. The former was unacceptable because it contained a plethora of toxic chemicals. The latter, completely safe and useful for laundry, worked well, she found after adding it to water, applying it with a brush, letting it sit fifteen minutes, scrubbing a bit, and then rinsing it off. I had bought it through the internet to use for cleaning the house cedar siding before restaining but hadn't had time to try it out.

Jason had stopped by while I was woodcutting to tell me the tank was down to 11'. I called Gary and since he would be over to Crane to read the meters on this first day of a new month, he could add time to the pumps. I walked the quarter of a mile to check the tank level and found that Jason had read the top, not the bottom of the indicator that moves up and down the outside of the tank wall, a depth scale behind it. The tank was at 12'. I called Gary again to let him know. He would put more time on the pumps anyway since the level actually should have been higher by now.

At dinner Yvonne told me Margaret had gone to the Orcas Center for the evening to see a broadcast of the NY Metropolitan Opera using their new projection equipment. We both agreed we'd see about doing that in the future, my last visit to the Met having been in 1965. And we talked about more potential house improvements. Yvonne wanted wood flooring everywhere — but that would be too expensive so she'd settle for new carpet in the living room. I wanted to see skylights in the studio. I'd made arrangements during the day for a plumber to come to Crane the next Tuesday to lower the closet flange in the guest bathroom so I could install the new toilet at a normal height, undoing what Iris and Dean had considered an improvement. On our circuit of the island we talked about why the island in particular and the Pacific Northwest in general looks so parklike — our tentative conclusion being that since the grass doesn't die back over the winter — it's green year round — it makes it difficult for weeds to gain a foothold except where the soil has been disturbed, a benefit of the gentle winter rains and moderate temperatures.

As we neared the dock a banged up pick-up came our way, Peter driving and cab and bed filled with family, a gray-muzzled golden retriever unenthusiastically loping along behind. We said hello and they went on but the pooch stopped, turned around and began to walk with us in the direction of the dock. Peter was soon back and they took the dog aboard. Brooks and Gretchen wouldn't be up for the weekend. Did he check his e-mail? Probably not. I had sent him a coming fiscal year budget draft for review. I'd have to give him a call.

Two-hundred-fifty-seven: Parade

"Parades are a testament to the power of community, a celebration of our shared history and our collective dreams for the future." - Barack Obama

Five minutes before six, the rising sun in the northeast just coming over the forest on Orcas above Hobie and Susan's house reflected in the glassy surface of the Salish Sea, the outgoing tide running through Pole Pass disturbing the surface that isn't moving on either side. The two hummingbird feeders are empty, the two lawn chairs below the house and under a patient juniper and a struggling madrona warm themselves in the morning light that enters Raven Cove, most of the day shaded by firs, madronas, maples, and willows on the south bank.

Later, at Massacre Bay we pass Jack's house (Jack a UU island character who had died of Alzheimer's a few years before, Yvonne and I having picked him up sometimes to go to a service), his son Andy having just sold it and moved out and then a yard sale being set up at what used to be a B&B but we don't have time to stop.

Traffic is picking up in Eastsound for the parade and parking will soon become scarce. Because I intend to drop off a computer and printer at the new Food Bank building on the grounds of the Community Church we pull into the lot there and look for a key, hidden somewhere Yvonne heard, but we can't find it so I take the 8' bamboo pole from the van, and advised by Yvonne not to poke anyone (Do I look like I'm gonna?) we walk through the Island Market lot, through the Home Grown Market passage between Plum Alley and North Beach Road and cross to the Village Green where the Farmers Market is open and bustling. Joyce's booth occupies the same spot as last year, her sewing products hung everywhere, colorful, cute, and conscientiously done. Larry will man the booth (heretofore, womaned, but no one gets it) while Joyce joins us with the Food Bank group, walking in the parade — our theme

Two-hundred-fifty-seven: Parade

— Thank you Orcas — and an invitation to attend the open house July 10th. Joyce has the banner Yvonne had made last year, we hang it on the bamboo pole and the three of us walk over to and up Prune Alley to School Road and find parade formation position 11 right behind the American Legion group. We're soon joined by two or three others but are then advised by a parade official that the sequence had been changed and we need to move to position 27, around the corner on Madrona. That doesn't seem to me like a very good way to run a parade. We're concerned about how others wanting to join the Food Bank group, will find us. We see a yellow "27" painted on the chip seal street and take our places, Yvonne explaining to me how we should hold the sign (Didn't we already do this last year? Did I forget?). The others find us, carrying thank you signs on sticks, and Sharon is soon telling me about her house for sale, how she has too many books, and so on. Yvonne and Joyce go back to location 11 on School Road to direct stragglers to our new spot and the other Food Bank marchers retreat to a spot in the shade, leaving me with Sharon. Undirected she will talk non-stop, jumping from topic to topic in free association, a monolog rather than conversation — so I keep moving the conversation back to topics I have some interest in, books and real estate, but I'm relieved when Yvonne and Joyce finally return, the other women come back to the street from the shade and someone else begins talking with Sharon.

Immediately ahead is the Orcas Chamber Music Festival group, directed by Victoria, who resigned as director of the Library before I joined the Board and just before the parade begins to move assembles the group and asks me to take the photo. One of their two antique cars is a 1941 Packard Woody that reminds me of the car my uncle John offered to sell my father — who reluctantly declined when he determined that it wouldn't fit in our garage on Washington Street, in Lombard, a Chicago suburb. The Orcas Center group would precede the Chamber Music Festival group and I'd been watching them attentively though I hoped unobtrusively because their exhibit was a team of younger rather than older leotard dressed women who were practicing a choreographed dance number accompanied by drum and saxophone. Though they all made the same moves they made them very differently, expressing, I supposed, differences in their personalities and I began to form theories about what they were and then the parade had begun.

Two-hundred-fifty-seven: Parade

257: July 2nd parade in Eastsound; Food Bank says thank you.

Most of the spectators gather at the intersection of North Beach Road and A Street, where the Orcas Band is playing, announcers are reviewing the entries as they pass by and expressing thanks to the Food Bank for its service to the community and to the community for contributing the funds to make the new building possible. Everyone is invited to the open house the 10th. Yvonne and I each see friends and acquaintances as we walk the route, the crowd congratulatory of the Food Bank and those of us representing it waving Thank You signs and saying so out loud. Earlier when we walk to the park to find Joyce and Larry, heart of the group, Yvonne and I talked about how much we had enjoyed our first Orcas Fourth of July Parade in 2001, being struck by the intimacy and smallness of it, a small town parade three blocks long with 400 people — with cars, bicycles, wagons, and floats, passing in front of maybe 1500 spectators.

When we reached Main Street and the end of the route, Yvonne doubled back to walk with the Garden Club and Joyce, her daughter and I walked back to the park so that Joyce could relieve Larry so he and I could go to the Food Bank building and bring in and set up the computer and printer. About the time I had made certain everything was working as it should (I created a page in Word and printed it out) and had introduced Larry to the system, Yvonne appeared. Connection to the internet would have to wait until the CenuryLink service person installed the DSL modem.

At Island Market I stopped to talk with Judith, she and Barbara home for the summer after teaching fall and spring semesters at Lewis and Clark in Portland. We'd have them over before they went back to school — and Judith was interested in doing an eNotated edition of U.S. law cases that changed history. We stopped briefly at the rental center on Enchanted Forest Road but they didn't carry or didn't know whether they had saw chains compatible with the Oregon S62 18" chain, what I was looking for. I had lots more cutting to do and wanted a spare chain or two. Nothing doing. We stopped to drop off John's rain jacket, forgotten after the tree felling session, and since he and Suzanne weren't home I hung it on their front door knob. Farther along we picked out a berry bowl at Orcas Pottery for Casey and Jodi, in Boulder, having just married and soon moving in with his father, Loren, my friend and former business partner, east of town. The Orcas Pottery site, in the sunshine, pottery on tables all over the lawn facing the Straight of Georgia and Vancouver — almost visible in the day and its lights evident at night — has a striking setting and beautiful pottery thrown by local artisans in the studio next to the shop. At the lumber yard, Island Hardware & Supply, I inquired about saw chains but what they had wouldn't work for me though I did buy a new pair of gloves, the rubber face on my old pair mostly gone. Kate and Ken pulled into the lot to buy gas. They'd spent Friday on San Juan Island facilitating the inspection of a house their client had made an offer on. Everything looked good for a closing soon. Their second client and offer were underway — and a third client had just made an offer. Good news.

On the way home, at Massacre Bay, an eight-year old boy waved a yard sale sign and we pulled off the road to visit the sale we passed on our way to Eastsound earlier in the day. Yvonne found some ceramic tile she'd mount as a back splash over the sinks in the pantry. I bought four six-inch dock cleats I thought I might be able to use with our treehouse project coming up with Borgfest, the family gathering beginning at the end of July. And then Michael came in with his truck to pick up a kennel, a wheeled trash can, and other odds and ends, including the rest of the cleats. I told him everyone had appreciated Kat's letter in the Sounder, acknowledging help and care from the community as she struggled with her mysterious illness and now her extended recovery — especially Howard and Sheila. Stuart and Liz were unloading at the Orcas dock. They'd be on Crane for the next six weeks. He was working on a new book on Mind and I told him I'd used material from his last book for a UU talk. We'd get together and visit. Liz and Yvonne would figure out a dinner occasion.

The sun on the studio deck, no longer entangled in the firs John had dropped on Wednesday, now fell on Yvonne, lying on her chaise lounge chair. She was in heaven. Not able to keep my eyes open, I snoozed on the living room love seat. So much excitement. I was exhausted.

Two-hundred-fifty-eight: Another Parade

"The only person you are destined to become is the person you decide to be." - Ralph Waldo Emerson

This would be our fourth Crane "Third of July parade," Molly's innovation five years before and this the sixth occasion. Margaret had responsibility for food for the picnic at Clark's cabin following the parade and I helped her take supplies over at 10:00, benefiting from having our F150 on Crane. Jim and Nancy had already set up their hot dog cart, Dick had mowed the lawn of what had once been a grass tennis court but would today serve as a game field. At 11:00, Yvonne, Margaret, and I walked to the dock parking lot. Dan would drive the fire truck and we'd drive the Fire and Rescue vehicle. Looking toward the dock I could see that it was swarming with people, already crowded with boats, with three more looking for space to moor. On the dock I began to consolidate boats and direct traffic and before long everyone could come ashore. Who were all these people I'd never seen before? From Double Island it turned out, in West Sound, legacy of the Kaiser presence, regular Crane parade attendees. Warren and Laurie arrived from the other side of Pole Pass, she expertly parking their fishing boat in a space with only a few feet to spare. Though I didn't count the all-ages crowd, I guessed it numbered just shy of 100, a big group for our little island, topped only by the 120 plus that appeared for the Crane Island Association 50th anniversary party the previous summer. Martha carried a bullhorn, welcomed everyone and then handed it to Jason — who recited the Pledge of Allegiance with Star Spangled Banner singing taking place at Clark's later. The parade would begin now.

Dan headed out with the fire engine, followed by a motley collection of vehicles of all sizes — from Gators to Tom H's restored army surplus supply truck, now labeled the Crane Island Civil Defense vehicle. Half a dozen spectators watched the rest of us pass by, and bringing up the rear we parked the Fire and Rescue vehicle at the Fire Station/Community Center, me concerned that it be able to make a service call should that be necessary without being tied up in traffic. We walked the next several hundred yards to Clark's, Margaret and I each carrying a big watermelon. Dick came up shortly with his van full, three men standing on the rear bumper that now nearly touched the ground. They'd take the melons to the picnic site.

258A: Assembling for the Crane July 3rd Parade

Peter acted as master of ceremonies, directing the games on the old grass tennis court. First up — the water balloon toss and Yvonne and I did pretty well until the ballon burst all over her when she was about 30' away. When only four or five couples were left, Peter substituted raw eggs for balloons, one making a mess on one of the catchers. With two couples left, 50 feet apart,

Peter declared them both winners. Two years before I'd fallen over backwards trying to catch the egg Yvonne had thrown over my head. Four years ago at our first picnic I'd joined the foot race group, coming in third to two teenage boys but not the last by any means. Peter led the group in three legged and sack races and a boat fender toss, the kids and their parents and sometimes grandparents participating while the rest of us watched.

258B: The parade begins

Seeing Stuart, I asked whether he had any comments on the budget draft I'd sent him for review. Only a question about the advisability of raising dues by $100 per lot. Why not just make smaller contributions to the reserves? If we needed more money we could just do a special assessment. Why not wait for a full reserve study before making any decision about dues? I acknowledged that he had a good point but that the board was operating on the principle of avoiding special assessments, which can be difficult to get agreement for and

Two-hundred-fifty-eight: Another Parade

hard for some people to pay, that the last long range plan advised putting away $30,000 per year and that the Board considered that its duty, that with costs rising and service fees declining (lower water use, less dock use) our revenue was inadequate for our normal operating expenses (like making a $3000 repair to the Orcas dock and $2000 repair to Crane roads). He wasn't convinced and turned to Jason to make his argument. The Board would talk this through at its meeting a week away. With Jason finishing his second consecutive three-year Board term, the last as President, we talked about who his successor might be, me not interested because of my water and treasurer duties and wanting to make improvements there, but we agreed that Martha would be effective — except then we'd loose her excellent services as Secretary of the Board. We both agreed that it was crucial the new president run effective meetings and keep the Board focused.

Later, sitting on the studio patio in the afternoon sun, Yvonne enjoyed a long conversation with Eric, catching him as he and his family headed to Bob's club for some pool time. They'd be leaving for Maui the next morning. She had watched our local raccoon come to her pond for a drink, from the side of the pond, not the rock peninsula with the snow lantern or the little dock I'd made. At dinner we talked about in-place lives and in-motion livesWe'd tried the latter years before, traveling between three different houses for a while and found it more frustrating than satisfying. Wherever we were we found we didn't have what we needed. It was at the other place. The travel between was time consuming and expensive. And we couldn't have a deep life, be really anywhere, when we were constantly coming and going. We would like to do more travel and perhaps in the future could manage some Elder Hostel trips, John M at the Crane picnic earlier in the day describing how much they'd enjoyed sessions in the U.S. and then this summer in France. I was convinced that when people of means don't know what to do with their time, have no real purpose for it, they fill their days with getting ready to go, going, settling in, and getting ready to go again, convincing themselves that they're actually doing something, that they're enjoying themselves. That wouldn't work for us, intent on having projects, on serving, on creating something worthwhile, on being with family and friends, on actually being where we were.

Yvonne would do more deck cleaning and I'd do windows in the morning so I walked to the community dock to retrieve our bottle of Boat Zoap, a dandy liquid cleaner you could use with salt water. I'd be cleaning the *Huginn* shortly but I'd found that Boat Zoap was especially effective cleaning our salt encrusted windows, especially those facing the water — otherwise getting the salt off without leaving streaks takes lots of fresh water, something on Crane we were careful not to waste.

258C: Egg toss excitement

The *Mud Puppy* was at the beach next to the community dock, its ramp down waiting for Dan to return from his house with a load to go to Orcas. At the picnic, Dan, Yvonne, Margaret and I had talked about the osprey pair nesting near his house, I finding I'd acquired some lore I could pass on to him. Wilma was at the helm of the *Mud Puppy*, a rusting landing craft, holding it to the beach and Gary and I continued our conversation about putting a remote pump switch into the tank, he explaining why trenching from well houses #5 and #6 to the tank, though expensive in the short run would be very useful in the long run, when we would want to put a transducer in the tank so that we could check the tank level and adjust the pumping remotely. That made a lot of sense.

In bed reading after 10:00, twilight outside, Yvonne and I could hear the fireworks in Deer Harbor. We'd watched them in the past, last year from the community dock and once from the *Gumption* on the water in Deer Harbor, when Morgan was a tot, but this evening we couldn't get interested enough to get out of bed. Gary and I had talked about fireworks earlier, both agreeing we could no longer generate much enthusiasm for them — except perhaps for occasions like the international competition Yvonne and I had seen with Loren and Janelle five years before on English Bay in Vancouver, BC, the Spanish team winning with an elaborate display I couldn't begin to imagine how they'd accomplished. I had begun to re-read Robinson's *Absence of Mind* now with a sharp pencil to underline key passages and make marginal note — imagining that Stuart K and I might talk about it later in the summer.

Two-hundred-fifty-nine: Fourth Open House

"The details are not the details. They make the design." - Charles Eames

About 9:00 a.m. I opened the studio gate in the deer fence to go next door to ask Margaret whether she would mind my running my chain saw — and there she was coming back from a walk with Moonie and about to ask whether I'd mind her running her chain saw. With Yvonne adding to the noise with her battery powered weed whacker, the three of us made quite a racket. I'd already cut up the tree that had fallen into Margaret's driveway. Now I worked on the tree that fell on our shared driveway that rises to the cul de sac of Eagle Lane. I cut the top 20' or so into sections light enough to lift into the cart and then began cutting 15" sections but my chainsaw wasn't cutting well. Was oil failing to reach the chain? I took the bar and chain off and cleaned around the clutch and oil feed but that made no difference. The chain was no longer sharp enough to cut the way it had when new just a few days before. I kept up the cutting anyway reducing the trunk to about 1/3 of its original length and then carted what I'd cut to the growing drying pile outside the deer fence in the front yard. Later when cleaning up I saw that one of the wood scraps I'd used to support the trunk when cutting had a nail in it and the nail had been scored by the chain. That explained why the almost new chain wasn't cutting well. I could hear Margaret's chain saw around her house all morning.

Yvonne had experimented with Stain Solver on the deck stairs and landing and was very pleased with the results: the green growth had disappeared and the opaque stain on the wood looked good, if not quite new. But she thought Stain Solver was too expensive so she tried detergent but even with lots of scrubbing the green growth remained. Stain Solver worked well for the rest of the deck but she had to work on her hands and knees and by 3:00 when

Two-hundred-fifty-nine: Fourth Open House

she finished she was tired. She'd used very little of the Stain Solver that I'd bought to clean the cedar siding on the house before putting on a new coat of translucent stain. I was eager to try it out but that would have to wait.

259: Busy Independence Day on the Crane Community dock at Pole Pass

We had been invited to join Chris and Lynn and Howard and Sheila and maybe some others in Reid Harbor on Stuart Island in a week. I'd been thinking of the *Huginn*, our 19' SeaSport as a marine truck — but it had a V-berth with an overhead hatch, reading lights, a sink with pressured water from a holding tank, a porta-potty, and lots of storage under the V-berth and on an overhead shelf. It never occurred to me that we could use the *Huginn* for boat camping (my expectations having been set by much bigger and better equipped boats we'd taken cruising). I cleared everything off the V-berth and

Two-hundred-fifty-nine: Fourth Open House

laid down. It would work. I'd clean up the *Huginn* and we'd take it to Reid Harbor and join our friends.

For some years I picked up spare life jackets of all sizes so we'd have plenty for our passengers of all sizes — but we wouldn't need all of them for this trip so I left six in the boat and stacked the balance in our dock cart — fifteen in all — and took them home, put them in a big plastic bag, and put it in our storage tent. Then I thoroughly cleaned the V-berth and cabin area, setting aside what belonged in the garbage. After a while Yvonne came down to the dock and found me cleaning the cabin floor — after I'd removed the carpeting, hung it over a fence, and beat it with our collapsable boat hook. We both got into the V-berth. It would still work. I pointed out all the storage locations to Yvonne so she could plan where to put what we'd take along. We still had some down sleeping bags we'd gotten 30 years before.

Now on the dock, Margaret asked me if I could take her latest yard sale acquisition to her house when I brought our dock cart home. Of course. Happy to.

About 5:00 Yvonne and I left Crane to attend Jens' and Susan's open house in Orcas Highlands. We met Jeorge, his younger brother who would return to Germany in two days. Jens and Susan had invited Chris and Lynn and a number of neighbor couples, most like them new to Orcas and a bit younger than us. I'd talked with Jeorge about the financial problems besetting the European Union and what he thought of American politics. I'd told those interested about Jens' Kafka ebook and passed around my Nook for them to exercise it. One techie liked the idea; a retired librarian said it would interfere with the reading process, and Jeorge was impressed with the clarity of the Nook screen. As the sun set behind Saturna, in Canada, fifteen miles north and west, Yvonne and I left the group and drove back to Deer Harbor and they watched the Eastsound, Lopez Village, Friday Harbor, and Roche Harbor fireworks from their perch on the flank of Mt. Constitution, 800' above East Sound. We passed through Eastsound as hundreds converged on the waterside park to watch fireworks up close, as we had done with Noah, Natasha, and Morgan years earlier. It was cool now with the sun gone and many carried blankets and wore jackets. As we drove along Massacre Bay, now about 10:10, the northwest horizon glowed red, with a sickle moon soon to follow the sun and crossing to Crane later from the dock on Orcas, the sky and reflected light on the water was bright enough that we didn't need a flashlight.

Two-hundred-sixty: Plumbing Help

"Our houses are our corners of the world...they are our first universe, a real cosmos in every sense of the word." - Gaston Bachelard

Yvonne was in a dither. She'd been asked to pick up plants for landscaping the new Food Bank building at the Christiansen Nursery near La Connor this day but no one had provided a list. Her plan had been to take the 8:50 ferry and return on the 12:30 and be home by 2:30. Because we'd moved our pickup to Crane she'd be using the van. But by the time we'd gone to bed the night before she'd heard nothing — she didn't have a list. Then this morning she came out of the bedroom before 7:00 to check her email. She'd gotten the list. She was going to America. I took her over to Orcas.

Ron, the plumber I'd talked to the week before would be at the Orcas dock at 10:00 and come to Crane to put a new closet flange on the toilet waste pipe in the guest bathroom, the current model now inappropriately sitting 3 1/2 inches off the floor — which the height the toilet I was replacing had been raised by Dean and Iris, the original owners. Ron was coming down the ramp as I pulled up to the dock in the *Huginn*. Because he couldn't drive his truck to our house he'd packed ABS parts into a tub and tools into two five gallon buckets.

Ron had never been to Crane but knew Steve G and his family since both families had participated in 4H. Who's big catamaran is that? Hobie A's. Yes, of course. And where is Warren M's house? Just to the right and Howard W Jr's house is right at Pole Pass. Ron had done work for or otherwise known about Mike S and I pointed out that Jim J owned property on Orcas he was now trying to sell. Why had we moved to Crane? Because we liked the house and wanted waterfront property and it was half-a-million dollars less expense on Crane compared to Orcas. Then Ron told me he'd been offered $1.8m for his 20 acres with 600 feet of waterfront near Orcas Pottery, property he'd bought in 1997 at what were now bargain prices. He'd moved his family to

Two-hundred-sixty: Plumbing Help

Orcas from King County but continued to work there until the 2008 crash when the real estate development firm where he managed two teams of plumbers laid off all 60 as well as their carpenters and everyone else and shut down the project. I was grateful he was available and willing to come to Crane Island.

I showed Ron the waste pipe and flange sticking up above the floor. I'd brought a hose in the house earlier in the day to clean it out, thinking that might be helpful to him or less gross but he didn't seem to care one way or another. Then he wanted to see the plumbing below the floor — in the crawl space — accessible from under the deck outside the dinning area. I'd left a halogen light on a long extension cord in the crawl space — always useful — but it wouldn't light — or the light on a switch by the access door. Hmm. Nothing off in the house circuit box. I disconnected the extension cord from an outdoor outlet near the dining room door that Yvonne had run to the pump in her little pond outside the deer fence — the pump having mysteriously stopped working the day before — and connected the halogen light to it. Nothing doing. Ah! The crawl space and outdoor outlets must be on the same circuit and the circuit must have a ground fault protection feature that has flipped off. I found the outlet inside and reset it. Light in the crawl space.

Ron and I crawled in and looked at the toilet plumbing from below. He described how he would cut out some of the connectors and then put everything back together, the closet flange then level with the floor above. But what about cutting the waste pipe at floor level in the bathroom and attaching a new closet flange to the shortened ABS pipe? I thought that might work. Back in the bathroom he cut the pipe down and then looking at it thought the flange would still be too high. I told him that I was going to put down a new floor and that would add 3/8" to the height of the floor and I got some Marmoleum scraps left over from doing the master bathroom floor from my shop and he thought that might work. He glued in the new closet flange and then told me he had accidentally made it too high. It was about 3/8" higher than the Marmoleum samples under it. But he'd make it right. He'd come back another day and rip it all out and do it over. I suggested we set the toilet on it to see whether the extra height would really matter. It didn't seem to. He thought it wouldn't leak though I might want to use a special sealing ring rather than wax. He was done — except then I remembered that I'd already bought a frost free sill cock to replace one that leaked (my guess was that a hose had been left attached during freezing temperatures) and he thought he could. I found some pipe glue and turned off the water. Ron returned to the crawl space, cut the feed line and glued on the shut off valve that should have been part of the sill cock system.

260: Summer salad

The existing sill cock passed through a 4" thick concrete house trim feature and whacking it with a hammer wouldn't dislodge it. I found some 3/4" pipe but the sill cock was 7/8" so the pipe was more or less useless. He tried a chisel I found in my shop but that was very slow going. I'd figure it out later and was happy that I could now work on the guest bathroom floor and new toilet. I paid Ron, thanked him and took him back to Orcas. I checked the UPS cabinet and found that the special retrofit Oatey closet flange had been delivered — and I was surprised because my email to the retailer asking for delivery information had never been responded to. I'd use it, perhaps, when installing a new, lowered toilet in the master bath.

Earlier in the day I ordered two new saw chains through Amazon but when Yvonne called saying she wouldn't be able to make the 12:30 ferry because the pick up process at Christiansen's was taking too much time and asked whether I wanted her to pick anything up I gave her the Oregon saw chains part number and suggested she look for it at Lowes' in Burlington. Later she called again when leaving Costco asking whether I could think of anything else. I sent her to Home Depot nearby to look for 7/8" OD pipe or metal rod. The store didn't carry anything like that. How about a 7/8" metal cutting drill bit — the sill cock pipe was made of copper and so it might be possible to drill it out. They did have a bit like that and she bought it.

The ferry line was crowded, the ferry was packed, and took forever to unload so she wasn't back in the Crane parking lot on Orcas until 5:30, tired and psychically depleted from her trip to America. I'd made a little progress putting down a new floor in the bathroom, taking my time to make it look nice. I had spare Marmoluem planks available and that was a good thing since I ruined two almost immediately. At dinner I told Yvonne I was concerned about the intersection of floor and tub but that I thought translucent caulking might work. Pointing out what a shoddy job I'd done last time I used it, she suggested, no insisted, that she do the caulking. Fine with me. She caught up on her email and then it was time for a Netflix Instaplay.

Two-hundred-sixty-one: Sympathy

"There is no grief like the grief that does not speak." - Henry Wordsworth

Another sunny day, deep blue sky, almost no clouds, calm dawn waters becoming frisky by afternoon. As I approached the Crane dock on my way to Howard's for a Greybeards session I saw a lone brown duck (female) in the shallow receding water and a small head bobbing toward the rocky shore — a mink it turned out — that was carrying a crab to some place private for breakfast.

As I entered Howard's honeymoon cottage, David was finishing a story about how Maxine was now questioning the wisdom of selling their house and moving off island — something she had suggested they do when David went through a period when he required hospitalization though he had been healthy since. They'd built their house so that they could live on one level and with a lower level that could accommodate live-in household help, should they need it. That had been a reasonable plan in the past. It could be a reasonable plan going forward. David was certain that at some point they'd need help to continue living on Orcas or have to move to someplace they could get it. Later, walking through Howard's garden we marveled at how much it had grown in the last few weeks. He'd collected two gallons of raspberries and looked forward to 30 (last year's crop) — the berry plants protected by netting. The potato plants (several different varieties) were flowering, beans were growing and squash would soon flower.

I stopped at the marina store to buy the *Seattle Times* and *Islands' Sounder* for Yvonne and to pick up the mail at the Deer Harbor Post Office. Over the weekend the marina had been packed. This morning a few slips were empty but would probably be filled by afternoon. Summer in the San Juans begins on the Fourth of July and ends on Labor Day, a short season of mostly dry, sunny, and warm but not hot days. I'd been aware of the substantial increase in traffic

Two-hundred-sixty-one: Sympathy

coming through Pole Pass from the east, at one point seeing a dozen boats in a line stretching from near Pole Pass to the Ferry Landing two miles to the east, with another ten boats, half under sail, with local itineraries. Pole Pass is a gateway to the Gulf Islands off the southeastern end of Vancouver Island and part of the same archipelago the San Juans belong to. Some of the boats would head farther north, to Desolation Sound or to Juneau, almost 1000 miles north through the Inside Passage.

Yvonne had a Food Bank board meeting at 2:00 and had volunteered us to help with the move into the new building beforehand. I would meet with Judith to talk about eNotation and her experience teaching law in Portland. George and another man were completing the shingling on the porch roofs sheltering the new building's two front doors, a trellis between them. He came down from the roof to help move potted plants Yvonne had picked up at Christiansen's the day before to a spot under a big maple on the church lawn. Roses would grow along one end of the trellis and wisteria the other. Larry handed me the DSL modem he'd received from CenturyLink, the local telephone service provider, a wireless mouse, and a cordless telephone with two additional handsets. I had set up the new computer and printer on Saturday and now added the connection to the internet. Because the DSL modem box hadn't included a filter for attaching a handset to the line I couldn't set up the telephone. I'd send one with Yvonne when she went to town the next day.

I met Jens and Judith in the Library foyer, introduced them to each other and gave Jens his stock certificate; he was now an owner of eNotated Classics. We were both pleased; and Judith and I walked the two short blocks to Enzo's to sit and talk, finding nowhere in the Library to sit. Enzo's was busy as well and while Judith and I sipped our ice teas, I brought her up to date on our project and showed her Jens' book on my Nook but mostly on my iPad and she immediately began to see applicability to the teaching of law, her vocation at Lewis and Clark in Portland. We'd collaborate on a prototype during the fall, Judith providing me with materials or telling me where to find them, including audio perhaps, and me experimenting with ways to present the material that would facilitate study. Afterwards, at the Library waiting for Yvonne to appear after her Food Bank Board meeting I talked with Phil, the Director, Holly, and Mary about what the Library was doing with ebooks and what it would really like to do.

Two-hundred-sixty-one: Sympathy

Crossing in the *Huginn* to Crane and home, Yvonne sat outside in the cockpit; the cabin was too warm in the afternoon sun, though the outside temperature wasn't more than 75. At 5:10 we returned to Orcas, Yvonne carrying a sack in each hand — one containing a fresh baked blueberry pie and the other fixings for a salad niçoise with poached salmon. I offered to carry one or both but my offer was declined. She didn't consider that safe.

261: Yvonne at Huginn's helm

Joan opened her front door with a smile, warm greetings and hugs for us, though her eyes were sad. Roger had been gone a week now, having lingered, unconscious in a Kalispell nursing facility nine days after suffering a vascular stroke in Glacier National Park on a sightseeing trip he very much wanted to

Two-hundred-sixty-one: Sympathy

do and that Joan suspected might be their last together. At 94, he'd become frail over the last two years, but had skied, boated, and played tennis, into his 90s. Wanting to talk about Roger and their life together, I reminded Joan that we'd first met them at Deep Cove Chateau, on the west side of the Saanich Peninsula, on Vancouver Island, during a Yacht Club cruise. We sat with Roger and Joan at dinner and much enjoyed their conversation. Roger's last days had brought the family together in Kalispell and they'd convene again in August for a memorial service in Eastsound we'd attend. Sue and Al had organized friends and neighbors to bring Joan dinners and company during this first difficult period. We continued our conversation at the table, the light, direct and reflected by the expanse of water that began not 30 feet from where we sat and extended west to Sydney by the Sea on Vancouver Island. Yvonne and I had been attracted by Roger and Joan's integrity — smart, caring, involved people that had little time and sympathy for nonsense. Back in the Crane parking lot, I took a sack in each hand and carried them, now lighter, to the *Huginn*, the sun nearing the horizon.

Two-hundred-sixty-two: Operational

"Your home should tell the story of who you are, and be a collection of what you love." - Nate Berkus

Yvonne took off for Orcas and Eastsound about 10:00, frustrated at having so much to do — clean the van, hair cut, work on the Community Club grounds. When are we going to start to have fun? But when she drove past the Community Club she saw that someone had trimmed all around the building — probably Taylor, and probably strongly encouraged by his mother Pam. She smiled and relaxed and told herself to get over being in a grumpy mood.

Time was running short. Our first batch of guests would appear in a week and we'd be gone some of that time to Reid Harbor and were committed to volunteer and social obligations that would absorb at least half those days. I needed to lay the new bathroom floor and install the toilet, cut and move five big trees to the firewood area, clean the *Huginn* cockpit, launch our daysailer, *Discovery*, prepare for the Crane Board meeting (in preparation for the Annual Meeting), and catch up on correspondence.

First — Crane business: I'd received the June water usage figures from Gary and was pleased to see that the difference between pumped and metered was only 2500 gallons, what it had been in May, a huge improvement over the beginning of the year when as much as 30,000 gallons per month was disappearing, more in fact, by far, than was actually being consumed. We had found the leak in the line from well house #4 to the main line and then Gary had laid new pipe to bypass the leak. Adding usage by meter to the June column of the annual water report I had only July to go to finish the year. That report, a spreadsheet, would provide input to the member bills that would go out in August. I sent the updated (as of June 30) water usage report to Martha for distribution to the Board. I'd had responses to the budget draft from all three Finance Committee members, one questioning the need to raise dues by $100 per lot, suggesting first that we could raise the water meter fee instead by

$100 — which would raise less new revenue but could be justified by the fact that the water system fees didn't pay its operating costs and second that if we couldn't make a $30,000 deposit to reserves by the end of the fiscal year it didn't really matter. We could always levy a special assessment in an emergency. I sent the current General Ledger and Cash report, along with the budget draft and discussion to Martha for distribution.

Now I could work on the bathroom. I'd removed the old toilet and wooden pedestal that raised it 3 1/2", disconnected the plumbing from the sink, and moved the unit into the hall, removed the trim and door, and pulled the vinyl flooring up. Ron, the plumber, had installed a new closet flange — a bit too high. Now I began putting the bathroom back together, starting with the Marmoleum flooring, a click-together, 12" x 36" plank with cork on the back and a linoleum-like floor covering on the front. There were only two problematic areas: the doorway/threshold and the closet flange. I had two spare pieces of flooring to substitute should I wreck any in the process. I'd laid down a row of planks with the closet flange (7" diameter) positioned equidistant from both sides of a plank and then started fitting the flooring at the door, moving toward the back of the room. When I got to the closet flange row, I measured to the center of the flange from the tub and from the last plank row, used a compass to draw a 7 1/2" circle on a plank and then cut out the circle so I could lay the plank over the flange — after I'd put some of the cutout under the flange to support it and then completed the last row of flooring. I screwed the flange to the floor, then put a wax ring around the hole in the bottom of the toilet, then placed the toilet on the flange (right side up of course), lined up the floor bolts and pushed the toilet down onto the wax ring, slowly tightening the floor bolts thus bringing the foot of the bowl down flat on the floor. As I expected, the flange wasn't too high. I fastened the tank to the back of the toilet bowl unit and attached the water feed hose to the bottom of the tank. Because the toilet was lower than the previous model, the feed hose was too long and leaked a bit. I applied pipe compound and that slowed but did not entirely stop the leak. I'd have to do something about that. Then I reinstalled the sink and cabinet and found that the sink wouldn't drain properly. Why not? The drain pipe was full of paper, now black. How had it gotten there? Someone would have had to pull out the drain stopper, put the paper into the drain pipe and then replaced the stopper. A mystery I'd probably never get to the bottom of.

262: Orcas Island Pottery treasures

I replaced a threshold piece that connected the laminate flooring in the hall with the new Marmoleum flooring in the bathroom, put the trim back (in a temporary way — I'd have to use my pneumatic brad gun to finish) and then put the door back in place — and it closed over the new floor without scraping (something I was reasonably but not completely confident about). I'd also need to put some kind of trim over the space between the edge of the flooring and the tub but the bathroom worked again. That was key.

And then Yvonne came home, her hair cut back into a bob (when she'd departed from that style a few months earlier she'd regretted it — I liked her in a bob best) and then washed and arranged it to her liking. She'd had a good day, along the way stopping at the new Food Bank building, volunteers busy stocking it with supplies from the Community Church basement 40 feet away, the current home of the Food Bank, and gave Larry a DSL filter I had so that the phone could be used simultaneously with internet access and found out that Larry and Joyce were frustrated because the Windows 7 standard time for the automatic log-off was too short. I'd have to find out how to change that setting. She'd washed and vacuumed the van, including cleaning all around the inside of the door frames, but not before being frustrated with the car wash next to the NAPA store and its unresponsive staff (who preferred talking to each other to talking to a customer — her — who had come into the store looking for help). She was very pleased with the new floor, a marbly carmel color that matched the dark brown antique (laminate) hickory flooring in the hall outside and the almost forest green walls inside.

We ate dinner early because I had been recruited by Margaret to be part of a team to bring her new, custom made, 200 pound birdbath from Orcas to Crane but about 5:45 she called to say that she and Steve had taken advantage of his versatile hand truck to do the move so Yvonne and I could use our found time to walk Circle Road, meeting Dan and Jan and their 14 week old labradoodle (black coat and white feet and tail tip) coming the other direction, and then Liv and her daughter, Liv, like John, happy to be back on Crane for the summer after their bouts with pneumonia. And then we were home in plenty of time to watch Sofia Coppola's new film, *Somewhere*. Though for each of us the day at its beginning looked uncomfortably daunting, now at its end we each had a sense of accomplishment — what we like to have when we're not having fun.

Two-hundred-sixty-three: The Details

"The wheel is come full circle." - William Shakespeare

Though the sky was cloudy at dawn by 9:00 the blue sky to the southwest now covered Crane and while Yvonne printed out certificates of appreciation for Food Bank fund drive contributors I walked to the community dock and began to clean the *Huginn*'s cockpit, the open area behind the cabin with the engine compartment cover in the rear center occupying about half the deck area. I hadn't cleaned the cockpit in more than a year — and during that time it had had a half dozen maintenance and repair sessions and had carried many loads of trash to Orcas for disposal at the County transfer station.

I'd already cleaned out the cabin, and it was now a much more pleasant place to be. Today my first focus was the black streaks and scratches on the white gelcoat, the smooth surface covering the fiberglass, the result of using the cockpit like the bed of a truck. I found a can of what looked like kitchen cleanser, a creamy white powder, and wet a rag with fresh water I'd carried to the boat and applied it to the a stain. Some rubbing and it was gone. Then I scrubbed some black gelcoat scratches and they came clean. I spent the next hour scrubbing every scratch and every stain. With the upper transom walls and the engine compartment clean, I dipped a five gallon bucket in sea water next to the boat, hauled it aboard, poured in some Boat Zoap, a cleaning product that worked in salt water as well as fresh and began to scrub the deck inside the cockpit. I rinsed the cockpit by dumping buckets of sea water into it, the water running out through ports on each side of the stern just above water line, protected from taking on sea water by ping pong ball check valves. The bow and cabin top were clean enough; I wouldn't spend any time on them. The green hull, on the other hand, needed cleaning, waxing, and buffing after thousands of dockings, not every one perfectly executed. And then it was time for an early lunch while Yvonne continued her Food Bank work on her old Mac iBook in the studio.

Two-hundred-sixty-three: The Details

After lunch I called Margaret to see whether she had any objections to my running my chain saw to cut up the 4 1/2 big trees lying in the backyard; she didn't but Yvonne did. She wanted to thoroughly clean the guest bathroom and I hadn't quite finished my work there. I needed to complete the re-installation of the trim, caulk around the toilet and along the edge of the tub and then somehow cover the caulked gap between flooring and tub, and cut down the floor bolts holding it to the closet flange so the caps would fit over them. I tried cutting the bolts using a metal blade in my Bosch jigsaw but the blade was too short for the constraints imposed by the structure of the toilet bowl so I took the slow route with a hacksaw. I found some tubes of Alex caulking and applied it next to the tub and 2' along the wall and then around the base of the toilet, very carefully wiping off the excess with a damp rag. I then wheeled my compressor from my shop to the house, carrying my brad gun, putting the compressor on the front porch and plugging it in. Once the tank was pressurized I secured the door and baseboard natural finish pine trim to the wall, pulling out finish nails Dean had used and I'd pounded in partially to temporarily hold the trim. I'd found a 6' piece of 1/2' concave pine molding and some teak stain in my shop (the can open along with another 20 cans of paint and stain I wanted to dry out so I could dispose of them) and cut it down to fit inside the trim at each end of the tub and then fastened it in place with the brad nailer. I called Yvonne in from her studio and she approved. I had one more task — to deal with occasional drips from the toilet water supply line but that would wait. By late afternoon Yvonne had cleaned the bathroom, put everything in its place and laid a new rug on the floor in front of the toilet and against the tub. Good work!

Now I could get to the tree trunks littering the yard. But as I brought all the tools and materials back to my shop that I'd used on the bathroom project to put them back I found I could no longer abide the mess in the shop so I spent a half hour arranging and discarding; not a complete job but good enough to withstand the casual scrutiny of our soon to arrive guests. Everything more or less put away and the shop floor swept, I put my chainsaw, gas, chain oil, wood scraps for blocking, and other tools in the cart and wheeled it to my next job site, the bottom half of the tree that fell up the driveway. I replaced the dull chain I was so frustrated with a few days before with a new one Yvonne had picked up a Lowes' when she was in America picking up plants for the Food Bank building landscaping. Since the 40' remaining lower half of the trunk lay flat on the ground I'd do the bucking by cutting 15" pieces 75% through, roll the log half over and finish the cuts. With the new chain, the saw created chips instead of dust, the chips pouring through the holes in the knees of my Levis and spilling down into my Muck shoes, my normal daily footwear. What a pleasure! Noise, the smell of two-cycle gasoline exhaust, a dangerous power tool, cleaning up the yard, and the prospect of a cozy fire later on. By 5:00, I'd cut and moved two trees to the wood pile. Three to go.

263: Yvonne tending her raised bed garden

Two-hundred-sixty-three: The Details

Don's suggestion that the Deer Harbor Community Club continue its potlucks through the summer so that seasonal residents could attend was being applied for the second time — now the second Friday in July. Howard, recently retired president, had suggested firing up the Club's grill for the event and by 6:30 most of the men attending were outside behind the kitchen either using or observing the grill. Yvonne had brought turkey burger patties, others had shish kabob, chicken, or steak. Bob, raised in Colorado, described spending summers on his uncles's ranch in North Park, near Steamboat Springs, where an entirely horse powered operation managed 1000 cattle, including cutting and stacking hay that would see the cattle through the brutal winters. The ranch operation is almost the same today except that elk and moose now feast on the hay stacks leaving less for the cattle. Phoenix newcomers Chuck and Diane had bought a house on Cayou Valley Road, up the hill from where we had lived and planned to spend summers on Orcas Island to get away from the insufferable summer heat in Arizona. Ken reported that their big sale was ready to close — no more contingencies — and would help them continue trying to make a living as realtors. During the official meeting portion after the meal Don, substituting for new president Becky, told everyone that Roger had passed away, though most already knew that and many were taking turns visiting and bringing meals to Joan.

Two-hundred-sixty-four: Short Strokes

"The more I contemplate the wonders of nature, the more I am convinced that the universe is not governed by chance but by a supreme intelligence." - Albert Einstein

While at the sink washing out my oatmeal pot after breakfast, I saw that a deer had walked down the wooden steps to the path that lead to the ramp that lead to our beach in Raven Cove — and the young buck, with velvet covered new antlers, was squatting and peeing on the path — and I was surprised — never having seen a deer pee — and half expected that the buck would lift one hind leg like a male dog. In the bright sunlight streaming down on the big studio deck and garden on either side after lunch, Yvonne and I each separately noticed a beautiful black and yellow butterfly, the shape of a down-pointing triangle flit through the space between gate and trellis, landing on a blue delphinium blossom, drinking the nectar, move to the next blossom, and then eventually flit away — only to return, Yvonne saw — to enjoy the neighboring day lilies that had opened a day or two before. The butterfly seemed to be a female eastern tiger swallowtail more than a thousand miles from its normal habitat. Later, in the afternoon, while in the kitchen Yvonne saw something moving outside the living room windows and realized that it was our local young raccoon walking along the porch railing on its way to the stairs that would take it down to the ground on its daily trip to the compost pile to look for treats. Then I saw a doe with two fawns come to Yvonne's little pond to drink. As we sat in the hot tub in the dusk I saw something fly from left to right and alight on a branch of the yew tree where Yvonne had harvested new, large Prince mushrooms earlier in the day, and I suspected that it was an owl. Yvonne got out of the tub for a better view. It was an owl, probably a barn owl, its face looking a bit like a cat with "ears" sticking up. Later she could hear it hooting outside the bedroom window — "Who cooks for you?"

Two-hundred-sixty-four: Short Strokes

264: Eastern tiger swallowtail

Before starting anything else I wrote my two sisters, replying, finally to their week-old emails, not having had the time or energy to do so earlier, excusing myself by describing in excruciating detail what all we had been doing, knowing that each of then would more likely think we were crazy than admire us for all we'd accomplished. Maybe so.

While Yvonne cleaned the outsides of all the windows — washing them with Boat Zoap and then removing the water with a squeegee, I sat through a productive 2 1/2 hour Crane Island Association Board meeting in the community building (that also served as the firehouse). Jason presided with Martha taking minutes and Dan, Dave, and I in attendance locally and Kate remotely through a telephone conferencing service and a conference phone on the picnic table we sat around. After reporting on the current financials (everyone had a the YTD general ledger and current cash report), I said that

Two-hundred-sixty-four: Short Strokes

overall we were on track to contribute our budgeted amount to reserves at year end. Then I reported that unaccounted for water remained minimal in June and that I was waiting for Gary to write a proposal for a tank float — pump shut off switch. Because Blair couldn't attend the meeting, I reported on progress with Waterfront Construction on repairing the rubber donut hinges that linked the breakwater float ("B") with the bottom of the U ("C") and Jason signed the contract I'd return to initiate the repair effort. The key focus for the meeting was acceptance of a budget for the coming fiscal year, beginning August 1st, to be approved at the members Annual Meeting August 20th. Rather than raise dues by $100, we'd raise the annual water access fee from $100 to $200, and consider the dues again after finishing the long range plan study the next spring, as Stu, a member of the Finance Committee had suggested. Dave led the discussion of the consolidated and updated policy document the members would also have to approve and Jason noticed the absence of airstrip policies. Dave pointed out that Jason hadn't submitted any and Jason replied that he would, immediately, if only to state clearly to the members that the runway was not a walking path, having seen a long-time family strolling there while he was working on his plane, and who told him they would do as they pleased after he asked them to vacate the grass airstrip. Deer are a problem. People who should know better are a worse problem. Then Dan complained that there were too many flights to and from the air strip, four, for instance on July 3rd, for the Island party. Jason, who would leave the Board after serving for the last six years, was eager to create a Crane website and I volunteered for the committee. I recounted how frustrating and expensive the bookkeeping services were and the group encouraged me to write up a recommendation for the next meeting.

Back home, the clean windows looked good and Yvonne had shampooed the carpet and by 4:00 wanted to take a break. I had picked up where I'd left off the day before, cutting up and moving the three remaining felled trees to a pile in the firewood area north of Yvonne's front garden. It was dirty, heavy work, though figuring out optimal strategies for dealing with each log in its particular setting (on top of another log, flat on the ground, gaps under some section, deep in the salal) was satisfying but I didn't think I could finish before dinner — but I did — deciding finally to throw away my old Levi's with open knees and now yellow stained from lichen-coated tree bark and I left them on the front walk before taking a shower before sitting down to dinner.

Two-hundred-sixty-four: Short Strokes

Mid-afternoon Margaret had interrupted my sawing to tell me she had found her septic tank, (the design drawing having nothing to do with reality), something she'd worked on for the last week and was worried about. She would be taking a homeowners septic system class on Orcas the coming week (as I had the previous year) so that she could report on her system to the County sanitation department, something all homeowners needed to do annually. I went to look. Her system was gravity-fed with a concrete tank and she'd found the lid, buried in about 18" of fill that had been excavated from the site of the addition she'd had added to her cabin some years ago. I was amazed she had been able to find it, the clue apparently a piece of PVC pipe placed upright when the lid had been covered.

Yvonne and I had worked very hard for the last several weeks and we had a bit more to do before our guests arrived on Thursday, but the house looked good and Yvonne continued to say how pleased she was with the new guest bathroom floor and toilet. I managed to stay awake until 10:00, tired but feeling very good physically. I knew it was true that hard physical work outdoors in the fresh air was a good thing but I was surprised in a way at how strong and younger I felt — except when I sat for any time and then found my joints frozen up. More to do of course but we now had two big piles of firewood to be split — though it would have to dry first — and the house was in the best shape ever. I was considering putting off cleaning and re-staining the siding until next summer — a big job. I'd see how I felt in mid-August after our guests had left.

Two-hundred-sixty-five: Grand Opening

"The only way to make sense of life is to grow into the belief that the world awaits your obedience, your loving service." - Ralph Waldo Emerson

Yvonne made cookies. I retrieved the porta-potti from the *Discovery*, sitting forlornly on its trailer in front of the Costco storage tent. At 2:00 the Food Bank was hosting an open house to introduce the community to its new building and to thank the individuals and groups that funded it. The next morning we'd make our way to Reid Harbor on Stuart Island in the *Huginn* to meet our friends and boat camp overnight.

The Thetford Porta-Potti had been a standard installed item on our 19' SeaSport, *Huginn*, but since we had no need for it there I took it out and put it in the hold of the Ranger, *Discovery*, our 20' day sailer, as an emergency resource for small children who might need it, though as far as I knew it hadn't been used. The *Discovery* was covered with two brown tarps stretched over its mast, the edges tied to the trailer, fore and aft, and to the other side of the tarp. I untied the lines holding down the starboard-aft corner and crawled under the tarp to find the porta-potti. Though covered, leaves had blown into the boat and it would need cleaning before launch. I brought the porta-potti back to the studio deck, separated the bowl from waste tank, rinsed both off and then because it turned out not to have been empty after all, poured the water from the latter into the toilet. When I removed the porta-potti from the *Huginn* I'd taken out the mounting brackets as well though couldn't remember what I'd done with them so I looked through my hardware inventory for alternatives but didn't find anything quite the right shape.

Two-hundred-sixty-five: Grand Opening

265A: At opening, Larry recounts the new Food Bank story

We left for Eastsound at 11:00, stopping at the marina store for the *Sunday Seattle Times* (all gone) and the Post Office to pick up the last several days of mail. Our first stop in Eastsound was Eastsound Sporting Goods, where Yvonne bought a crabbing license (the season would begin in five days), then Ray's Pharmacy where she picked up two bunches of helium filled balloons, and then Home Grown Market where she bought an ounce of dill. I stayed in the van and managed a short nap, still worn out, I suppose from all the sawing and carting I'd done the day before. Now close to noon, we parked in the Community Church parking lot in front of the Food Bank building and when Larry and Joyce appeared and unlocked the doors, I turned on their new computer, made some setting changes — so it would wait 30 minutes with no activity before engaging the screen saver and turning off the option to show the logon form after waking it up from the screen saver.

Two-hundred-sixty-five: Grand Opening

265B: Joyce beams with satisfaction at a job well done

Then I added new photos Yvonne had taken of the process of setting up the interior, created a slide show — from groundbreaking through set up, started it playing in a loop, and explained what I'd done to Larry and to Joyce. The slide show would play in the office where visitors taking a tour of the facility later could watch it.

While Yvonne and the others set up tables and began placing food on tables outside in preparation for the party, I went to Ace Hardware to shop for project needs I was missing. I found a pair of nylon (I think) curtain rod hangers and a 4' dowel rod that fit, Thetford holding tank powder, and picture hanging hardware I thought might do to hold the porta potti in place as substitutes for the retraining hardware I'd carelessly misplaced.

Back at the Food Bank building I helped with set up and soon guests began to appear. Yvonne had arranged one table with framed and unframed certificates of appreciation that she had prepared over the previous couple weeks. Suzanne brought a plate of homemade wheat-free cookies that were awfully good. Yvonne heated up some Costco spring rolls as an addition to her homemade cookies.

Two-hundred-sixty-five: Grand Opening

265C: Yvonne describes community support

Craig, looking bishoply, said hello and talked to Suzanne for awhile, both on the Orcas Interfaith Council, a group I had belonged to when the idea of a new facility for the Food Bank was first being discussed.

One table held coffee, lemonade, and dark chocolate cupcakes. Every square inch of the other three tables held a plate with some kind of treat — mostly sweet. About 2:30 Larry introduced himself to the 100 or so attendees, talked briefly about the project, and then invited Yvonne (who thanked the volunteers and pointed out the certificates for pick up) and then Joyce (who thanked Yvonne for never saying "No" when Joyce needed help and me for putting their new computer system together, and many others for their contributions) and then George (who had taken care of the everything to do with the building being designed, installed, and improved — with a clever trellis/door rain protection structure and who now talked about all the people that were drawn into the project and gave their time to this community effort). When I asked Yvonne what she was most proud of with the project she pointed to how the board members each reached out to their circles, bringing in donations, volunteers, and enthusiasm, so that the project really was community wide, an element of life in the Islands that we admired and resonated with. Larry and Lina (she and Dave had started the Food Bank decades ago) cut the yellow ribbon and invited the crowd into the building for a tour.

265D: A community celebration

Two-hundred-sixty-five: Grand Opening

265E: What the inside looks like

Later, at Madrona Grill, Joyce and Larry, Yvonne and I refreshed ourselves and talked about the project and the future. They saw themselves as playing a transitional role, of having physically moved the Food Bank from very inadequate facilities, minimal funding, and unpredictable food supplies, to a practical, clean, and efficient facility, subscription funding, and food supplies from four major sources. Once the Food Bank was running smoothly, now with the change in venue and time for reform of process, they saw themselves as playing a less operational role. Though I hadn't done much, Yvonne had, and I felt satisfaction being connected with a community service that in my mind was clearly a good thing — feeding the hungry who for whatever reason couldn't for the moment afford to feed themselves.

Two-hundred-sixty-six: Reid Harbor

"The sea, once it casts its spell, holds one in its net of wonder forever." - Jacques Yves Cousteau

The plan was to leave for Reid Harbor by 8:30. With Margaret's help the day before I'd taken the Livingston off its stand on our beach, put it in the water and rowed north to Pole Pass and then once through it turning left and docked the dingy behind our SeaSport. About 6:00 a.m. I went back to the community dock, tied a bridle across the stern of the SeaSport through the eyes — port and starboard, and then put another line through the bow eye on the Livingston and then doubled back to the bridle and tied a bowline loop around the bridle so the tow line could slide on the bridle. I took the car battery I'd charged overnight, the electric motor we'd bought for the Livingston the year before, sleeping bags, and everything else ready to go. By 8:20, Yvonne was up and ready to leave, taking with a dozen homemade apricot scones and a thermos with hot water. On our way toward Jones Island, Yvonne had breakfast and I sipped tea from a mug decorated with portrait photos of Morgan and Opal. Not much wind and not much sun.

Our route took us past Reef Island and then through North Pass and south of Jones Island, a state park we had visited and hiked on with Corrina and Kelly, then quite pregnant, in the spring. Crossing the intersection of San Juan and Speiden Channels, an area of whirlpools and standing waves (see NOAA chart 18421), we continued through New Channel up the northwest side of Speiden Island, Flattop and Cactus to the right and eventually Johns and Stuart Islands, split by Johns Pass. We entered shallow Reid Harbor, found our friends moored to a float and once Yvonne pulled the Livingston in close to the stern of the SeaSport I docked at the space they'd saved for us behind two power boats. Because we were towing the Livingston I couldn't take the SeaSport up on plane, so we moseyed along averaging a bit over 7 knots or almost 8 mph. The Crane/Stuart cruise had taken 90 minutes.

266A: At the keeper's house

By 11:00 we were ready for our walk to the lighthouse and we crossed to the beach at the head of Reid Harbor and the concrete ramp at the end of the county road in three dinghies — Howard with us and Sheila with Lynn and Chris. Since it was near low tide we helped each other carry the dinghies across the beach to the bare logs left by winter storms accompanied by especially high tides, securing the dinghies so they wouldn't drift off when the tide came in over the next two hours.

We walked up the county road, past the school house and then at the road to the county dock turned left for the Turn Point Lighthouse, our destination for the five mile round trip walk Yvonne and I had made at least a dozen times before. Years ago, island children were boated off island for school, then a sinking and drowning of the children resulted in building a local school though now it had few if any students. The last fifth of the walk is along headlands above the north end of Harrow Straight through which shipping passes when bound for the Pacific out through the Straight of Juan de Fuca or when bound for Vancouver, B.C. along Boundary Passage and then the Straight of Georgia.

266B: Turn Point

At the top of Stuart Island the shipping channel off the island turns almost 90 degrees so it's called Turn Point and just as we arrived at the restored lighthouse buildings a northbound freighter made a right turn into Boundary Channel. The shipping lanes follow the international border here. We were almost on the Canadian border and well north of Victoria, to the south and west on Vancouver Island, facing the Straight of Juan de Fuca and the Washington Peninsula and Olympic Mountains across the way. The sunlight forced itself through breaks in the clouds while we ate our sandwiches, took photos, and toured the grounds. The museum was closed unfortunately today though we had all been through it before. Turn Point is extraordinarily beautiful and we'd enjoyed it both from land and sea, once before having encountered Orca whales a mile north of Stuart Island.

Back in Reid Harbor we retired to our respective boats for reading and napping, appearing on the float just before 5:00 with wine bottles, glasses, and snacks of various kinds. For the next three hours we enjoyed a blackened tuna, fresh from the garden green salad, roasted vegetables, homemade nut bread, and dill sprinkled boiled potatoes. A feast. By 8:00 it began to sprinkle a bit and we returned to our boats until Howard came by to invite us to the *Eileen B.*, a green-hulled Mercator he and Sheila had lovingly restored. Sheila served tea and we sat and talked until 10:00 when Howard began to nod off so we thanked our hosts and crawled into the slightly too small but otherwise comfortable V berth on the *Huginn* and read for a few minutes before entering the Land of Nod.

Two-hundred-sixty-six: Reid Harbor

266C: New technology takes over

Two-hundred-sixty-seven: No Winds

"The world is indeed comic, but the joke is on mankind." - H. P. Lovecraft

Though I woke up a few times I slept well in too-small SeaSport V berth and about 7:00 turned on my reading light and returned to my second and more careful reading of Marilyn Robinson's *Absence of Mind*, underlining and making notes in the margins. Because of her writing style and abstract subject matter, not an easy book to read, but an important one as an open minded and educated response to writers like Hawkins and Dennett, who have made a popular case for ignoring mind, that is art, history, culture, since from their point of view mind doesn't exist or is at best a highly unreliable witness. Not long after 8:00 Yvonne woke up and the first order of business was to take the Livingston to the State Park dock and use the comfort facility. Back on the float, Yvonne unpacked her scones and we joined Sheila and Howard hosting Nancy and Steve in the cockpit of the *Eileen B*. I'd made tea with water from the thermos Yvonne had filled 24 hours before and though still hot it wasn't quite hot enough. Yvonne accepted the offer of hot water from Sheila and made herself a cup of coffee trying out what amounted to a packet of instant coffee — which she declared quite good. Not being a coffee drinker but having watched my father make himself instant coffee years ago and then drink it, I couldn't imagine instant coffee could be satisfying — but Yvonne, very particular about her coffee said it could — now, anyway. Isn't science wonderful? Yvonne's apricot scones made the rounds and were soon gone. Lynn and Chris would have to look out for themselves.

The *Huginn* and the other boats were wet — more from overnight dew than rain and the overcast was gray, but not uniformly, suggesting it would clear later, at least partially. The little wind had blown itself out, as had the big wind the first night we spent in Reid Harbor in our first boat, a 26' Macgregor, twelve years before. The cruise from Orcas, under power, had been slightly less than terrifying, as we encountered the whirlpools, waves, and wakes, now, in a much smaller boat we barely noticed.

267: Reid Harbor the first time

That evening Yvonne had grilled chicken and served it with peanut butter sauce with a cabbage and crisp noodle salad. Reid Harbor was full of boats, at least a 100 compared to the 50 we'd seen this trip. With the county dock and mooring buoys all occupied I dropped the anchor in a spot not far from the dock, since we'd want to get to land from time to time — Yvonne, James, and I — and our little black mutt Samantha. Our experienced sailor friend, Dick, had told me the anchor rode (the length of the anchor line) should be five times the depth of the water. I thought that excessive, especially because in 30 feet of water we'd have to allow for a circle around the boat with a diameter of almost 300 feet to avoid colliding with other boats or tangling lines. Before going to bed I noted the position of the county dock and other boats around us — especially their anchor lights, which often was all I could see. Worried about the anchor and generally about the boat inexplicably sinking with us aboard ("Family Drowns in Tragic Accident; Dog Somehow Survives Cold Water"), I awoke every hour or so to make sure all was well. About 2:00 a.m., the wind having changed direction, now blowing hard from the north and the head of Reid Harbor rather than the south, I couldn't recognize our position or any of the boats around us. I could see the County dock but it was now far to the north. We were moving south, rapidly, dragging anchor and though we hadn't hit another boat yet or tangled anchor lines we were headed for a power boat. I woke Yvonne and jumped out on deck in my underwear and started the outboard. Yvonne, in a nightgown, in the howling wind and almost total darkness made her way to the bow to pull up the anchor, something we had to do before moving. James, age fourteen, came up on deck and took a position on deck between me and Yvonne so that he could relay information back and forth — since I didn't want to disturb the other boats by yelling, on the one hand, but Yvonne and I couldn't hear because of the wind on the other. A shout of complaint came from the power boat we nearly collided with and I pushed off with a boat hook. The anchor was free. Now we had to make our way in the darkness through a maze of boats and anchor lines to — where? Not to deeper water surely. That hadn't worked, so I headed the boat north to the head of the harbor. Yvonne had a flashlight now and would call out "port" or "starboard" and then "left" or "right" and James would relay her message to me. Not confident about anchoring again, I decided to run the boat up on the beach. Since the Macgregor had a centerboard (we'd pulled up) instead of a keel and used water for ballast (the tank was empty because we'd come to Reid Harbor under power) beaching really wasn't dangerous for us or the boat. The tide was in, so I could bring the boat close to the massive tree trunks left by past storms, and I secured a bow line to a thick branch extending from a nearby log. We were safe. The boat wouldn't sink and it wouldn't cause trouble for other boaters. We went to sleep soothed by waves lapping the hull. And then there was no sound of lapping waves. About 8:30 a.m. I stuck my head out of the cockpit hatch and saw that the *Simrishamn* was high and dry, the water 50' feet south. But the boat was upright because the aft portion of the hull was flat for planing under power. We had only to wait for the tide to come back in to float us free of the beach and we could return home. Since we had little food aboard because we had planned to leave early and now couldn't, Yvonne found crackers and other snacks to tide us over and I used the opportunity of having the hull conveniently exposed to do some routine maintenance. But the boating community was interested at seeing a sailboat stranded out of the water and a steady stream of gawkers strolled by expressing their sympathy that we'd had a mishap — assuming the keel was buried in the sand — so I found it necessary to explain that we were there by design not accident — trying to salvage what I could of what was left of my dignity. About noon, the tide having flooded the beach, two strong young men helped me push the bow off the beach, Yvonne, James, and Samantha in the stern to bring the bow up. And then we were afloat, returning to Cayou Quay Marina, me under a cloud, wiser about anchoring but not for the first or last time chagrined at ignoring studied advice.

Now, years later, we'd had no wind and tied to a float so it wouldn't have mattered anyway. But now it was time to go home, so I tied the long floating polypropylene line to the Livingston, doubled it back to the bridle I'd tied to the stern of the *Huginn*, and with Yvonne holding the line so that the dingy was close by and then letting the line out as we cleared the other boats in the harbor, we headed back to Crane Island by the same route we'd come the day before, Yvonne quickly retiring to the V berth to catch up on the sleep she'd missed the night before, leaving me to the green islands, gray and brown rocky shore, blue water and my thoughts of past, present, and future.

Two-hundred-sixty-eight: It's the Berries!

"The land knows no boundaries, yet it is the root of all identity." - Wallace Stegner

David was traveling and Chris and Brian were each aboard their sailboats so it was left to Howard and me to carry on with the Greybeards at our weekly Wednesday morning convocation in his honeymoon cottage at the edge of his fenced vegetable garden. We talked about the Reid Harbor cruise briefly and then, at Howard's prompting, turned to a topic we'd touched on several times recently — he and I doing an eNotated version of one of Thomas Hardy's novels — both of us having read most of them and both big fans. Hardy, the son of a stone mason, wrote knowingly of the lives and vocations of the lower and middle classes in south central England, an area he called Wessex in his books. Hardy writes with extraordinary detail about farming and forestry, heath, village, and town life in Wessex, evoking a world that was nearly gone but that lingered here and there in certain respects until the 1950's. Howard, trained in agriculture in England, knew men who still tended hedgerows or created and sold charcoal and were the sons and grandsons of the people Hardy knew. The plan was for Howard to focus on providing historic background Hardy assumed his readers knew to today's readers that certainly don't and for me to focus on Hardy's life and literary topics. We tentatively chose *Tess of the d'Urbervilles* as the book we'd start with, beginning work in September once his harvest was mostly in.

And then he handed me a quart bucket and invited me to pick raspberries with him, the bushes begging for attention since he'd been absent for three days. His berry patch was inside a fenced and covered area safe from birds and raccoons — who would otherwise pick the bushes bare before he could get to them. Howard showed me where he left off and how to identify the ripe berries (slightly different shade and very easy to pull from seed and stem — which would remain hanging from the branch. Once he'd harvested this first crop he'd cut back the older shoots and the bush would flower and produce berries for a second time later in the season. His technique came from his father who mastered berry cultivation in England through reading and experimentation. Howard had studied agriculture, practiced it, then taught it and practical arts generally, migrating in search of opportunity to the US and eventually teaching at a high school in Oregon and finally in Alaska in an Inuit village with Sheila for nine years (excepting summers when they'd vacation in Deer Harbor).

268: Yvonne picks blackberries in the Crane lot on Orcas (August 2009)

After picking up the mail at the Post Office and buying the *Seattle Times* and *Islands' Sounder* for Yvonne I ran into Sheldon at the marina and we talked about his father-in-law, Brian, now on his boat with his son Bart and Bart's friend. Sheldon said Brian was driving again, much to the dismay of Sheldon and Dawn but neither the sheriff nor a counselor could help. I told Sheldon how after being prompted for suggestions by Brian the Greybeard's had suggested Brian rent out the cabin next to his house and use that revenue to fund transportation from professional sources rather than frustrate himself and others with ad hoc requests of family and friends to chauffeur him around Orcas. Sheldon like the suggestion.

After cutting down five of the six stumps left in the yard from the Douglas fir massacre and then running out of bar and chain oil, I retired to the shower and got ready to go to dinner at Caroline and Kenneth's in Victorian Valley near the ferry landing. We each knew Caroline a little bit, from her visits and talk to the Unitarian group and for Yvonne, her association with the Garden Club. Neither of us had met Kenneth. He had studied mechanical engineering at the University of Texas in Austin, the two of them had done the interior work on their Lindal home, a very meticulous job I could see. Caroline was a painter and Kenneth a serious photographer and he showed Yvonne and me some prints he'd made after spending hundreds of hours adjusting pixels in the image files. He was most proud of his 16" x 45" picture of a peak in the Cascades in the early spring, the snow still sitting at the base of the basalt cliffs. He had stitched the picture together from perhaps a dozen individual shots, at least two per section of the mountain, choosing the best images of the cliffs and best images of the snow beneath them. The level of detail was stunning. As he pointed out — with his prints there was no best viewing spot. The picture looked good as close as you could get and at a distance. After feeling overwhelmed with things to do before our guests arrived the next day and getting a stiff back because of it I relaxed with Caroline and Kenneth's hospitality and friendliness and by the time we headed home toward Pole Pass in the twilight just before 10:00 I felt more hopeful about the future of the world.

What's Next?

Crane Island Journal is a four-volume covering October 19, 2010 through October 18, 2011. This is *Vor (Spring)*, the third volume of *Crane Island Journal*.

Find information about *Haust (Autumn)*, *Vetur (Winter)*, and *Sumar (Summer)* on the Journal's website, www.craneislandjournal.com.

www.ingramcontent.com/pod-product-compliance
Lightning Source LLC
Chambersburg PA
CBHW070418010526
44118CB00014B/1812